The Crisis of the

American South

The Crisis of the American South

A Critical Examination of the Economic and Moral
Failures of a Slave-Holding Society

Hinton Rowan Helper

Edited by Paul Dennis Sporer

QUANTERNESS PRESS

ANZA PUBLISHING, Chester, NY 10918
Quanterness Press is an imprint of Anza Publishing

This work is a new edition of *The Impending Crisis of the South: How to Meet It*, by Hinton Rowan Helper, originally published in 1857.

Library of Congress Cataloguing-in-Publication Data
Helper, Hinton Rowan, 1829-1909.
  [Impending crisis of the South]
  The crisis of the American South / Hinton Rowan Helper ; edited by Paul Dennis Sporer.
    p. cm.
  Includes index.
  ISBN 1-932490-36-1 (hardcover : alk. paper)
  1. Slavery--United States.   2. Slavery--Southern States.   3. Slavery--Southern States--Quotations, maxims, etc.   4. United States--Politics and government--1857-1861. I. Sporer, Paul D. II. Title.
  E449.H483 2005
  973.7'114--dc22   2005021782

Visit AnzaPublishing.com for more information on outstanding authors and titles. Please support our efforts to restore great literature to a place of prominence in our culture.

∞ This book is printed on acid-free paper.

ISBN 1-932490-36-1

Contents

Tables

Editor's Preface

Although Harriet Beecher Stowe's *Uncle Tom's Cabin* is considered to be the book that most motivated a nation against slavery, it was not a work of fiction, but rather a sociological treatise that perhaps should take that honor. Hinton Rowan Helper, a slaveholder's son, wrote a well-researched and persuasive indictment of slavery, which not only became widely known but also had a major impact on American politics. In fact, it was instrumental in helping Abraham Lincoln win the Presidential election of 1860. However, this work, *The Crisis of the American South*, is complex, and it would be a mistake to look at it solely as anti-slavery propaganda.

Helper, as other authors, argued that the basic injustices within the institution of slavery were a heinous offence against Christian principles. Yet, he went much further than others to document the harm that was actually being done to society by this institution. For example, Helper claimed that slavery was keeping the South backwards agriculturally and industrially, that it was destroying land prices, and hindering railroad building. In addition, he brought much needed attention to key cultural aspects that were usually ignored, such as the dependence of Southerners on the products of Northern industry, a lack of patriotism amongst the Southern elite, and the inability of the illiterate poor whites of the South to express their desires and aims.

It is clear from his writing, that although Helper was sympathetic to the plight of blacks, he empathized most with the downtrodden whites of the South. Interestingly, he concludes that the South's economic and social ills should not be blamed on the North, but on a small group of very powerful white slaveholders, who were manipulating society for their own purposes. Ultimately, Helper's larger goal was to provoke a type of socialist revolution, and the emancipation of slaves was only one aspect of this.

Hinton Rowan Helper (1829-1909) was born and raised in North Carolina, his father dying only a year after his birth. His family owned a few slaves, working them on a small farm. After a wasted three years in California during the "gold rush", he apparently contemplated a work that would address the economic problems in his own section of the country, the South. He spent some time writing and attempting to publish this work. However, to Helper's great fortune, his book was officially adopted by the Republican party as providing key support for their political policies. They distributed, in abridged form, over 100,000 copies of it as part of their 1860 Presidential campaign.

Subsequent to receiving these accolades, Helper went on to live in South America, being appointed by President Lincoln as U.S. consul to Buenos Aires. Although respected as a scholar for his landmark anti-slavery work, his later writings became strident and polemical. Through various publications, he warned Americans about the threat that blacks and other non-white races posed for American society. His erstwhile supporters came to regard his post-war views with distaste, and they could not allow themselves to be associated with his program of nativism.

The Crisis of the American South contains a painstaking and extensive statistical treatment of social issues, unusual for its time. All the calculations in the book were done by hand, truly an arduous task before the age of computational devices. However, we do find errors in the totals in certain tables. Since we do not have the original documents Helper used, we cannot say whether the error was in transcription, or in the calculation itself. Thus, we have provided the true total (marked "Corrected") *only* if there is a difference between the edition's total and the actual sum. As for textual changes and alterations, we have removed three chapters, as they are largely irrelevant to the central themes. We have also added a comprehensive index.

PAUL DENNIS SPORER

Chapter 1

Comparison Between Free and Slave States

IT IS NOT OUR INTENTION in this chapter to enter into an elaborate ethnographical essay, to establish peculiarities of difference, mental, moral, and physical, in the great family of man. Neither is it our design to launch into a philosophical disquisition on the laws and principles of light and darkness, with a view of educing any additional evidence of the fact, that as a general rule, the rays of the sun are more fructifying and congenial than the shades of night. Nor yet is it our purpose, by writing a formal treatise on ethics, to draw a broad line of distinction between right and wrong, to point out the propriety of morality and its advantages over immorality, nor to waste time in pressing a universally admitted truism—that virtue is preferable to vice. Self-evident truths require no argumentative demonstration.

What we mean to do is simply this: to take a survey of the relative position and importance of the several states of this confederacy, from the adoption of the national compact; and when, of two sections of the country starting under the same auspices, and with equal natural advantages, we find the one rising to a degree of almost unexampled power and eminence, and the other sinking into a state of comparative imbecility and obscurity, it is our determination to trace out the causes which have led to the elevation of the former, and the depression of the latter, and to use our most earnest and honest endeavors to utterly extirpate whatever opposes the progress and prosperity of any portion of the union.

This survey we have already made; we have also instituted an impartial comparison between the cardinal sections of the country, north, south, east, and west; and as a true hearted southerner, whose ancestors have resided in North Carolina between one and two hundred years, and as one who would rather have his native clime excel than be excelled, we feel constrained to confess that we are deeply abashed and chagrined at the disclosures of the comparison thus instituted. At the time of the adoption of the Constitution, in 1789, we commenced an even race with the North. All things considered, if either the North or the South had the advantage, it was the latter. In proof of this, let us introduce a few statistics, beginning with the states of:

NEW YORK AND VIRGINIA

In 1790, when the first census was taken, New York contained 340,120 inhabitants; at the same time the population of Virginia was 748,308, being more than twice the number of New York. Just sixty years afterward, as we learn from the census of 1850, New York had a population of 3,097,394; while that of Virginia was only 1,421,661, being less than half the number of New York!

In 1791, the exports of New York amounted to $2,505,465; the exports of Virginia amounted to $3,130,865. In 1852, the exports of New York amounted to $87,484,456; the exports of Virginia, during the same year, amounted to only $2,724,657. In 1790, the imports of New York and Virginia were about equal; in 1853, the imports of New York amounted to the enormous sum of $178,270,999; while those of Virginia, for the same period, amounted to the pitiful sum of only $399,004. In 1850, the products of manufactures, mining and the mechanic arts in New York amounted to $237,597,249; those of Virginia amounted to only $29,705,387. At the taking of the last census, the value of real and personal property in Virginia, including negroes, was $391,646,438; that of New York, exclusive of any monetary valuation of human beings, was $1,080,309,216.

In August 1856, the real and personal estate assessed in the City of New York amounted in valuation to $511,740,491, showing that New York City alone is worth far more than the whole State of Virginia.

What says one of Virginia's own sons? He still lives; hear him speak. Says Gov. Wise:

"It may be painful, but nevertheless, profitable, to recur occasionally to the history of the past; to listen to the admonitions of experience, and learn lessons of wisdom from the efforts and actions of those who have preceded us in the drama of human life. The records of former days show that at a period not very remote, Virginia stood preeminently the first commercial State in the Union; when her commerce exceeded in amount that of all the New England States combined; when the City of Norfolk owned more than one hundred trading ships, and her direct foreign trade exceeded that of the City of New York, now the centre of trade and the great emporium of North America. At the period of the war of independence, the commerce of Virginia was four times larger than that of New York."

The cash value of all the farms, farming implements and machinery in Virginia, in 1850, was $223,423,315; the value of the same in New York, in the same year, was $576,631,568. In about the same ratio does the value of the agricultural products and live stock of New York exceed the value of the agricultural products and live stock of Virginia. But we will pursue this comparison no further. With feelings mingled with indignation and disgust, we turn from the picture, and will now pay our respects to two other states.

MASSACHUSETTS AND NORTH CAROLINA

In 1790, Massachusetts contained 378,717 inhabitants; in the same year North Carolina contained 393,751; in 1850, the population of Massachusetts was 994,514, all freemen; while that of North Carolina was only 869,039, of whom 288,548 were slaves. Massachusetts has an area of only 7,800 square miles; the area of North Carolina is 50,704 square miles, which, though less than Virginia, is considerably larger than the State of New York. Massachusetts and North Carolina each have a harbor, Boston and Beaufort, which harbors, with the States that back them, are, by nature, possessed of about equal capacities and advantages for commercial and manufacturing enterprise. Boston has grown to be the second commercial city in the Union; her ships, freighted with the useful and unique inventions and manufactures of her ingenious artisans and mechanics, and bearing upon their stalwart arms the majestic flag of our country, glide triumphantly through the winds and over the waves of every ocean. She has done, and is now doing, great honor to herself, her State and the nation, and her name and fame are spoken with reverence in the remotest regions of the earth.

How is it with Beaufort, in North Carolina, whose harbor is said to be the safest and most commodious anywhere to be found on the Atlantic coast south of the harbor of New York, and but little inferior to that? Has anybody ever heard of her? Do the masts of her ships ever cast a shadow on foreign waters? Upon what distant or benighted shore have her merchants and mariners ever hoisted our national ensign, or spread the arts of civilization and peaceful industry? What changes worthy of note have taken place in the physical features of her superficies since "the evening and the morning were the third day?" But we will make no further attempt to draw a comparison between the populous, wealthy, and renowned city of Boston and the obscure, despicable little village of Beaufort, which, notwithstanding "the placid bosom of its deep and well-protected harbor," has no place in the annals or records of the country, and has scarcely ever been heard of fifty miles from home.

In 1853, the exports of Massachusetts amounted to $16,895,304, and her imports to $41,367,956; during the same time, and indeed during all the time, from the period of the formation of the government up to the year 1853, inclusive, the exports and imports of North Carolina were so utterly insignificant that we are ashamed to record them. In 1850, the products of manufactures, mining and the mechanic arts in Massachusetts, amounted to $151,137,145; those of North Carolina, to only $9,111,245. In 1856, the products of these industrial pursuits in Massachusetts had increased to something over $288,000,000, a sum more than twice the value of the entire cotton crop of all the Southern States! In 1850, the cash value of all the farms, farming implements and machinery in Massachusetts, was $112,285,931; the value of the same in North Carolina, in the same year, was only $71,823,298. In 1850, the value of all the real and personal estate in Massachusetts, without recognizing property in man, or setting a monetary price on the head of a single citizen, white or black, amounted to $573,342,286; the value of the same in North Carolina, including negroes, amounted to only $226,800,472. In 1856, the real and personal estate assessed in the City of Boston amounted in valuation to within a fraction of $250,000,000, showing conclusively that so far as dollars and cents are concerned, that single city could buy the whole State of North Carolina, and by right of purchase, if sanctioned by the Constitution of the United States, and by State Constitutions, hold her as a province. In 1850, there were in Massachusetts 1,861 native white and free colored persons over twenty years of age who could not read and write; in the same year, the same class of persons in North Carolina numbered 80,083; while her 288,548 slaves were, by legislative enactments, kept in a state of absolute ignorance and unconditional subordination.

Hoping, however, and believing, that a large majority of the most respectable and patriotic citizens of North Carolina have resolved, or will soon resolve, with unyielding purpose, to cast aside the great obstacle that impedes their progress, and bring into action a new policy which will lead them from poverty and ignorance to wealth and intellectual greatness, and which will shield them not only from the rebukes of their own consciences, but also from the just reproaches of the civilized world, we will, for the present, in deference to their feelings, forbear the further enumeration of these degrading disparities, and turn our attention to:

PENNSYLVANIA AND SOUTH CAROLINA

An old gentleman, now residing in Charleston, told us, but a few months since, that he had a distinct recollection of the time when

Charleston imported foreign fabrics for the Philadelphia trade, and when, on a certain occasion, his mother went into a store on Market-street to select a silk dress for herself, the merchant, unable to please her fancy, persuaded her to postpone the selection for a few days, or until the arrival of a new stock of superb styles and fashions which he had recently purchased in the metropolis of South Carolina. This was all very proper Charleston had a spacious harbor, a central position, and a mild climate; and from priority of settlement and business connections, to say nothing of other advantages, she enjoyed greater facilities for commercial transactions than Philadelphia. She had a right to get custom wherever she could find it, and in securing so valuable a customer as the Quaker City, she exhibited no small degree of laudable enterprise. But why did she not maintain her supremacy? If the answer to this query is not already in the reader's mind, it will suggest itself before he peruses the whole of this work. For the present, suffice it to say, that the cause of her shameful insignificance and decline is essentially the same that has thrown every other Southern city and State in the rear of progress, and rendered them tributary, in a commercial and manufacturing point of view, almost entirely tributary, to the more sagacious and enterprising States and cities of the North.

A most unfortunate day was that for the Palmetto State, and indeed for the whole South, when the course of trade was changed, and she found herself the retailer of foreign and domestic goods, imported and vended by wholesale merchants at the North. Philadelphia ladies no longer look to the South for late fashions, and fine silks and satins; no Quaker dame now wears drab apparel of Charleston importation. Like all other 'niggervilles' in our disreputable part of the confederacy, the commercial emporium of South Carolina is sick and impoverished; her silver cord has been loosed; her golden bowl has been broken; and her unhappy people, without proper or profitable employment, poor in pocket, and few in number, go mourning or loafing about the streets. Her annual importations are actually less now than they were a century ago, when

South Carolina was the second commercial province on the continent, Virginia being the first.

In 1760, as we learn from Mr. Benton's "Thirty Years' View," the foreign imports into Charleston were $2,662,000; in 1855, they amounted to only $1,750,000! In 1854, the imports into Philadelphia, which, in foreign trade, ranks at present but fourth among the commercial cities of the union, were $21,963,021. In 1850, the products of manufactures, mining, and the mechanic arts, in Pennsylvania, amounted to $155,044,910; the products of the same in South Carolina, amounted to only $7,063,513.

As shown by the census report of 1850, which was prepared under the superintendence of a native of South Carolina, who certainly will not be suspected of injustice to his own section of the country, the Southern states, the cash value of all the farms, farming implements, and machinery in Pennsylvania, was $422,598,640; the value of the same in South Carolina, in the same year, was only $86,518,038. From a compendium of the same census, we learn that the value of all the real and personal property in Pennsylvania, actual property, no slaves, amounted to $729,144,998; the value of the same in South Carolina, including the estimated — we were about to say fictitious—value of 384,925 negroes, amounted to only $288,257,694. We have not been able to obtain the figures necessary to show the exact value of the real and personal estate in Philadelphia, but the amount is estimated to be not less than $300,000,000; and as, in 1850, there were 408,762 free inhabitants in the single city of Philadelphia, against 283,544 of the same class, in the whole state of South Carolina, it is quite evident that the former is more powerful than the latter, and far ahead of her in all the elements of genuine and permanent superiority. In Pennsylvania, in 1850, the annual income of public schools amounted to $1,348,249; the same in South Carolina, in the same year, amounted to only $200,600; in the former state there were 393 libraries other than private, in the latter only 26; in Pennsylvania 310 newspapers and periodicals were published, circulating 84,898,672 copies annually; in South Carolina only 46 newspapers and periodicals were published, circulating but 7,145,930 copies per annum.

The incontrovertible facts we have thus far presented are, we think, amply sufficient, both in number and magnitude, to bring conviction to the mind of every candid reader, that there is something wrong, socially, politically and morally wrong, in the policy under which the South has so long loitered and languished. Else, how is it that the North, under the operations of a policy directly the opposite of ours, has surpassed us in almost everything great and good, and left us standing before the world, an object of merited reprehension and derision?

For one, we are heartily ashamed of the inexcusable weakness, inertia and dilapidation everywhere so manifest throughout our native section; but the blame properly attaches itself to an usurping minority of the people, and we are determined that it shall rest where it belongs. More on this subject, however, after a brief but general survey of the inequalities and disparities that exist between those two grand divisions of the country, which, without reference to the situation that any part of their territory bears to the cardinal points, are every day becoming more familiarly known by the appropriate appellation of:

THE FREE AND THE SLAVE STATES

It is a fact well known to every intelligent Southerner that we are compelled to go to the North for almost every article of utility and adornment, from matches, shoepegs and paintings up to cotton-mills, steamships and statuary; that we have no foreign trade, no princely merchants, nor respectable artists; that, in comparison with the free states, we contribute nothing to the literature, polite arts and inventions of the age; that, for want of profitable employment at home, large numbers of our native population find themselves necessitated to emigrate to the West, whilst the free states retain not only the larger proportion of those born within their own limits, but induce, annually, hundreds of thousands of foreigners to settle and remain amongst them; that almost everything produced at the North meets with ready sale, while, at the same time, there is no demand, even among our own citizens, for the productions of Southern industry; that, owing to the absence of a proper system of business amongst us, the North becomes, in one way or another, the proprietor and dispenser of all our floating wealth, and that we are dependent on Northern capitalists for the means necessary to build our railroads, canals and other public improvements; that if we want to visit a foreign country, even though it may lie directly South of us, we find no convenient way of getting there except by taking passage through a Northern port; and that nearly all the profits arising from the exchange of commodities, from insurance and shipping offices, and from the thousand and one industrial pursuits of the country, accrue to the North, and are there invested in the erection of those magnificent cities and stupendous works of art which dazzle the eyes of the South, and attest the superiority of free institutions!

The North is the Mecca of our merchants, and to it they must and do make two pilgrimages per annum—one in the spring and one in the fall. All our commercial, mechanical, manufactural, and literary supplies come from there. We want Bibles, brooms, buckets and books, and we go to the North; we want pens, ink, paper, wafers and envelopes, and we go to the North; we want shoes, hats, handkerchiefs, umbrellas and pocket knives, and we go to the North; we want furniture, crockery, glassware and pianos, and we go to the North; we want toys, primers, school books, fashionable apparel, machinery, medicines, tombstones, and a thousand other things, and we go to the North for them all. Instead of keeping our money in circulation at home, by patronizing our own mechanics, manufacturers, and laborers, we send it all away to the North, and there it remains; it never falls into our hands again.

In one way or another we are more or less subservient to the North every day of our lives. In infancy we are swaddled in Northern muslin; in childhood we are humored with Northern gewgaws;

in youth we are instructed out of Northern books; at the age of maturity we sow our "wild oats" on Northern soil; in middle-life we exhaust our wealth, energies and talents in the dishonorable vocation of entailing our dependence on our children and on our children's children, and, to the neglect of our own interests and the interests of those around us, in giving aid and succor to every department of Northern power; in the decline of life we remedy our eye-sight with Northren spectacles, and support our infirmities with Northern canes; in old age we are drugged with Northern physic; and, finally, when we die, our inanimate bodies, shrouded in Northern cambric, are stretched upon the bier, borne to the grave in a Northern carriage, entombed with a Northern spade, and memorized with a Northern slab!

But it can hardly be necessary to say more in illustration of this unmanly and unnational dependence, which is so glaring that it cannot fail to be apparent to even the most careless and superficial observer. All the world sees, or ought to see, that in a commercial, mechanical, manufactural, financial, and literary point of view, we are as helpless as babes; that, in comparison with the Free States, our agricultural resources have been greatly exaggerated, misunderstood and mismanaged; and that, instead of cultivating among ourselves a wise policy of mutual assistance and cooperation with respect to individuals, and of self-reliance with respect to the South at large, instead of giving countenance and encouragement to the industrial enterprises projected in our midst, and instead of building up, aggrandizing and beautifying our own States, cities and towns, we have been spending our substance at the North, and are daily augmenting and strengthening the very power which now has us so completely under its thumb.

It thus appears, in view of the preceding statistical facts and arguments, that the South, at one time the superior of the North in almost all the ennobling pursuits and conditions of life, has fallen far behind her competitor, and now ranks more as the dependency of a mother country than as the equal confederate of free and inde-

pendent States. Following the order of our task, the next duty that
devolves upon us is to trace out the causes which have conspired
to bring about this important change, and to place on record the
reasons, as we understand them:

WHY THE NORTH HAS SURPASSED THE SOUTH

And now that we have come to the very heart and soul of our
subject, we feel no disposition to mince matters, but mean to speak
plainly, and to the point, without any equivocation, mental reserva-
tion, or secret evasion whatever. The son of a venerated parent,
who, while he lived, was a considerate and merciful slaveholder, a
native of the South, born and bred in North Carolina, of a family
whose home has been in the valley of the Yadkin for nearly a century and a half, a Southerner by instinct and by all the influences
of thought, habits, and kindred, and with the desire and fixed purpose to reside permanently within the limits of the South, and with
the expectation of dying there also—we feel that we have the right
to express our opinion, however humble or unimportant it may be,
on any and every question that affects the public good; and, so help
us God, "sink or swim, live or die, survive or perish," we are determined to exercise that right with manly firmness, and without fear,
favor or affection.

And now to the point. In our opinion, an opinion which has been
formed from data obtained by assiduous researches, and comparisons, from laborious investigation, logical reasoning, and earnest
reflection, the causes which have impeded the progress and prosperity of the South, which have dwindled our commerce, and other
similar pursuits, into the most contemptible insignificance; sunk a
large majority of our people in galling poverty and ignorance, rendered a small minority conceited and tyrannical, and driven the rest
away from their homes; entailed upon us a humiliating dependence
on the Free States; disgraced us in the recesses of our own souls,
and brought us under reproach in the eyes of all civilized and enlightened nations—may all be traced to one common source, and

there find solution in the most hateful and horrible word, that was ever incorporated into the vocabulary of human economy—*Slavery!*

Reared amidst the institution of slavery, believing it to be wrong both in principle and in practice, and having seen and felt its evil influences upon individuals, communities and states, we deem it a duty, no less than a privilege, to enter our protest against it, and to use our most strenuous efforts to overturn and abolish it! Then we are an abolitionist? Yes! not merely a freesoiler, but an abolitionist, in the fullest sense of the term. We are not only in favor of keeping slavery out of the territories, but, carrying our opposition to the institution a step further, we here unhesitatingly declare ourself in favor of its immediate and unconditional abolition, in every state in this confederacy, where it now exists! Patriotism makes us a freesoiler; state pride makes us an emancipationist; a profound sense of duty to the South makes us an abolitionist; a reasonable degree of fellow feeling for the negro, makes us a colonizationist. With the free state men in Kansas and Nebraska, we sympathize with all our heart We love the whole country, the great family of states and territories, one and inseparable, and would have the word Liberty engraved as an appropriate and truthful motto, on the escutcheon of every member of the confederacy. We love freedom, we hate slavery, and rather than give up the one or submit to the other, we will forfeit the pound of flesh nearest our heart. Is this sufficiently explicit and categorical? If not, we hold ourself in readiness at all times, to return a prompt reply to any proper question that may be put forward.

Our repugnance to the institution of slavery, springs from no one-sided idea, or sickly sentimentality. We have not been hasty in making up our mind on the subject; we have jumped at no conclusions; we have acted with perfect calmness and deliberation; we have carefully considered, and examined the reasons for and against the institution, and have also taken into account the probable consequences of our decision. The more we investigate the matter, the deeper becomes the conviction that we are right; and with this to impel and sustain us, we pursue our labor with love, with hope, and with constantly renewing vigor.

That we shall encounter opposition we consider as certain; perhaps we may even be subjected to insult and violence. From the conceited and cruel oligarchy of the South, we could look for nothing less. But we shall shrink from no responsibility, and do nothing unbecoming a man; we know how to repel indignity, and if assaulted, shall not fail to make the blow recoil upon the aggressor's head. The road we have to travel may be a rough one, but no impediment shall cause us to falter in our course. The line of our duty is clearly defined, and it is our intention to follow it faithfully, or die in the attempt.

But, we have no ominous forebodings of the result of the contest now pending between Liberty and Slavery in this confederacy. Though neither a prophet nor the son of a prophet, our vision is sufficiently penetrative to divine the future so far as to be able to see that the "peculiar institution" has but a short, and as heretofore, inglorious existence before it. Time, the righter of every wrong, is ripening events for the desired consummation of our labors and the fulfillment of our cherished hopes. Each revolving year brings nearer the inevitable crisis. The sooner it comes the better; may heaven, through our humble efforts, hasten its advent.

The first and most sacred duty of every Southerner, who has the honor and the interest of his country at heart, is to declare himself an unqualified and uncompromising abolitionist. No conditional or half-way declaration will avail; no mere threatening demonstration will succeed. With those who desire to be instrumental in bringing about the triumph of liberty over slavery, there should be neither evasion, vacillation, nor equivocation. We should listen to no modifying terms or compromises that may be proposed by the proprietors of the unprofitable and ungodly institution. Nothing short of the complete abolition of slavery can save the South from falling into the vortex of utter ruin. Too long have we yielded a submissive obedience to the tyrannical domination of an inflated oligarchy; too

long have we tolerated their arrogance and self-conceit; too long
have we submitted to their unjust and savage exactions. Let us now
wrest from them the sceptre of power, establish liberty and equal
rights throughout the land, and henceforth and forever guard our
legislative halls from the pollutions and usurpations of proslavery
demagogues.

We have stated, in a cursory manner, the reasons, as we understand them, why the North has surpassed the South, and have
endeavored to show, we think successfully, that the political salvation of the South depends upon the speedy and unconditional abolition of slavery. We will not, however, rest the case exclusively on
our own arguments, but will again appeal to incontrovertible facts
and statistics to sustain us in our conclusions. But before we do so,
we desire to fortify ourself against a charge that is too frequently
made by careless and superficial readers. We allude to the objections so often urged against the use of tabular statements and statistical facts. It is worthy of note, however, that those objections never
come from thorough scholars or profound thinkers. Among the
majority of mankind, the science of statistics is only beginning to
be appreciated; when well understood, it will be recognized as one
of the most important branches of knowledge, and, as a matter of
course, be introduced and taught as an indispensable element of
practical education in all our principal institutions of learning. One
of the most vigorous and popular transatlantic writers of the day,
Wm. C. Taylor, LL.D., of Dublin, says:

"The cultivation of statistics must be the source of all future
improvement in the science of political economy, because it is to the
table of the statistician that the economist must look for his facts;
and all speculations not founded upon facts, though they may be
admired and applauded when first propounded, will, in the end,
assuredly be forgotten. Statistical science may almost be regarded
as the creation of this age. The word statistics was invented in the
middle of the last century by a German professor (Achenwall, a
native of Elbing, Prussia. Born 1719, died 1792), to express a sum-

mary view of the physical, moral, and social conditions of States; he justly remarked, that a numerical statement of the extent, density of population, imports, exports, revenues, etc., of a country, more perfectly explained its social condition than general statements, however graphic or however accurate. When such statements began to be collected, and exhibited in a popular form, it was soon discovered that the political and economical sciences were likely to gain the position of physical sciences; that is to say, they were about to obtain records of observation, which would test the accuracy of recognized principles, and lead to the discovery of new modes of action. But the great object of this new science is to lead to the knowledge of human nature; that is, to ascertain the general course of operation of man's mental and moral faculties, and to furnish us with a correct standard of judgement, by enabling us to determine the average amount of the past as a guide to the average probabilities of the future. This science is yet in its infancy, but has already produced the most beneficial effects. The accuracy of the tables of life have rendered the calculations of rates of insurance a matter of much greater certainty than they were heretofore; the system of keeping the public accounts has been simplified and improved; and finally, the experimental sciences of medicine and political economy, have been fixed on a firmer foundation than could be anticipated in the last century. Even in private life this science is likely to prove of immense advantage, by directing attention to the collection and registration of facts, and thus preventing the formation of hasty judgments and erroneous conclusions."

The compiler, or rather the superintendent of the seventh United States census, Prof. De Bow, a gentleman of more than ordinary industry and practical learning, who, in his excellent Review, has, from time to time, displayed much commendable zeal in his efforts to develop the industrial resources of the Southern and South-western states, and who is, perhaps, the greatest statistician in the country, says:

"Statistics are far from being the barren array of figures

ingeniously and laboriously combined into columns and tables, which many persons are apt to suppose them. They constitute rather the ledger of a nation, in which, like the merchant in his books, the citizen can read, at one view, all of the results of a year or of a period of years, as compared with other periods, and deduce the profit or the loss which has been made, in morals, education, wealth or power."

Impressed with a sense of the propriety of introducing, in this as well as in the succeeding chapters of our work, a number of tabular statements exhibiting the comparative growth and prosperity of the free and slave states, we have deemed it eminently proper to adduce the testimony of these distinguished authors in support of the claims which official facts and accurate statistics lay to our consideration. And here we may remark that the statistics which we propose to offer, like those already given, have been obtained from official sources, and may, therefore, be relied on as correct. The object we have in view in making a free use of facts and figures, if not already apparent, will soon be understood. It is not so much in its moral and religious aspects that we propose to discuss the question of slavery, as in its social and political character and influences. To say nothing of the sin and the shame of slavery, we believe it is a most expensive and unprofitable institution; and if our brethren of the South will but throw aside their unfounded prejudices and preconceived opinions, and give us a fair and patient hearing, we feel confident, that we can bring them to the same conclusion. Indeed, we believe we shall be enabled — not alone by our own contributions, but with the aid of incontestable facts and arguments which we shall introduce from other sources—to convince all true-hearted, candid and intelligent Southerners, who may chance to read our book, (and we hope their name may be legion) that slavery, and nothing but slavery, has retarded the progress and prosperity of our portion of the Union; depopulated and impoverished our cities by forcing the more industrious and enterprising natives of the soil to emigrate to the free states; brought our domain under a sparse and inert population by preventing foreign immigration; made us tributary to the North, and reduced us to the humiliating condition of mere provincial subjects in fact, though not in name. We believe, moreover, that every patriotic Southerner thus convinced will feel it a duty he owes to himself, to his country, and to his God, to become a thorough, inflexible, practical abolitionist. So might it be!

Now to our figures. Few persons have an adequate idea of the important part the cardinal numbers are now playing in the cause of Liberty. They are working wonders in the South. Intelligent, business men, from the Chesapeake to the Rio Grande, are beginning to see that slavery, even in a mercenary point of view, is impolitic, because it is unprofitable. Those unique, mysterious little Arabic sentinels on the watch-towers of political economy, 1, 2, 3, 4, 5, 6, 7, 8, 9, 0, have joined forces, allied themselves to the powers of freedom, and are hemming in and combatting the institution with the most signal success. If let alone, we have no doubt the digits themselves would soon terminate the existence of slavery; but we do not mean to let them alone; they must not have all the honor of annihilating the monstrous iniquity. We want to become an auxiliary in the good work, and facilitate it. The liberation of five millions of "poor white trash" from the second degree of slavery, and of three millions of miserable kidnapped negroes from the first degree, cannot be accomplished too soon. That it was not accomplished many years ago is our misfortune. It now behooves us to take a bold and determined stand in defence of the inalienable rights of ourselves and of our fellow men, and to avenge the multiplicity of wrongs, social and political, which we have suffered at the hands of a villainous oligarchy. It is madness to delay. We cannot be too hasty in carrying out our designs. Precipitance in this matter is an utter impossibility. If today we could emancipate all the slaves in the Union, we would do it, and the country and everybody in it would be vastly better off tomorrow. Now is the time for action; let us work.

By taking a sort of inventory of the agricultural products of the free and slave States in 1850, we now propose to correct a most extraordinary and mischievous error into which the people of the South have unconsciously fallen. Agriculture, it is well known, is the sole boast of the South; and, strange to say, many pro-slavery Southerners, who, in our latitude, pass for intelligent men, are so puffed up with the idea of our importance in this respect, that they speak of the North as a sterile region, unfit for cultivation, and quite dependent on the South for the necessaries of life! We can prove that the North produces greater quantities of bread-stuffs than the South! Figures shall show the facts. Properly, the South has nothing left to boast of; the North has surpassed her in everything, and is going farther and farther ahead of her every day.

We ask the reader's careful attention to the following tables, which we have prepared at no little cost of time and trouble, and which, when duly considered in connection with the foregoing and subsequent portions of our work, will, we believe, carry conviction to the mind that the downward tendency of the South can be arrested only by the abolition of slavery.

Table No. I

Agricultural Products of the Free States — 1850

	Wheat, bushels	Oats, bushels	Indian Corn, bushels
California	17,228		12,236
Connecticut	41,762	1,258,738	1,935,043
Illinois	9,414,575	10,087,241	57,646,984
Indiana	6,214,458	5,655,014	52,964,863
Iowa	1,530,581	1,524,345	8,656,799
Maine	296,259	2,181,037	1,750,056
Massachusetts	31,211	1,165,146	2,345,490
Michigan	4,925,889	2,866,056	5,641,420
New Hampshire	185,658	973,381	1,573,670
New Jersey	1,601,190	3,378,063	8,759,704
New York	13,121,498	26,552,814	17,858,400
Ohio	14,487,351	13,472,742	59,078,695
Pennsylvania	15,367,691	21,538,156	19,835,214
Rhode Island	49	215,232	539,201
Vermont	535,955	2,307,734	2,032,396
Wisconsin	4,286,131	3,414,672	1,988,979
TOTAL	72,157,486	96,590,371	242,618,650
*Corrected**	*72,057,486*		*242,619,150*

[* for the meaning of this row, refer to the Editor's Preface]

Table No. II.

Agricultural Products of the Slave States — 1850

	Wheat, bushels	Oats, bushels	Indian Corn, bushels
Alabama	294,044	2,965,696	28,754,048
Arkansas	199,639	656,183	8,893,939
Delaware	482,511	604,518	3,145,542
Florida	1,027	66,586	1,996,809
Georgia	1,088,534	3,820,044	30,080,099
Kentucky	2,142,822	8,201,311	58,672,591
Louisiana	417	89,637	10,266,373
Maryland	4,494,680	2,242,151	10,749,858
Mississippi	137,990	1,503,288	22,446,552
Missouri	2,981,652	5,278,079	36,214,537
North Carolina	2,130,102	4,052,078	27,941,051
South Carolina	1,066,277	2,322,155	16,271,454
Tennessee	1,619,386	7,703,086	52,276,223
Texas	41,729	199,017	6,028,876
Virginia	11,212,616	10,179,144	35,254,319
TOTAL	27,904,476	49,882,979	348,992,282
Corrected	*27,893,426*		*348,992,271*

Table No. III.

Agricultural Products of the Free States — 1850

	Potatoes, (I. & S.) bushels	Rye, bushels	Barley, bushels
California	10,292		9,712
Connecticut	2,689,805	600,893	19,099
Illinois	2,672,294	83,364	110,795
Indiana	2,285,048	78,792	45,483
Iowa	282,363	19,916	25,093
Maine	3,436,040	102,916	151,731
Massachusetts	3,585,384	481,021	112,385
Michigan	2,361,074	105,871	75,249
New Hampshire	4,307,919	183,117	70,256
New Jersey	3,715,251	1,255,578	6,492
New York	15,403,997	4,148,182	3,585,059
Ohio	5,245,760	425,918	354,358
Pennsylvania	6,032,904	4,805,160	165,584
Rhode Island	651,029	26,409	18,875
Vermont	4,951,014	176,233	42,150
Wisconsin	1,402,956	81,253	209,692
TOTAL	59,033,170	12,574,623	5,002,013

Table No. IV.

Agricultural Products of the Slave States — 1850

	Potatoes, (I. & S.) bushels	Rye, bushels	Barley, bushels
Alabama	5,721,205	17,261	3,958
Arkansas	981,981	8,047	177
Delaware	305,985	8,066	56
Florida	765,054	1,152	
Georgia	7,213,807	53,750	11,501
Kentucky	2,490,666	415,073	95,343
Louisiana	1,524,085	475	
Maryland	973,932	226,014	745
Mississippi	5,003,277	9,606	228
Missouri	1,274,511	44,268	9,631
North Carolina	5,716,027	229,563	2,735
South Carolina	4,473,960	43,790	4,583
Tennessee	3,845,560	89,137	2,737
Texas	1,426,803	3,108	4,776
Virginia	3,130,567	458,930	25,437
TOTAL	44,847,420	1,608,240	161,907

Table No. V.
Agricultural Products of the Free States — 1850

	Buckwheat, bushels	Beans & Peas, bushels	Clov. & Grass seeds, bushels
California		2,292	
Connecticut	229,297	19,090	30,469
Illinois	184,509	82,814	17,807
Indiana	149,740	35,773	30,271
Iowa	52,516	4,475	2,438
Maine	104,523	205,541	18,311
Massachusetts	105,895	43,709	6,087
Michigan	472,917	74,254	26,274
New Hampshire	65,265	70,856	8,900
New Jersey	878,934	14,174	91,331
New York	3,183,955	741,546	184,715
Ohio	638,060	60,168	140,501
Pennsylvania	2,193,692	55,231	178,943
Rhode Island	1,245	6,846	5,036
Vermont	209,819	104,649	15,696
Wisconsin	79,878	20,657	5,486
TOTAL	8,550,245	1,542,295	762,265
Corrected		*1,542,075*	

Table No. VI.

Agricultural Products of the Slave States — 1850

	Buckwheat, bushels	Beans & Peas, bushels	Clov. & Grass seeds, bushels
Alabama	348	892,701	685
Arkansas	175	285,738	526
Delaware	8,615	4,120	3,928
Florida	55	135,359	2
Georgia	250	1,142,011	560
Kentucky	16,097	202,574	24,711
Louisiana	3	161,732	99
Maryland	103,671	12,816	17,778
Mississippi	1,121	1,072,757	617
Missouri	23,641	46,017	4,965
North Carolina	16,704	1,584,252	1,851
South Carolina	283	1,026,900	406
Tennessee	19,427	369,321	14,214
Texas	59	179,351	10
Virginia	214,898	521,579	53,155
TOTAL	405,357	7,637,227	123,517
Corrected	*405,347*		*123,507*

Table No. VII.
Agricultural Products of the Free States — 1850

	Flaxseed, bushels	Val. of Garden products	Val. of Orchard products
California		$75,275	$17,700
Connecticut	703	196,874	175,118
Illinois	10,787	127,494	446,049
Indiana	36,888	72,864	324,940
Iowa	1,959	8,848	8,434
Maine	580	122,387	342,865
Massachusetts	72	600,020	463,995
Michigan	519	14,738	132,650
New Hampshire	189	56,810	248,560
New Jersey	16,525	475,242	607,268
New York	57,963	912,047	1,761,950
Ohio	188,880	214,004	695,921
Pennsylvania	41,728	688,714	723,389
Rhode Island		98,298	63,994
Vermont	939	18,853	315,255
Wisconsin	1,191	32,142	4,823
TOTAL	358,923	$3,714,605	$6,332,914
Corrected		*$3,714,610*	*$6,332,911*

Table No. VIII.

Agricultural Products of the Slave States — 1850

	Flaxseed, bushels	Val. of Garden products	Val. of Orchard products
Alabama	69	$84,821	$15,408
Arkansas	321	17,150	40,141
Delaware	904	12,714	46,574
Florida		8,721	1,280
Georgia	622	76,500	92,776
Kentucky	75,801	303,120	106,230
Louisiana		148,329	22,259
Maryland	2,446	200,869	164,051
Mississippi	26	46,250	50,405
Missouri	13,696	99,454	514,711
North Carolina	38,196	39,462	34,348
South Carolina	55	47,286	35,108
Tennessee	18,904	97,183	52,894
Texas	26	12,354	12,505
Virginia	52,318	183,047	177,137
TOTAL	203,484	$1,377,260	$1,355,827
Corrected	*203,384*		*$1,365,827*

Recapitulation—Free States

Wheat	72,157,486 bush.	@	2	$108,236,229
Oats	96,590,371 bush	@	40	38,636,148
Indian Corn	242,618,650 bush.	@	60	145,571,190
Potatoes (I. & S.).	59,033,170 bush.	@	38	22,432,604
Rye	12,574,623 bush.	@	1	12,574,623
Barley	5,002,013 bush.	@	90	4,501,811
Buckwheat	8,550,245 bush.	@	50	4,275,122
Beans & Peas	1,542,295 bush.	@	2	2,699,015
Clov. & Grass seeds	762,265 bush.	@	3	2,286,795
Flax Seeds	358,923 bush.	@	1	448,647
Garden Products				3,714,605
Orchard Products				6,332,914
TOTAL	499,190,041	bushels, valued as above, at		$351,709,703

Recapitulation—Slave States

Wheat	27,904,476 bush.	@	1.5	$ 41,856,714
Oats	49,882,799 bush.	@	40	19,953,191
Indian Corn	348,992,282 bush.	@	60	209,395,369
Potatoes (I. & S.).	44,847,420 bush.	@	38	17,042,019
Rye	1,608,240 bush.	@	1	1,608,240
Barley	161,907 bush.	@	90	145,716
Buckwheat	405,357 bush.	@	50	202,678
Beans & Peas	7,637,227 bush.	@	1.75	13,365,147
Clov. & Grass seeds	123,517 bush.	@	3	370,551
Flax Seeds	203,484 bush.	@	1.25	254,355
Garden Products				1,377,260
Orchard Products				1,355,827
TOTAL	481,766,889	bushels, valued as above, at		$306,927,067

Total Difference — Bushel-measure Products

	Bushels		Value
Free States	499,190,041		$351,709,703
Slave States	481,766,889		306,927,067
Balance in bushels	17,423,152	Difference in value	$44,782,636

So much for the boasted agricultural superiority of the South! Mark well the balance in bushels, and the difference in value! Is either in favor of the South? No! Are both in favor of the North? Yes! Here we have unquestionable proof that of all the bushel-measure products of the nation, the free states produce far more than one-half; and it is worthy of particular mention, that *the excess of Northern products is of the most valuable kind.* The account shows a balance against the South, in favor of the North, of *seventeen million four hundred and twenty-three thousand one hundred and fifty-two bushels,* and a difference in value of *forty-four million seven hundred and eighty-two thousand six hundred and thirty-six dollars.* Please bear these facts in mind, for, in order to show positively how the free and slave States do stand upon the great and important subject of rural economy, we intend to take an account of all the other products of the soil, of the live-stock upon farms, of the animals slaughtered, and, in fact, of every item of husbandry of the two sections; and if, in bringing our tabular exercises to a close, we find slavery gaining upon freedom—a thing it has never yet been known to do—we shall, as a matter of course, see that the above amount is transferred to the credit of the side to which it of right belongs.

In making up these tables we have two objects in view; the first is to open the eyes of the non-slaveholders of the South, to the system of deception, that has so long been practiced upon them, and the second is to show slaveholders themselves—we have reference only to those who are not too perverse, ignorant, to perceive naked truths—that free labor is far more respectable, profitable, and productive, than slave labor. In the South, unfortunately, no kind of labor is either free or respectable. Every white man who is under the necessity of earning his bread, by the sweat of his brow, or by manual labor, in any capacity, no matter how unassuming in deportment, or exemplary in morals, is treated as if he was a loathsome beast, and shunned with the utmost disdain. His soul may be the very seat of honor and integrity, yet without slaves—himself a slave—he is accounted as nobody, and would be deemed intolerably presumptuous, if he dared to open his mouth, even so wide as to give faint utterance to a three-lettered monosyllable, like yea or nay, in the presence of an august knight of the whip and the lash.

There are few Southerners who will not be astonished at the disclosures of these statistical comparisons, between the free and the slave States. That the astonishment of the more intelligent and patriotic non-slaveholders will be mingled with indignation, is no more than we anticipate. We confess our own surprise, and deep chagrin, at the result of our investigations. Until we examined into the matter, we thought and hoped the South was really ahead of the North in *one* particular, that of agriculture; but our thoughts have been changed, and our hopes frustrated, for instead of finding ourselves the possessors of a single advantage, we behold our dear native South stripped of every laurel, and sinking deeper and deeper in the depths of poverty and shame; while, at the same time, we see the North, our successful rival, extracting and absorbing the few elements of wealth yet remaining amongst us, and rising higher and higher in the scale of fame, fortune, and invulnerable power. Thus our disappointment gives way to a feeling of intense mortification, and our soul involuntarily, but justly, we believe, cries out for retribution against the treacherous, slavedriving legislators, who have so basely and unpatriotically neglected the interests of their poor white constituents and bargained away the rights of posterity. Notwithstanding the fact that the white non-slaveholders of the South, are in the majority, as five to one, they have never yet had any part or lot in framing the laws under which they live. There is no legislation except for the benefit of slavery, and slaveholders. As a general rule, poor white persons are regarded with less esteem and attention than negroes, and though the condition of the latter is wretched beyond description, vast numbers of the former are infinitely worse off. A cunningly devised mockery of freedom is guarantied to them, and that is all. To all intents and purposes they are disfranchised, and outlawed, and the only privilege extended to them, is a shallow and circumscribed participation in the political movements that usher slaveholders into office.

We have not breathed away seven and twenty years in the South, without becoming acquainted with the demagogical manoeuverings of the oligarchy. Their intrigues and tricks of legerdemain are as familiar to us as household words; in vain might the world be ransacked for a more precious junto of flatterers and cajolers. It is amusing to ignorance, amazing to credulity, and insulting to intelligence, to hear them in their efforts to mystify and pervert the sacred principles of liberty, and turn the curse of slavery into a blessing. To the illiterate poor whites — made poor and ignorant by the system of slavery — they hold out the idea that slavery is the very bulwark of our liberties, and the foundation of American independence! For hours at a time, day after day, will they expatiate upon the inexpressible beauties and excellencies of this great, *free* and *independent* nation; and finally, with the most extravagant gesticulations and rhetorical flourishes, conclude their nonsensical ravings, by attributing all the glory and prosperity of the country, from Maine to Texas, and from Georgia to California, to the "invaluable institutions of the South!" With what patience we could command, we have frequently listened to the incoherent and truth-murdering declamations of these champions of slavery, and, in the absence of a more politic method of giving vent to our disgust and indignation, have involuntarily bit our lips into blisters.

The slave-holders are not only absolute masters of the blacks, who are bought and sold, and driven about like so many cattle, but they are also the oracles and arbiters of all non-slaveholding whites, whose freedom is merely nominal, and whose unparalleled illiteracy and degradation is purposely and fiendishly perpetuated. How little the "poor white trash," the great majority of the Southern people, know of the real condition of the country is, indeed, sadly astonishing. The truth is, they know nothing of public measures, and little of private affairs, except what their imperious masters, the slave-drivers, condescend to tell, and that is but precious little, and even that little, always garbled and one-sided, is never told except in public harangues; for the haughty cavaliers of shackles and handcuffs will not degrade themselves by holding private converse with those who have neither dimes nor hereditary rights in human flesh.

Whenever it pleases, and to the extent it pleases, a slaveholder to become communicative, poor whites may hear with fear and trembling, but not speak. They must be as mum as dumb brutes, and stand in awe of their august superiors, or be crushed with stern rebukes, cruel oppressions, or downright violence. If they dare to think for themselves, their thoughts must be forever concealed. The expression of any sentiment at all conflicting with the gospel of slavery, dooms them at once in the community in which they live, and then, whether willing or unwilling, they are obliged to become heroes, martyrs, or exiles. They may thirst for knowledge, but there is no Moses among them to smite it out of the rocks of Horeb. The black veil, through whose almost impenetrable meshes light seldom gleams, has long been pendent over their eyes, and there, with fiendish jealousy, the slave-driving ruffians sedulously guard it. Non-slaveholders are not only kept in ignorance of what is transpiring at the North, but they are continually misinformed of what is going on even in the South. Never were the poorer classes of a people, and those classes so largely in the majority, and all inhabiting the same country, so basely duped, so adroitly swindled, or so damnably outraged.

It is expected that the stupid and sequacious masses, the white victims of slavery, will believe, and, as a general thing, they do believe, whatever the slaveholders tell them; and thus it is that they are cajoled into the notion that they are the freest, happiest and most intelligent people in the world, and are taught to look with prejudice and disapprobation upon every new principle or progressive movement. Thus it is that the South, woefully inert and inventionless, has lagged behind the North, and is now weltering in the cesspool of ignorance and degradation.

We have already intimated that the opinion is prevalent throughout the South that the free States are quite sterile and unproductive, and that they are mainly dependent on us for breadstuffs and other provisions. So far as the cereals, fruits, garden vegetables and esculent roots are concerned, we have, in the preceding tables, shown the utter falsity of this opinion; and we now propose to show that it is equally erroneous in other particulars, and very far from the truth in the general reckoning. We can prove, and we intend to prove, from facts in our possession, that the hay crop of the free States is worth considerably more in dollars and cents than all the cotton, tobacco, rice, hay and hemp produced in the fifteen slave States. This statement may strike some of our readers with amazement, and others may, for the moment, regard it as quite incredible; but it is true, nevertheless, and we shall soon proceed to confirm it. The single free State of New York produces more than *three times* the quantity of hay that is produced in all the slave States. Ohio produces a larger number of tons than all the Southern and Southwestern States, and so does Pennsylvania. Vermont, little and unpretending as she is, does the same thing, with the exception of Virginia. Look at the facts as presented in the tables, and let your own eyes, physical and intellectual, confirm you in the truth.

And yet, the slave-driving oligarchy would whip us into the belief that agriculture is not one of the leading and lucrative pursuits of the free States, that the soil there is an uninterrupted barren waste, and that our Northern brethren, having the advantage in nothing except wealth, population, inland and foreign commerce, manufactures, mechanism, inventions, literature, the arts and sciences, and their concomitant branches of profitable industry, — miserable objects of charity — are dependent on us for the necessaries of life.

Next to Virginia, Maryland is the greatest Southern hay-producing State; and yet, it is the opinion of several of the most extensive hay and grain dealers in Baltimore, with whom we have conversed on the subject, that the domestic crop is scarcely equal to one-third the demand, and that the balance required for home consumption, about two-thirds, is chiefly brought from New York, Pennsylvania and Massachusetts. At this rate, Maryland receives and consumes not less than three hundred and fifteen thousand tons of Northern hay every year; and this, as we are informed by the dealers above-mentioned, at an average cost to the last purchaser, by the time it is stowed in the mow, of at least twenty-five dollars per ton; it would thus appear that this most popular and valuable provender, one of the staple commodities of the North, commands a market in a single slave State, to the amount of seven million eight hundred and seventy-five thousand dollars per annum.

In this same State of Maryland, less than one million of dollar's worth of cotton finds a market, the whole number of bales sold here in 1850 amounting to only twenty-three thousand three hundred and twenty-five, valued at seven hundred and forty-six thousand four hundred dollars. Briefly, then, and in round numbers, we may state the case thus: Maryland buys annually seven millions of dollars worth of hay from the North, and one million of dollars worth of cotton from the South. Let slaveholders and their fawning defenders read, ponder and compare.

The exact quantities of Northern hay, rye, and buck-wheat flour, Irish potatoes, fruits, clover and grass seeds, and other products of the soil, received and consumed in all the slaveholding States, we have no means of ascertaining; but for all practical purposes, we can arrive sufficiently near to the amount by inference from the above data, and from what we see with our eyes and hear with our ears wherever we go. Food from the North for man or for beast, or for both, is for sale in every market in the South. Even in the most insignificant little villages in the interior of the slave States, where books, newspapers and other mediums of intelligence are unknown, where the poor whites and the negroes are alike bowed down in heathenish ignorance and barbarism, and where the news is received but once a week, and then only in a Northern-built stage-coach, drawn by horses in Northern harness, in charge of a driver dressed head to foot in Northern clothing, and with a Northern whip in his hand, — the agricultural products of the North, either crude, prepared, pickled or preserved, are ever to be found.

Mortifying as the acknowledgment of the fact is to us, it is our unbiased opinion — an opinion which will, we believe, be endorsed by every intelligent person who goes into a careful examination and comparison of all the facts in the case — that the profits arising to the North from the sale of provender and provisions to the South, are far greater than those arising to the South from the sale of cotton, tobacco and breadstuffs to the North. It follows, then, that the agricultural interests of the North being not only equal but actually superior to those of the South, the hundreds of millions of dollars which the commerce and manufactures of the former annually yield, is just so much clear and independent gain over the letter. It follows, also, from a corresponding train or system of deduction, and with all the foregoing facts in view, that the difference between freedom and slavery is simply the difference between sense and nonsense, wisdom and folly, good and evil, right and wrong.

Any observant American, from whatever point of the compass he may hail, who will take the trouble to pass through the Southern markets, both great and small, as we have done, and inquire where this article, that and the other came from, will be utterly astonished at the variety and quantity of Northern agricultural productions kept for sale. And this state of things is growing worse and worse every year. Exclusively agricultural as the South is in her industrial pursuits, she is barely able to support her sparse and degenerate population. Her men and her domestic animals, both dwarfed into shabby objects of commiseration under the blighting effects of slavery, are constantly feeding on the multifarious products of Northern soil. And if the whole truth must be told, we may here add, that these products, like all other articles of merchandise purchased at the North, are generally bought on a credit, and, in a great number of instances, by far too many, never paid for—not, as a general rule, because the purchasers are dishonest or unwilling to pay, but because they are impoverished and depressed by the retrogressive and deadening operations of slavery, that most unprofitable and pernicious institution under which they live.

To show how well we are sustained in our remarks upon hay and other special products of the soil, as well as to give circulation to other facts of equal significance, we quote a single passage from an address by Paul C. Cameron, before the Agricultural Society of Orange County, North Carolina. This production is, in the main, so powerfully conceived, so correct and plausible in its statements and conclusions, and so well calculated, though, perhaps, not intended, to arouse the old North State to a sense of her natural greatness and acquired shame, that we could wish to see it published in pamphlet form, and circulated throughout the length and breadth of that unfortunate and degraded heritage of slavery. Mr. Cameron says:

"I know not when I have been more humiliated, as a North Carolina farmer, than when, a few weeks ago, at a railroad depot at the very doors of our State capital, I saw wagons drawn by Kentucky mules, loading with Northern hay, for the supply not only of the town, but to be taken to the country. Such a sight at the capital of a State whose population is almost exclusively devoted to agriculture, is a most humiliating exhibition. Let us cease to use every thing, as far as it is practicable, that is not the product of our own soil and workshops—not an axe, or a broom, or bucket, from Connecticut. By every consideration of self-preservation, we are called to make better efforts to expel the Northern grocer from the State with his butter, and the Ohio and Kentucky horse, mule and hog driver, from our county at least. It is a reproach on us as farmers, and no little deduction from our wealth, that we suffer the population of our towns and villages to supply themselves with butter from another Orange County in New York."

We have promised to prove that the hay crop of the free states is worth considerably more than all the cotton, tobacco, rice, hay and hemp produced in the fifteen slave States. The compilers of the last census, as we learn from Prof. De Bow, the able and courteous superintendent, in making up the hay-tables, allowed two thousand two hundred and forty pounds to the ton. The price per ton at which we should estimate its value has puzzled us to some extent. Dealers in the article in Baltimore think it will average twenty-five dollars, in their market. Four or five months ago they sold it at thirty dollars per ton. At the very time we write, though there is less activity in the article than usual, we learn, from an examination of sundry prices-current and commercial journals, that hay is selling in Savannah at $33 per ton; in Mobile and New Orleans at $26; in Charleston at $25; in Louisville at $24; and in Cincinnati at $23. The average of these prices is *twenty-six dollars sixteen and two-third cents;* and we suppose it would be fair to employ the figures which would indicate this amount, the net value of a single ton, in calculating the total market value of the entire crop. Were we to do this—and, with the foregoing facts in view, we submit to intelligent men whether we would not be justifiable in doing it,—the hay crop of the free states, 12,690,982 tons, in 1850, would amount in valuation to the enormous sum of $331,081,695—more than four times the value of all the cotton produced in the United States during the same period!

But we shall not make the calculation at what we have found to be the average value per ton throughout the country. What rate, then, shall be agreed upon as a basis of comparison between the value of the hay crop of the North and that of the South, and as a means of testing the truth of our declaration — that the former exceeds the aggregate value of all the cotton, tobacco, rice, hay and hemp produced in the fifteen slave States? Suppose we take $13.08 1/3—just half the average value—as the multiplier in this arithmetical exercise. This we can well afford to do; indeed, we might reduce the amount per ton to much less than half the average value, and still have a large margin left for triumphant demonstration. It is not our purpose, however, to make an overwhelming display of the incomparable greatness of the free States.

In estimating the value of the various agricultural products of the two great sections of the country, we have been guided by prices emanating from the Bureau of Agriculture in Washington; and in a catalogue of those prices now before us, we perceive that the average value of hay throughout the nation is supposed to be not more than half a cent per pound—$11.20 per ton—which, as we have seen above, is considerably less than half the present market value;—and this, too, in the face of the fact that prices generally rule higher than they do just now. It will be admitted on all sides, however, that the prices fixed upon by the Bureau of Agriculture, taken as a whole, are as fair for one section of the country as for the other, and that we cannot blamelessly deviate from them in one particular without deviating from them in another. Eleven dollars and twenty cents ($11.20) per ton shall therefore be the price; and, notwithstanding these greatly reduced figures, we now renew, with an addendum, our declaration and promise, that—*We can prove, and we shall now proceed to prove, that the annual hay crop of the free States is worth considerably more in dollars and cents than all the cotton, tobacco, rice, hay, hemp and cane sugar annually produced in the fifteen slave States.*

Hay Crop of the Free States—1850
12,690,982 tons @ $11.20 $142,138,998

Sundry Products of the Slave States—1850

Cotton	2445779 bales	@	3200	$78,264,928
Tobacco	185023906 lbs.	@	10	18,502,390
Rice (rough)	215313497 lbs.	@	4	8,612,539
Hay	1137784 tons	@	1120	12,743,180

Hemp	34673 tons	@	11200	3,883,376
Cane Sugar	237133000 lbs.	@	7	16,599,310
TOTAL				$138,605,723

Recapitulation:

Hay crop of the free States	$142,138,998
Sundry products of the slave States	$138,605,723
Balance in favor of the free States	$3,533,275

There is the account; look at it, and let it stand in attestation of the exalted virtues and surpassing powers of freedom. Scan it well, lords of the lash, and learn from it new lessons of the utter inefficiency, and despicable imbecility of slavery. Examine it minutely, liberty loving patriots of the North, and behold in it additional evidences of the beauty, grandeur, and super-excellence of free institutions. Treasure it up in your minds, outraged friends and non-slaveholders of the South, and let the recollection of it arouse you to an inflexible determination to extirpate the monstrous enemy that stalks abroad in your land, and to recover the inalienable rights and liberties, which have been filched from you by an unprincipled oligarchy.

In deference to truth, decency and good sense, it is to be hoped that negro-driving politicians will never more have the effrontery to open their mouths in extolling the agricultural achievements of slave labor. Especially is it desirable, that, as a simple act of justice to a basely deceived populace, they may cease their stale and senseless harangues on the importance of cotton. The value of cotton to the South, to the North, to the nation, and to the world, has been so grossly exaggerated, and so extensive have been the evils which have resulted in consequence of the extraordinary misrepresentations concerning it, that we should feel constrained to reproach ourself for remissness of duty, if we failed to make an attempt to explode the popular error. The figures above show what it is, and what it is not. Recur to them, and learn the facts.

So hyperbolically has the importance of cotton been magnified by certain pro-slavery politicians of the South, that the person who would give credence to all their pretentious banality and bombast, would be under the necessity of believing that the very existence of almost everything, in the heaven above, in the earth beneath, and in the water under the earth, depended on it. The truth is, however, that the cotton crop is of but little value to the South. New England and Old England, by their superior enterprise and sagacity, turn it chiefly to their own advantage. It is carried in their ships, spun in their factories, woven in their looms, insured in their offices, returned again in their own vessels, and, with double freight and cost of manufacturing added, purchased by the South at a high premium. Of all the parties engaged or interested in its transportation and manufacture, the South is the only one that does not make a profit. Nor does she, as a general thing, make a profit by producing it.

We are credibly informed that many of the farmers in the immediate vicinity of Baltimore, where we now write, have turned their attention exclusively to hay, and that from one acre they frequently gather two tons, for which they receive fifty dollars. Let us now inquire how many dollars may be expected from an acre planted in cotton. Mr. Cameron, from whose able address before the Agricultural Society of Orange County, North Carolina, we have already gleaned some interesting particulars, informs us, that the cotton planters in his part of the country, "have contented themselves with a crop yielding only *ten or twelve dollars per acre*," and that "the summing up of a large surface gives but a living result." An intelligent resident of the Palmetto State, writing in De Bows Review, not long since, advances the opinion that the cotton planters of South Carolina are not realizing more than one per cent on the amount of capital they have invested. While in Virginia, very recently, an elderly slaveholder, whose religious walk and conversation had recommended and promoted him to an eldership in the Presbyterian church, and who supports himself and family by raising blacks and tobacco, told us that, for the last eight or ten years, aside from the increase of his human chattels, he felt quite confident he had not cleared as much even as one per cent. per annum on the amount of his investment. The real and personal property of this aged *Christian* consists chiefly in a large tract of land and about thirty negroes, most of whom, according to his own confession, are more expensive than profitable. The proceeds arising from the sale of the tobacco they produce, are all absorbed in the purchase of meat and bread for home consumption, and when the crop is stunted by drought, frost, or otherwise cut short, one of the negroes must be sold to raise funds for the support of the others. Such are the agricultural achievements of slave labor; such are the results of "the sum of all villainies." The diabolical institution subsists on its own flesh. At one time children are sold to procure food for the parents, at another, parents are sold to procure food for the children. Within its pestilential atmosphere, nothing succeeds; progress and prosperity are unknown; inanition and slothfulness ensue; everything becomes dull, dismal and unprofitable; wretchedness and desolation run riot throughout the land; an aspect of most melancholy inactivity and dilapidation broods over every city and town; ignorance and prejudice sit enthroned over the minds of the people; usurping despots wield the sceptre of power; everywhere, and in everything, between Delaware Bay and the Gulf of Mexico, are the multitudinous evils of slavery apparent.

The soil itself soon sickens and dies beneath the unnatural tread of the slave. Hear what the Hon. C. C. Clay, of Alabama, has to say upon the subject. His testimony is eminently suggestive, well-timed, and truthful; and we heartily commend it to the careful consideration of every spirited Southerner who loves his country, and desires to see it rescued from the fatal grasp of "the mother of harlots:" Says he:

"I can show you, with sorrow, in the older portions of Alabama, and in my native county of Madison, the sad memorials of the artless and exhausting culture of cotton. Our small planters, after taking the cream off their lands, unable to restore them by rest, manures, or otherwise, are going further West and South, in search of other virgin lands, which they may and will despoil and impoverish in like manner. Our wealthier planters, with greater means and no more skill, are buying out their poorer neighbors, extending their plantations, and adding to their slave force. The wealthy few, who are able to live on smaller profits, and to give their blasted fields some rest, are thus pushing off the many who are merely independent. Of the $20,000,000 annually realized from the sales of the cotton crop of Alabama, nearly all not expended in supporting the producers, is re-invested in land and negroes. Thus the white population has decreased and the slave increased almost *pari passu* in several counties of our State. In 1825, Madison county cast about 3,000 votes; now, she cannot cast exceeding 2,300. In traversing that county, one will discover numerous farm-houses, once the abode of industrious and intelligent freemen, now occupied by slaves, or tenantless, deserted and dilapidated; he will observe fields, once fertile, now unfenced, abandoned, and covered with those evil harbingers, fox-tail and broomsedge; he will see the moss growing on the mouldering walls of once thrifty villages, and will find 'one only master grasps the whole domain,' that once furnished happy homes for a dozen white families. Indeed, a country in its infancy, where fifty years ago scarce a forest tree had been felled by the axe of the pioneer, is already exhibiting the painful signs of senility and decay, apparent in Virginia and the Carolinas."

Some one has said that "an honest confession is good for the soul," and if the adage be true, as we have no doubt it is, we think Mr. C. C. Clay is entitled to a quiet conscience on one score at least. In the extract quoted above, he gives us a graphic description of the ruinous operations and influences of slavery in the Southwest; and we, as a native of Carolina, and a traveler through Virginia, are ready to bear testimony to the fitness of his remarks when he referred to those States as examples of senility and decay. With equal propriety, however, he might have stopped nearer home for a subject of comparison. Either of the States bordering upon Alabama, or, indeed, any other slave States, would have answered his purpose quite as well as Virginia and the Carolinas. Wherever slavery exists there he may find parallels to the destruction that is sweeping with such deadly influence over his own unfortunate State.

As for examples of vigorous, industrious and thrifty communities, they can be found anywhere beyond the poisonous shadow of slavery — nowhere else. New York and Massachusetts, which, by nature, are confessedly far inferior to Virginia and the Carolinas, have, by the more liberal and equitable policy which they have pursued, in substituting liberty for slavery, attained a degree of eminence and prosperity altogether unknown in the slave States.

Amidst all the hyperbole and cajolery of slave-driving politicians who as we have already seen, are the books, the arts, the academies, that show, contain, and govern all the South, we are rejoiced to see that Mr. Clay, Mr. Cameron, and a few others, have had the boldness and honesty to step forward and proclaim the truth. All such frank admissions are to be hailed as good omens for the South. Nothing good can come from any attempt to conceal the unconcealable evidences of poverty and desolation everywhere trailing in the wake of slavery. Let the truth be told on all occasions, of the North as well as of the South, and the people will soon begin to discover the egregiousness of their errors, to draw just comparisons, to inquire into cause and effect, and to adopt the more until measures, manners and customs of their wiser contemporaries.

In wilfully traducing and decrying everything North of Mason and Dixon's line, and in excessively magnifying the importance of everything South of it, the oligarchy have, in the eyes of all liberal and intelligent men, only made an exhibition of their uncommon folly and dishonesty. For a long time, it is true, they have succeeded in deceiving the people, in keeping them humbled in the murky sloughs of poverty and ignorance, and in instilling into their untutored minds passions and prejudices expressly calculated to strengthen and protect the accursed institution of slavery; but, thanks to heaven, their inglorious reign is fast drawing to a close; with irresistible brilliancy, and in spite of the interdict of tyrants, light from the pure fountain of knowledge is now streaming over the dark places of our land, and, before long—mark our words—there will ascend from Delaware, and from Texas, and from all the intermediate States, a cheer for Freedom and for Equal Rights, that will utterly confound the friends of despotism, set at defiance the authority of usurpers, and carry consternation to the heart of every slavery-propagandist.

To undeceive the people of the South, to bring them to a knowledge of the inferior and disreputable position which they occupy as a component part of the Union, and to give prominence and popularity to those plans which, if adopted, will elevate us to an equality, socially, morally, intellectually, industrially, politically, and financially, with the most flourishing and refined nation in the world, and, if possible, to place us in the van of even that, is the object of this work. Slaveholders, either from ignorance or from a wilful disposition to propagate error, contend that the South has nothing to be ashamed of, that slavery has proved a blessing to her, and that her superiority over the North in an agricultural point of view makes amends for all her short-comings in other respects. On the other hand, we contend that many years of continual blushing and severe penance would not suffice to cancel or annul the shame and disgrace that justly attaches to the South in consequence of slavery —the direst evil that ever befell the land—that the South bears nothing like even a respectable approximation to the North in navigation, commerce, or manufactures, and that, contrary to the opinion entertained by ninety-nine hundredths of her people, she is far behind the free States in the only thing of which she has ever dared to boast—agriculture. We submit the question to the arbitration of figures, which, it is said, do not lie. With regard to the bushel-measure products of the soil, of which we have already taken an inventory, we have seen that there is a balance against the South in favor of the North of *seventeen million four hundred and twenty-three thousand one hundred and fifty-two bushels,* and a difference in the value of the same, also in favor of the North, of *forty-four million seven hundred and eighty-two thousand six hundred and thirty-six dollars.* It is certainly a most novel kind of agricultural superiority that the South claims on that score!

Our attention shall now be directed to the twelve principal pound-measure products of the free and of the slave States—hay, cotton, butter and cheese, tobacco, cane, sugar, wool, rice, hemp, maple sugar, beeswax and honey, flax, and hops—and in taking an account of them, we shall, in order to show the exact quantity produced in each State, and for the convenience of future reference, pursue the same plan as that adopted in the preceding tables. Whether slavery will appear to better advantage on the scales than it did in the half-bushel, remains to be seen. It is possible that the rickety monster may make a better show on a new track; if it makes a more ridiculous display, we shall not be surprised. A careful examination of its precedents, has taught us the folly of expecting anything good to issue from it in any manner whatever. It has no disposition to emulate the magnanimity of its betters, and as for a laudable ambition to excel, that is a characteristic altogether foreign to its nature. Languor and inertia are the insalutary viands upon which it delights to satiate its morbid appetite; and "from bad to worse" is the ill-omened motto under which, in all its feeble efforts and achievements, it ekes out a most miserable and deleterious existence.

Table No. IX.
Agricultural Products of the Free States — 1850

	Hay, tons	Hemp, tons	Hops, lbs.
California	2,038		
Connecticut	516,131		554
Illinois	601,952		3,551
Indiana	403,230		92,796
Iowa	89,055		8,242
Maine	755,889		40,120
Massachusetts	651,807		121,595
Michigan	404,934		10,663
New Hampshire	598,854		257,174
New Jersey	435,950		2,133
New York	3,728,797	4	2,536,299
Ohio	1,443,142	150	63,731
Pennsylvania	1,842,970	44	22,088
Rhode Island	74,418		277
Vermont	866,153		288,023
Wisconsin	275,662		15,930
TOTAL	12,690,982	198	3,463,176

Table No. X.

Agricultural Products of the Slave States—1850

	Hay, tons	Hemp, tons	Hops, lbs.
Alabama	32,685		276
Arkansas	3,976	15	157
Delaware	30,159		348
Florida	2,510		14
Georgia	23,449		261
Kentucky	113,747	17,787	4,309
Louisiana	25,752		125
Maryland	157,956	63	1,870
Mississippi	12,504	7	473
Missouri	116,925	16,028	4,130
North Carolina	145,653	39	9,246
South Carolina	20,925		26
Tennessee	74,091	595	1,032
Texas	8,354		7
Virginia	369,098	139	11,506
TOTAL	1,137,784	34,673	33,780

Table No. XI.
Agricultural Products of the Free States—1850

	Flax, lbs	Maple Sugar, lbs	Tobacco, lbs
California			1,000
Connecticut	17,928	50,796	1,267,624
Illinois	160,063	248,904	841,394
Indiana	584,469	2,921,192	1,044,620
Iowa	62,660	78,407	6,041
Maine	17,081	93,542	
Massachusetts	1,162	795,525	138,246
Michigan	7,152	2,439,794	1,245
New Hampshire	7,652	1,298,863	50
New Jersey	182,965	2,197	310
New York	940,577	10,357,484	83,189
Ohio	446,932	4,588,209	10,454,449
Pennsylvania	530,307	2,326,525	912,651
Rhode Island	85	28	
Vermont	20,852	6,349,357	
Wisconsin	68,393	610,976	1,268
TOTAL	3,048,278	32,161,799	14,752,087

Table No. XII.

Agricultural Products of the Slave States — 1850

	Flax, lbs	Maple Sugar, lbs	Tobacco, lbs
Alabama	3,921	643	164,990
Arkansas	12,291	9,330	218,936
Delaware	17,174		
Florida	50		998,614
Georgia	5,387	50	423,924
Kentucky	2,100,116	437,405	55,501,196
Louisiana		255	26,878
Maryland	35,686	47,740	21,407,497
Mississippi	665		49,960
Missouri	627,160	178,910	17,113,784
North Carolina	593,796	27,932	11,984,786
South Carolina	333	200	74,285
Tennessee	368,131	158,557	20,148,932
Texas	1,048		66,897
Virginia	1,000,450	1,227,665	56,803,227
TOTAL	4,768,198	2,088,687	185,023,906
Corrected	*4,766,208*		*184,983,906*

Table No. XIII.
Animal Products of the Free States — 1850

	Wool, lbs	Butter and Cheese, lbs	Beeswax and Honey, lbs
California	5,520	855	
Connecticut	497,454	11,861,396	93,304
Illinois	2,150,113	13,804,768	869,444
Indiana	2,610,287	13,506,099	935,329
Iowa	373,898	2,381,028	321,711
Maine	1,364,034	11,678,265	189,618
Massachusetts	585,136	15,159,512	59,508
Michigan	2,043,283	8,077,390	359,232
New Hampshire	1,108,476	10,173,619	117,140
New Jersey	375,396	9,852,966	156,694
New York	10,071,301	129,507,507	1,755,830
Ohio	10,196,371	55,268,921	804,275
Pennsylvania	4,481,570	42,383,452	839,509
Rhode Island	129,692	1,312,178	6,347
Vermont	3,400,717	20,858,814	249,422
Wisconsin	253,963	4,034,033	131,005
TOTAL	39,617,211	349,860,783	6,888,368
Corrected	*39,647,211*	*349,860,803*	

Table No. XIV.

Animal Products of the Slave States — 1850

	Wool, lbs	Butter and Cheese, lbs	Beeswax and Honey, lbs
Alabama	657,118	4,040,223	897,021
Arkansas	182,595	1,884,327	192,338
Delaware	57,768	1,058,495	41,248
Florida	23,247	389,513	18,971
Georgia	990,019	4,687,535	732,514
Kentucky	2,297,433	10,161,477	1,158,019
Louisiana	109,897	685,026	96,701
Maryland	477,438	3,810,135	74,802
Mississippi	559,619	4,367,425	397,460
Missouri	1,627,164	8,037,931	1,328,972
North Carolina	970,738	4,242,211	512,289
South Carolina	487,233	2,986,820	216,281
Tennessee	1,364,378	8,317,266	1,036,572
Texas	131,917	2,440,199	380,825
Virginia	2,860,765	11,525,651	880,767
TOTAL	12,797,329	68,634,224	7,964,760

Table No. XV.
Agricultural Products of the Slave States — 1850

	Cotton, bales of 400 lbs	Cane Sugar, hhds. 1000 lbs	Rough Rice, lbs
Alabama	564,429	87	2,312,252
Arkansas	65,344		63,179
Delaware			
Florida	45,131	2,750	1,075,090
Georgia	499,091	846	38,950,691
Kentucky	758	10	5,688
Louisiana	178,737	226,001	4,425,349
Maryland			
Mississippi	484,292	8	2,719,856
Missouri			700
North Carolina	50,545		5,465,868
South Carolina	300,901	77	159,930,613
Tennessee	194,532	3	258,854
Texas	58,072	7,351	88,203
Virginia	3,947		17,154
TOTAL	2,445,779	237,133	215,313,497

Recapitulation—Free States

Hay	28,427,799,680	lbs. @	1-2 c.	$142,138,998
Hemp	443,520	lbs. @	5 c.	22,176
Hops	3,463,176	lbs. @	15 c.	519,476
Flax	3,048,278	lbs. @	10 c.	304,827
Maple Sugar	32,161,799	lbs. @	8 c.	2,572,943
Tobacco	14,752,087	lbs. @	10 c.	1,475,208
Wool	39,647,211	lbs. @	35 c.	13,876,523
Butter and Cheese	349,860,783	lbs. @	15 c.	52,479,117
Beeswax and Honey	6,888,368	lbs. @	15 c.	1,033,255
TOTAL	28,878,064,902	lbs., valued at		$214,422,523

Recapitulation—Slave States

Hay	2,548,636,160	lbs. @	2 c.	$12,743,180
Hemp	77,667,520	lbs. @	5 c.	3,883,376
Hops	33,780	lbs. @	15 c.	5,067
Flax	4,766,198	lbs. @	10 c.	476,619
Maple Sugar	2,088,687	lbs. @	8 c.	167,094
Tobacco	185,023,906	lbs. @	10 c.	18,502,390
Wool	12,797,329	lbs. @	35 c.	4,479,065
Butter and Cheese	68,634,224	lbs. @	15 c.	10,295,133
Beeswax and Honey	7,964,760	lbs. @	15 c.	1,194,714
Cotton	978,311,600	lbs. @	8 c.	78,264,928
Cane Sugar	237,133,000	lbs. @	7 c.	16,599,310
Rice (rough)	215,313,497	lbs. @	4 c.	8,612,539
TOTAL	4,338,370,661	lbs. valued at		$155,223,415

Total Difference — pound-measure Products

	Pounds	Value
Free States	28,878,064,902	$214,422,523
Slave States	4,338,370,661	155,223,415
	Balance in pounds:	Difference in value:
	24,539,694,241	$59,199,108

Both quantity and value again in favor of the North! See also the enormousness of the difference! In this comparison with the South, neither hundreds, thousands, nor millions, according to the regular method of computation, are sufficient to exhibit the excess of the pound-measure products of the North. Recourse must be had to an almost inconceivable number: billions must be called into play; and there are the figures telling us, with unmistakable emphasis and distinctness, that, in this department of agriculture, as in every other, the North is vastly the superior of the South — the figures showing a total balance in favor of the former of *twenty-four billion five hundred and thirty-nine million six hundred and ninety-four thousand two hundred and forty-one pounds,* valued at *fifty-nine million one hundred and ninety-nine thousand one hundred and eight dollars.* And yet, the North is a poor, God-forsaken country, bleak, inhospitable, and unproductive!

What next? Is it necessary to adduce other facts in order to prove that the rural wealth of the free States is far greater than that of the slave States? Shall we make a further demonstration of the fertility of northern soil, or bring forward new evidences of the inefficient and desolating system of terra-culture in the South? Will nothing less than "confirmations strong as proofs of holy writ," suffice to convince the South that she is standing in her own light, and ruining both body and soul by the retention of slavery? Whatever duty and expedience require to be done, we are willing to do. Additional

proofs are at hand. Slaveholders and slave-breeders shall be convinced, confuted, convicted, and converted. They shall, in their
hearts and consciences, if not with their tongues and pens, bear
testimony to the triumphant achievements of free labor. In the two
tables which immediately follow these remarks, they shall see how
much more vigorous and fruitful the soil is when under the prudent
management of free white husbandmen, than it is when under the
rude and nature-murdering tillage of enslaved negroes; and in two
subsequent tables they shall find that the live stock, slaughtered
animals, farms, and farming implements and machinery, in the free
States, are worth at least *one thousand million of dollars* more than
the market value of the same in the slave States! In the face, however, of all these most significant and incontrovertible facts, the
oligarchy have the unparalleled audacity to tell us that the South
is the greatest agricultural country in the world, and that the North
is a dreary waste, unfit for cultivation, and quite dependent on us
for the necessaries of life. How preposterously false all such babble
is, the following tables will show:

Table No. XVI.

Actual Crops per Acre on the Average in the Free States — 1850

	Wheat, bushels.	Oats, bushels.	Rye. bushels.	Ind. Corn, bushels	Irish Potatoes, bushels
Connecticut		21		40	85
Illinois	11	29	14	33	115
Indiana	12	20	18	33	100
Iowa	14	36		32	100
Maine	10			27	120
Massachusetts	16	26	13	31	170
Michigan	10	26		32	140
New Hampshire	11	30		30	220
New Jersey	11	26		33	
New York	12	25	17	27	100
Ohio	12	21	25	36	
Pennsylvania	15			20	75
Rhode Island		30			100
Vermont	13		20	32	178
Wisconsin	14	35		30	
TOTAL	161	325	107	436	1,503

Table No. XVII.

Actual Crops per Acre on the Average in the Slave States — 1850

	Wheat, bushels	Oats, bushels	Rye, bushels	Ind. Corn, bushels	Irish Potatoes, bushels
Alabama	5	12		15	60
Arkansas		18		22	
Delaware	11	20		20	
Florida	15				175
Georgia	5	18	7	16	125
Kentucky	8	18	11	24	130
Louisiana				16	
Maryland	13	21	18	23	75
Mississippi	9	12		18	105
Missouri	11	26		34	110
North Carolina	7	10	15	17	65
South Carolina	8	12		11	70
Tennessee	7	19	7	21	120
Texas	15			20	250
Virginia	7	13	5	18	75
TOTAL	121	199	63	275	1,360

Recapitulation of Actual Crops per Acre on the Average — 1850

Free States

Wheat	12	bushels per acre
Oats	27	bushels per acre
Rye	18	bushels per acre
Indian Corn	31	bushels per acre
Irish Potatoes	125	bushels per acre

Slave States

Wheat	9	bushels per acre
Oats	17	bushels per acre
Rye	11	bushels per acre
Indian Corn	20	bushels per acre
Irish Potatoes	113	bushels per acre

What an obvious contrast between the vigor of Liberty and the impotence of Slavery! What an unanswerable argument in favor of free labor! Add up the two columns of figures above, and what is the result? Two hundred and thirteen bushels as the products of five acres in the North, and only one hundred and seventy bushels as the products of five acres in the South. Look at each item separately, and you will find that the average crop per acre of every article enumerated is greater in the free States than it is in the slave States. Examine the table at large, and you will perceive that while Massachusetts produces sixteen bushels of wheat to the acre, Virginia produces only seven; that Pennsylvania produces fifteen and Georgia only five: that while Iowa produces thirty-six bushels of oats to the acre, Mississippi produces only twelve; that Rhode Island produces thirty, and North Carolina only ten: that while Ohio produces twenty-five bushels of rye to the acre, Kentucky produces only eleven; that Vermont produces twenty, and Tennessee only seven: that while Connecticut produces forty bushels of Indian corn to the acre, Texas produces only twenty; that New Jersey produces thirty-three, and South Carolina only eleven: that while New Hampshire produces two hundred and twenty bushels of Irish potatoes to the acre, Maryland produces only seventy-five; that Michigan produces one hundred and forty, and Alabama only sixty. Now for other beauties of slavery in another table.

Table No. XVIII.

Value of Farms and Domestic Animals in the Free States—1850

	Value of Live Stock	Val. of Animals Slaughtered	Cash Val. of Farms, Farm. Imp. & Mac.
California	$3,351,058	$107,173	$3,977,524
Connecticut	7,467,490	2,202,266	74,618,963
Illinois	24,209,258	4,972,286	102,538,851
Indiana	22,478,555	6,567,935	143,089,617
Iowa	3,689,275	821,164	17,830,436
Maine	9,705,726	1,646,773	57,146,305
Massachusetts	9,647,710	2,500,924	112,285,931
Michigan	8,008,734	1,328,327	54,763,817
New Hampshire	8,871,901	1,522,873	57,560,122
New Jersey	10,679,291	2,638,552	124,663,014
New York	73,570,499	13,573,883	576,631,568
Ohio	44,121,741	7,439,243	371,509,188
Pennsylvania	41,500,053	8,219,848	422,598,640
Rhode Island	1,532,637	667,486	17,568,003
Vermont	12,643,228	1,861,336	66,106,509
Wisconsin	4,897,385	920,178	30,170,131
TOTAL	$286,376,541	$56,990,237	$2,233,058,619

Table No. XIX.

Value of Farms and Domestic Animals in the Slave States — 1850

	Value of Live Stock	Val. of Animals Slaughtered	Cash Val. of Farms, Farm. Imp. & Mac.
Alabama	$21,690,112	$4,823,485	$69,448,887
Arkansas	6,647,969	1,163,313	16,866,541
Delaware	1,849,281	373,665	19,390,310
Florida	2,880,058	514,685	6,981,904
Georgia	25,728,416	6,339,762	101,647,595
Kentucky	29,661,436	6,462,598	160,190,299
Louisiana	11,152,275	1,458,990	87,391,336
Maryland	7,997,634	1,954,800	89,641,988
Mississippi	19,403,662	3,636,582	60,501,561
Missouri	19,887,580	3,367,106	67,207,068
North Carolina	17,717,647	5,767,866	71,823,298
South Carolina	15,060,015	3,502,637	86,568,038
Tennessee	29,978,016	6,401,765	103,211,422
Texas	10,412,927	1,116,137	18,701,712
Virginia	33,656,659	7,502,986	223,423,315
TOTAL	$253,723,687	$54,388,377	$1,183,995,274
Corrected		*$54,386,377*	*$1,182,995,274*

Recapitulation—Free States

Value of Live Stock	$286,376,541
Value of Animals slaughtered,	56,990,237
Value of Farms, Farming-Implements and Machinery	2,233,058,619
	$2,576,425,397

Recapitulation—Slave States

Value of Live Stock	$253,723,687
Value of Animals slaughtered	54,388,377
Value of Farms, Farming Implements and Machinery	1,183,995,274
	$1,492,107,338

Difference in Value—Farms and Domestic Animals

Free States	$2,576,425,397
Slave States	1,492,107,338
Balance in favor of the Free States	$1,084,318,059

By adding to this last balance in favor of the free States the differences in value which we found in their favor in our account of the bushel-and-pound-measure products, we shall have a very correct idea of the extent to which the undivided agricultural interests of the free States preponderate over those of the slave States. Let us add the differences, and see the balances all in favor of the North.

Difference in the value of bushel-measure products	$44,782,636
Difference in the value of pound-measure products	59,199,108
Difference in the value of farms and domestic animals	1,084,318,059
TOTAL	$1,188,299,803

No figures of rhetoric can add emphasis or significance to these figures of arithmetic. They demonstrate conclusively the great moral triumph of Liberty over Slavery. They show unequivocally, in spite of all the boasting of slave-driving politicians, that the entire value of all the agricultural interests of the free States is very nearly twice as great as the entire value of all the agricultural interests of the slave States — the value of those interests in the former being twenty-five hundred million of dollars, that of those in the latter only fourteen hundred million, leaving a balance in favor of the free States of *one billion one hundred and eighty-eight million two hundred and ninety-nine thousand eight hundred and three dollars!* That is what we call a full, fair and complete vindication of Free Labor. Would we not be correct in calling it a total eclipse of the Black Orb? Can it be possible that the slavocracy will ever have the hardihood to open their mouths again on the subject of terra-culture in the South? Dare they ever think of cotton again? Ought they not, as a befitting confession of their crimes and misdemeanors, and as a reasonable expiation for the countless evils which they have inflicted on society, to clothe themselves in sackcloth, and, after a suitable season of contrition and severe penance, follow the example of one Judas Iscariot, and go and hang themselves?

It will be observed that we have omitted the Territories and the District of Columbia in all the preceding tables. We did this purposely. Our object was to draw an equitable comparison between the value of free and slave labor in the thirty-one sovereign States, where the two systems, comparatively unaffected by the wrangling of politicians, and, as a matter of course, free from the interference of the general government, have had the fullest opportunities to exert their influence, to exhibit their virtues, and to commend themselves to the sober judgments of enlightened and discriminating minds. Had we counted the Territories on the side of the North, and the District of Columbia on the side of the South, the result would have been still greater in behalf of free labor. Though "the sum of all villanies" has but a mere nominal existence in Delaware and

Maryland, we have invariably counted those States on the side of the South; and the consequence is, that, in many particulars, the hopeless fortunes of slavery have been propped up and sustained by an imposing array of figures which of right ought to be regarded as the property of freedom. But we like to be generous to an unfortunate foe, and would utterly disdain the use of any unfair means of attack or defence.

We shall take no undue advantage of slavery. It shall have a fair trial, and be judged according to its deserts. Already has it been weighed in the balance, and found wanting; it has been measured in the half-bushel, and found wanting; it has been apprized in the field, and found wanting. Whatever redeeming traits or qualities it may possess, if any, shall be brought to light by subjecting it to other tests.

It was our desire and intention to furnish a correct table of the gallon-measure products of the several States of the Union; but we have not been successful in our attempt to procure the necessary statistics. Enough is known, however, to satisfy us that the value of the milk, wine, ardent spirits, malt liquors, fluids, oils, and molasses, annually produced and sold in the free States, is at east fifty millions of dollars greater than the value of the same articles annually produced and sold in the slave States. Of sweet milk alone, it is estimated that the monthly sales in three Northern cities, New York, Philadelphia and Boston, amount to a larger sum than the marketable value of all the rosin, tar, pitch, and turpentine, annually produced in the Southern States.

Our efforts to obtain reliable information respecting another very important branch of profitable industry, the lumber business, have also proved unavailing; and we are left to conjecture as to the amount of revenue annually derived from it in the two grand divisions of our country. The person whose curiosity prompts him to take an account of the immense piles of Northern lumber now lying on the wharves and houseless lots in Baltimore, Richmond, and other slaveholding cities, will not, we imagine, form a very flattering opinion of the products of Southern forests. Let it be remembered that nearly all the clippers, steamers, and small craft, are built at the North; that large cargoes of Eastern lumber are exported to foreign countries; that nine-tenths of the wooden-ware used in the Southern States is manufactured in New England; that, in outrageous disregard of the natural rights and claims of Southern mechanics, the markets of the South are forever filled with Northern furniture, vehicles, ax helves, walking canes, yard-sticks, clothespins and pen-holders; that the extraordinary number of factories, steam-engines, forges and machine-shops in the free States, require an extraordinary quantity of cord-wood; that a large majority of the magnificent edifices and other structures, both private and public, in which timber, in its various forms, is extensively used, are to be found in the free States — we say, let all these things be remembered, and the truth will at once flash across the mind that the forests of the North are a source of far greater income than those of the South. The difference is simply this: At the North everything is turned to advantage. When a tree is cut down, the main body is sold or used for lumber, railing or paling, the stump for matches and shoepegs, the knees for ship-building, and the branches for fuel. At the South everything is either neglected or mismanaged. Whole forests are felled by the ruthless hand of slavery, the trees are cut into logs, rolled into heaps, covered with the limbs and brush, and then burned on the identical soil that gave them birth. The land itself next falls a prey to the fell destroyer, and that which was once a beautiful, fertile and luxuriant woodland, is soon despoiled of all its treasures, and converted into an eye-offending desert.

Were we to go beneath the soil and collect all the mineral and lapidarious wealth of the free States, we should find it so much greater than the corresponding wealth of the slave States, that no ordinary combination of figures would suffice to express the difference. To say nothing of the gold and quicksilver of California, the iron and coal of Pennsylvania, the copper of Michigan, the lead of

Illinois, or the salt of New York, *the marble and free-stone quarries of New England are, incredible as it may seem to those unacquainted with the facts, far more important sources of revenue than all the subterranean deposits in the slave States.* From the most reliable statistics within our reach, we are led to the inference that the total value of all the precious metals, rocks, minerals, and medicinal waters, annually extracted from the bowels of the free States, is not less than eighty-five million of dollars; the whole value of the same substances annually brought up from beneath the surface of the slave States does not exceed twelve millions. In this respect to what is our poverty ascribable? To the same cause that has impoverished and dishonored us in all other respects — the thriftless and degrading institution of slavery.

Nature has been kind to us in all things. The strata and substrata of the South are profusely enriched with gold and silver, and precious stones, and from the natural orificies and aqueducts in Virginia and North Carolina, flow the purest healing waters in the world. But of what avail is all this latent wealth? Of what avail will it ever be, so long as slavery is permitted to play the dog in the manger? To these queries there can be but one reply. Slavery must be suppressed; the South, so great and so glorious by nature, must be reclaimed from her infamy and degradation; our cities, fields and forests, must be kept intact from the unsparing monster; the various and ample resources of our vast domain, subterraneous as well as superficial, must be developed, and made to contribute to our pleasures and to the necessities of the world.

A very significant chapter, and one particularly pertinent to many of the preceding pages, might be written on the Decline of Agriculture in the Slave States; but as the press of other subjects admonishes us to be concise upon this point, we shall present only a few of the more striking instances. In the first place, let us compare the crops of wheat and rye in Kentucky, in 1850, with the corresponding crops in the same State in 1840—after which, we will apply a similar rule of comparison to two or three other slaveholding states.

KENTUCKY

	Wheat, bus.		Rye, bus.
Crop of 1840	4,803,152		1,321,373
Crop of 1850	2,142,822		415,073
Decrease (bus.)	2,660,330	Decrease (bus.)	906,300

TENNESSEE

	Wheat, bus.		Tobacco, lbs.
Crop of 1840	4,569,692		29,550,432
Crop of 1850	1,619,386		20,148,932
Decrease (bus.)	2,950,306	Decrease (lbs.)	9,401,500

VIRGINIA

	Rye, bus.		Tobacco, lbs.
Crop of 1840	1,482,799		75,347,106
Crop of 1850	458,930		56,803,227
Decrease (bus.)	1,023,869	Decrease (lbs.)	18,543,879

ALABAMA

	Wheat, bus.		Rye, bus.
Crop of 1840	838,052		51,000
Crop of 1850	294,044		17,261
Decrease (bus.)	544,008	Decrease (bus.)	33,739

The story of these figures is too intelligible to require words of explanation; we shall, therefore, drop this part of our subject, and proceed to compile a couple of tables that will exhibit on a single page the wealth, revenue and expenditure, of the several states of the confederacy. Let it be distinctly understood, however, that, in the compilation of these tables, three million two hundred and four thousand three hundred and thirteen negroes are valued as personal property, and credited to the Southern States as if they were so many horses and asses, or bridles and blankets — and that no monetary valuation whatever is placed on any creature, of any age, color, sex or condition, that bears the upright form of man in the free States.

Table No. XX.

Wealth, Revenue and Expenditure of the Free States — 1850

	Real and Personal property	Revenue	Expenditure
California	$22,161,872	$366,825	$925,625
Connecticut	155,707,980	150,189	137,326
Illinois	156,265,006	736,030	192,940
Indiana	202,650,264	1,283,064	1,061,605
Iowa	23,714,638	139,681	131,631
Maine	122,777,571	744,879	624,101
Massachusetts	573,342,286	598,170	674,622
Michigan	59,787,255	548,326	431,918
New Hampshire	103,652,835	141,686	149,890
New Jersey	153,151,619	139,166	180,614
New York	1,080,309,216	2,698,310	2,520,932
Ohio	504,726,120	3,016,403	2,736,060
Pennsylvania	729,144,998	7,716,552	6,876,480
Rhode Island	80,508,794	124,944	115,835
Vermont	92,205,049	185,830	183,058
Wisconsin	42,056,595	135,155	136,096
TOTAL	$4,102,172,108	$18,725,211	$17,076,733
Corrected	*$4,102,162,098*	*$18,725,210*	

Table No. XXI.

Wealth, Revenue and Expenditure of the Slave States — 1850

	Real and Personal property	Revenue	Expenditure
Alabama	$228,204,332	$658,976	$513,559
Arkansas	39,841,025	68,412	74,076
Delaware	18,855,863		
Florida	23,198,734	60,619	55,234
Georgia	335,425,714	1,142,405	597,882
Kentucky	301,628,456	779,293	674,697
Louisiana	233,998,764	1,146,568	1,098,911
Maryland	219,217,364	1,279,953	1,360,458
Mississippi	228,951,130	221,200	223,637
Missouri	137,247,707	326,579	207,656
North Carolina	226,800,472	219,000	228,173
South Carolina	288,257,694	532,152	463,021
Tennessee	207,454,704	502,126	623,625
Texas	55,362,340	140,688	156,622
TOTAL	$2,936,090,737	$8,343,715	$7,549,933
Corrected	*$2,544,444,299*	*$7,077,971*	*$6,277,551*

[Table is missing Virginia]

Entire Wealth of the Free States	$4,102,172,108
Entire Wealth of the Slave States, including Slaves	$2,036,090,737
Balance in favor of the Free States	$1,166,081,371

What a towering monument to the beauty and glory of Free Labor! What irrefragable evidence of the unequaled efficacy and grandeur of free institutions! These figures are, indeed, too full of meaning to be passed by without comment. The two tables from which they are borrowed are at least a volume within themselves; and, after all the pains we have taken to compile them, we shall, perhaps, feel somewhat disappointed if the reader fails to avail himself of the important information they impart.

Human life, in all ages, has been made up of a series of adventures and experiments, and even at this stage of the world's existence, we are almost as destitute of a perfect rule of action, secular or religious, as were the erratic contemporaries of Noah. It is true, however, that we have made some progress in the right direction; and as it seems to be the tendency of the world to correct itself, we may suppose that future generations will be enabled, by intuition, to discriminate between the true and the false, the good and the bad, and that with the development of this faculty of the mind, error and discord will begin to wane, and finally cease to exist. Of all the experiments that have been tried by the people in America, slavery has proved the most fatal; and the sooner it is abolished the better it will be for us, for posterity, and for the world. One of the evils resulting from it, and that not the least, is apparent in the figures above. Indeed, the *unprofitableness* of slavery is a monstrous evil, when considered in all its bearings; it makes us poor; poverty makes us ignorant; ignorance makes us wretched; wretchedness makes us wicked, and wickedness leads to the devil!

"Ignorance is the curse of God, Knowledge the wing wherewith we fly to heaven."

Facts truly astounding are disclosed in the two last tables, and we could heartily wish that every intelligent American would commit them to memory. The total value of all the real and personal property of the free States, with an area of only 612,597 square miles, is one billion one hundred and sixty-six million eighty-one thousand three hundred and seventy-one dollars greater than the total value of all the real and personal property, including the price of 3,204,313 negroes, of the slave States, which have an area of 851,508 square miles! But extra-ordinary as this difference is in favor of the North, it is much less than the true amount. *On the authority of Southerners themselves, it is demonstrable beyond the possibility of refutation that the intrinsic value of all the property in the free States is more than three times greater than the intrinsic value of all the property in the slave States.*

James Madison, a Southern man, fourth President of the United States, a most correct thinker, and one of the greatest statesmen the country has produced, "thought it wrong to admit the idea that there could be property in man," and we indorse, to the fullest extent, this opinion of the profound editor of the *Federalist*. We shall not recognize property in man; the slaves of the South are not worth a groat in any civilized community; no man of genuine decency and refinement would hold them as property on any terms; in the eyes of all enlightened nations and individuals, they are men, not merchandise. Southern pro-slavery politicians, some of whom have not hesitated to buy and sell their own sons and daughters, boast that the slaves of the South are worth sixteen hundred million of dollars, and we have seen the amount estimated as high as two thousand million. Mr. De Bow, the Southern superintendent of the seventh census, informs us that the value of all the property in the slave States, real and personal, including slaves, was, in 1850, only $2,936,090,737; while, according to the same authority, the value of all the real and personal property in the free States, genuine property, property that is everywhere recognized as property, was, at the same time, $4,102,172,108. Now all we have to do in order to ascertain the real value of all the property of the South, independent of negroes, whose value, if valuable at all, is of a local and precarious character, is to subtract from the sum total of Mr. De Bow's return of the entire wealth of the slave States the estimated value of the slaves themselves; and then, by deducting the difference from the intrinsic value of all the property in the free States, we shall have the exact amount of the overplus of wealth in the glorious land of free soil, free labor, free speech, free presses, and free schools. And now to the task.

Entire Wealth of the Slave States, including Slaves	$2,936,090,737
Estimated Value of the Slaves	$1,600,000,000
True Wealth of the Slave States	$1,336,090,737
True Wealth of the Free States	$4,102,172,108
True Wealth of the Slave States	$1,336,090,737
Balance in favor of the Free States	$2,766,081,371

There, friends of the South and of the North, you have the conclusion of the whole matter. Liberty and slavery are before you; choose which you will have; as for us, in the memorable language of the immortal Henry, we say, "give us liberty, or give us death!" In the great struggle for wealth that has been going on between the two rival systems of free and slave labor, the balance above exhibits the net profits of the former. The struggle on the one side has been calm, laudable, and eminently successful; on the other, it has been attended by tumult, unutterable cruelties and disgraceful failure. We have given the slave drivers every conceivable opportunity to vindicate their domestic policy, but for them to do it is a moral impossibility.

Less than three-quarters of a century ago—say in 1789, for that was about the average time of the abolition of slavery in the Northern States — the South, with advantages in soil, climate, rivers, harbors, minerals, forests, and, indeed, almost every other natural resource, began an even race with the North in all the important pursuits of life; and now, in the brief space of scarce three score years and ten, we find her completely distanced, enervated, dejected and dishonored. Slave-drivers are the sole authors of her disgrace; as they have sown so let them reap.

As we have seen above, a careful and correct inventory of all the real and personal *property* in the two grand divisions of the country, discloses the astounding fact that, in 1850, the free States were worth precisely *two thousand seven hundred and sixty-six million eighty-one thousand three hundred and seventy-one dollars* more than the slave States! Twenty-seven hundred and sixty-six million of dollars! — Think of it! What a vast and desirable sum, and how much better off the South would be with it than without it! Such is the enormous amount out of which slavery has defrauded us during the space of sixty-one years—from 1789 to 1850—being an average of about forty-five million three hundred and fifty thousand dollars per annum. During the last twenty-five or thirty years, however, our annual losses have been far greater than they were formerly. There has been a gradual increase every year, and now the ratio of increase is almost incredible. No patriotic Southerner can become conversant with the facts without experiencing a feeling of alarm and indignation. Until the North abolished slavery, she had no advantage of us whatever; the South was more than her equal in every respect. But no sooner had she got rid of that hampering and pernicious institution than she began to absorb our wealth, and now it is confidently believed that the merchants and negro-driving pleasure-seekers of the South annually pour one hundred and twenty million of dollars into her coffers! Taking into account, then, the probable amount of money that has been drawn from the South and invested in the North within the last six years, and adding it to the grand balance above — the net profits of the North up to 1850

— it may be safely assumed that, in the present year of grace, 1857, *the free States are worth at least thirty-four hundred million of dollars more than the slave States!* Let him who dares, gainsay these remarks and calculations; no truthful tongue will deny them; no honorable pen can controvert them.

One more word now as to the valuation of negroes. Were our nature so degraded, or our conscience so elastic as to permit us to set a price upon men, as we would set a price upon cattle and corn, we should be content to abide by the appraisement of the slaves of the South, and would then enter into a calculation to ascertain the value of foreigners to the North. Not long since, it was declared in the South that "one free laborer is equal to five slaves," and as there are two million five hundred thousand Europeans in the free States, all of whom are free laborers, we might bring Southern authority to back us in estimating their value at *sixty-two hundred million of dollars* — a handsome sum wherewithal to offset the account of *sixteen hundred million of dollars,* brought forward as the value of Southern slaves! It is obvious, therefore, that if we were disposed to follow the barbarian example of the traffickers in human flesh, we could prove the North vastly richer than the South in bone and sinew—to say nothing of mind and morals, which shall receive our attention hereafter. The North has just as good a right to appraise the Irish immigrant, as the South has to set a price on the African slave. But as it would be wrong to do either, we shall do neither. It is not our business to think of man as a merchantable commodity; and we will not, even by implication, admit "the wild and guilty fantasy," that the condition of chattelhood may rightfully attach to sentient and immortal beings.

In this connection, we would direct the special attention of the reader to the following eloquent passage, exhibiting the philosophy of free and slave labor, from the facile pen of the editor of the *North American and United States Gazette:*

"In the very nature of things, the freeman must produce more than the slave. There is no conclusion of science more certain.

Under a system which gives to a laboring man the fruit of his toil, there is every motive to render him diligent and assiduous. If he relies on being employed by others, his wages rise with his reputation for industry, skill, and faithfulness. And as owner of the soil, there is every assurance that he will do what he can to cultivate it to the best advantage, and develop its latent wealth. Self-interest will call forth what powers of intellect and of invention he has to aid him in his work, and employ his physical strength to the greatest possible advantage. Free labor receives an immediate reward, which cheers and invigorates it; and above all, it has that chief spring of exertion, hope, whose bow always spans the heaven before it. It has an inviolate hearth; it has a home. But it looks forward to a still better condition, to brighter prospects in the future, to which its efforts all contribute. The children in such a household are chief inducements to nerve the arm of labor, that they may be properly cared for, fed, clothed, educated, accomplished, instructed in some useful and honorable calling, and provided for when they shall go out upon the world. All its sentiments, religious and otherwise, all its affections for parents and kindred, all its tastes are so many impelling and stimulating forces. It is disposed to read, to ornament its home, to travel, to enjoy social intercourse, and to attain these ends, it rises to higher exertions and a stricter economy of time; it explores every path of employment, and is, therefore, in the highest degree productive.

"How different is it with slave labor! The slave toils for another, and not for himself. Whether he does little or much, whether his work is well or ill performed, he has a subsistence, nothing less, nothing more; and why should he toil beyond necessity? He cannot accumulate any property for the decline of his years, or to leave to his children when he is departed. No, he cannot toil to better the present condition of his children. They belong to another, and not to him. He cannot supply his hut with comforts, or embellish it with the adornments of taste. He does not read. He does not journey for pleasure. inducements to exertion, he has none. That he may adapt

himself to his condition, and enjoy the present hour, he deadens
those aspirations that must always be baffled in his case, and sinks
down into ease and sensuality. His mind is unlighted and untutored;
dark with ignorance. Among those who value him most, he is pro-
verbially indolent, thievish, and neglectful of his master's interests.
It is common for even the advocates of slavery to declare that one
freeman is worth half a dozen slaves. With every cord to exertion
thus sundered, the mind benighted, the man nearly lost in the animal, it requires no deep philosophy to see why labor cannot be near
as productive as it would be were these conditions all reversed.
Though ever so well directed by the superior skill, and urged forward by the strong arm of the master, slave labor is necessarily a
blight to the soil—sterility follows in its steps, and not afar off.

"What a difference, plain and heaven-wide, between the outward
and interior life of a slave and of a free community, resulting directly and palpably from this difference in its labor. The cottage-
home, amid trees and shrubbery, its apartments well adorned and
furnished, books on its shelves, and the passing literature of the day
scattered around; the few, perhaps, but well-tilled acres, belonging
to the man who tills them; the happy children with sunny prospects;
the frequent school; the church arrayed with beauty; the thriving,
handsome village; the flourishing cities and prosperous marts of
trade; the busy factories; railroads, traffic, travel—where free labor
tills the ground, how beautiful it all is in contrast to the forlorn and
dreary aspect of a country tilled by slaves. The villages of such a
country are mainly groups of miserable huts. Its comparatively few
churches are too often dilapidated and unsightly. The common
school-house, the poor man's college, is hardly known, showing
how little interest is felt in the chief treasures of the State, the immortal minds of the multitude who are not born to wealth. The signs
of premature old age are visibly impressed upon everything that
meets the eye. The fields present a dread monotony. Everywhere
you see lands that are worn out, barren and deserted, in consequence of slave tillage, left for more fertile lands in newer regions,

which are also, in their turn, to be smitten with sterility and forsaken. The free community may increase its population almost without limit.

The capacity of slave countries to sustain a population is soon at an end, and then it diminishes. In all the elements of essential prosperity, in all that elevates man, how striking the contrast between the region that is tilled by slave, and the region that is tilled by free labor."

For the purpose of showing what Virginia, once the richest, most populous, and most powerful of the States, has become under the blight of slavery, we shall now introduce an extract from one of the speeches delivered by Henry A. Wise, during the last gubernatorial campaign in that degraded commonwealth. Addressing a Virginia audience, in language as graphic as it is truthful, he says:

"Commerce has long ago spread her sails, and sailed away from you. You have not, as yet, dug more than coal enough to warm yourselves at your own hearths; you have set no tilt-hammer of Vulcan to strike blows worthy of gods in your own iron-foundries; you have not yet spun more than coarse cotton enough, in the way of manufacture, to clothe your own slaves. You have no commerce, no mining, no manufactures. You have relied alone on the single power of agriculture, and *such agriculture!* Your sedge-patches outshine the sun. Your inattention to your only source of wealth, has seared the very bosom of mother earth. Instead of having to feed cattle on a thousand hills, you have had to chase the stumptailed steer through the sedge-patches to procure a tough beefsteak. The present condition of things has existed too long in Virginia. The landlord has skinned the tenant, and the tenant has skinned the land, until all have grown poor together."

With tears in its eyes, and truth on its lips, for the first time after an interval of twenty years, the *Richmond Enquirer* helps to paint the melancholy picture. In 1852, that journal thus bewailed the condition of Virginia:

"We have cause to feel deeply for our situation. Philadelphia

herself contains a population far greater than the whole free population of Eastern Virginia. The little State of Massachusetts has an
aggregate wealth exceeding that of Virginia by more than
$126,000,000."

Just a score of years before these words were penned, the same
paper, then edited by the elder Ritchie, made a most earnest appeal
to the intelligence and patriotism of Virginia, to adopt an effectual
measure for the speedy overthrow of the damnable institution of
human bondage Here is an extract from an article which appeared
in its editorial column under date of January 7th, 1832:

"Something must be done, and it is the part of no honest man to
deny it — of no free press to affect to conceal it. When this dark
population is growing upon us; when every new census is but gathering its appalling numbers upon us; when, within a period equal
to that in which this Federal Constitution has been in existence,
these numbers will increase to more than two millions within Virginia; when our sister States are closing their doors upon our blacks
for sale, and when our whites are moving westwardly in greater
numbers than we like to hear of; when this, the fairest land on all
this continent, for soil, and climate, and situation, combined, might
become a sort of garden spot, if it were worked by the hands of
white men alone, can we, ought we, to sit quietly down, fold our
arms, and say to each other, 'Well, well; this thing will not come to
the worst in our days; we will leave it to our children, and our
grandchildren, and great-grandchildren, to take care of themselves,
and to brave the storm!' Is this to act like wise men? Means, sure
but gradual, systematic but discreet, ought to be adopted, for reduc-
ing the mass of evil which is pressing upon the South, and will still
more press upon her, the longer it is put off. We say now, in the
utmost sincerity of our hearts, that our wisest men cannot give too
much of their attention to this subject, nor can they give it too
soon."

Better abolition doctrine than this is seldom heard. Why did not
the *Enqurier* continue to preach it? What potent influence hushed

its clarion voice, just as it began to be lifted in behalf of a liberal policy and an enlightened humanity? Had Mr. Ritchie continued to press the truth home to the hearts of the people, as he should have done, Virginia, instead of being worth only $392,000,000 in 1850—negroes and all—would have been worth at least $800,000,000 in genuine property; and if the State had emancipated her slaves at the time of the adoption of the Constitution, the last census would no doubt have reported her wealth, and correctly, at a sum exceeding a thousand millions of dollars.

Listen now to the statement of a momentous fact. The value of all the property, real and personal, including slaves, in seven slave States, Virginia, North Carolina, Tennessee, Missouri, Arkansas, Florida and Texas, is less than the real and personal estate, which is unquestionable property, in the single State of New York. No, worse; if eight entire slave States, Arkansas, Delaware, Florida, Maryland, Missouri, Mississippi, Tennessee and Texas, and the District of Columbia—with all their hordes of human merchandise—were put up at auction, New York could buy them all, and then have one hundred and thirty-three millions of dollars left in her pocket! Such is the amazing contrast between freedom and slavery, even in a pecuniary point of view. When we come to compare the North with the South in regard to literature, general intelligence, inventive genius, moral and religious enterprises, the discoveries in medicine, and the progress in the arts and sciences, we shall, in every instance, find the contrast equally great on the side of Liberty.

It gives us no pleasure to say hard things of the Old Dominion, the mother of Washington, Jefferson, Henry, and other illustrious patriots, who, as we shall prove hereafter, were genuine abolitionists. But the policy which she has pursued has been so utterly inexcusable, so unjust to the non-slaveholding whites, so cruel to the negroes, and so disregardful of the rights of humanity at large, that it becomes the solemn duty of every one who makes allusion to her history, to expose her follies, her crimes, and her poverty, and to publish every fact, of whatever nature, that would be instrumental in determining others to eschew her bad example. She has wilfully departed from the faith of the founders of this Republic. She has not only turned a deaf ear to the counsel of wise men from other States in the Union, but she has, in like manner, ignored the teachings of the great warriors and statesmen who have sprung from her own soil. In a subsequent chapter, we expect to show that all, or nearly all, the distinguished Virginians, whose bodies have been consigned to the grave, but whose names have been given to history, and whose memoirs have a place in the hearts of their countrymen, were the friends and advocates of universal freedom — that they were inflexibly opposed to the extension of slavery into the Territories, devised measures for its restriction, and, with hopeful anxiety, looked forward to the time when it should be eradicated from the States themselves. With them, the rescue of our country from British domination, and the establishment of the General Government upon a firm basis, were considerations of paramount importance; they supposed, and no doubt earnestly desired, that the States, in their sovereign capacities, would soon abolish an institution which was so palpably in conflict with the principles enunciated in the Declaration of Independence. Indeed, it would seem that, among the framers of that immortal instrument and its equally immortal sequel, the Constitution of the United States, there was a tacit understanding to this effect; and the Northern States, true to their implied faith, abolished it within a short period after our national independence had been secured. Not so with the South. She has pertinaciously refused to perform her duty. She has apostatized from the faith of her greatest men, and even at this very moment repudiates the sacred principle that "all men are endowed by their Creator with certain unalienable rights," among which "are life, liberty, and the pursuit of happiness." It is evident, therefore, that the free States are the only members of this confederacy that have established republican forms of government based upon the theories of Washington, Jefferson, Madison, Henry, and other eminent statesmen of Virginia.

The great revolutionary movement which was set on foot in Charlotte, Mecklenburg county, North Carolina, on the 20th day of May, 1775, has not yet been terminated, nor will it be, until every slave in the United States is freed from the tyranny of his master. Every victim of the vile institution, whether white or black, must be reinvested with the sacred rights and privileges of which he has been deprived by an inhuman oligarchy. What our noble sires of the revolution left unfinished it is our duty to complete. They did all that true valor and patriotism could accomplish. Not one iota did they swerve from their plighted faith; the self-sacrificing spirit which they evinced will command the applause of every succeeding age. Not in vindication of their own personal rights merely, but of the rights of humanity; not for their own generation and age simply, but for all ages to the end of time, they gave their toil, their treasure and their blood, nor deemed them all too great a price to pay for the establishment of so comprehensive and beneficent a principle. Let their posterity emulate their courage, their disinterestedness, and their zeal, and especially remember that it is the duty of every existing generation so to provide for its individual interests, as to confer superior advantages on that which is to follow.

To this principle the North has adhered with the strictest fidelity. How has it been with the South? Has she imitated the praiseworthy example of our illustrious ancestors? No! She has treated it with the utmost contempt; she has been extremely selfish — so selfish, indeed, that she has robbed posterity of its natural rights. From the period of the formation of the government down to the present moment, her policy has been downright suicidal, and, as a matter of course, wholly indefensible. She has hugged a viper to her breast; her whole system has been paralyzed, her conscience is seared, and she is becoming callous to every principle of justice and magnanimity. Except among the non-slaveholders, who, besides being kept in the grossest ignorance, are under the restraint of all manner of iniquitous laws, patriotism has ceased to exist within her borders. And here we desire to be distinctly understood, for we shall have occasion to refer to this matter again. We repeat, therefore, the substance of our averment, that, at this day, there is not a grain of patriotism in the South, except among the non-slaveholders. Subsequent pages shall testify to the truth of this assertion. Here and there, it is true, a slaveholder, disgusted with the institution, becomes ashamed of himself, emancipates his negroes, and enters upon the walks of honorable life; but these cases are exceedingly rare, and do not, in any manner, disprove the general correctness of our remark. All persons who do voluntarily manumit their slaves, as mentioned above, are undeniably actuated by principles of pure patriotism, justice and humanity; and so believing, we delight to do them honor.

Once more to the Old Dominion. At her door we lay the bulk of the evils of slavery. The first African sold in America was sold on James River, in that State, on the 20th of August, 1620; and although the institution was fastened upon her and the other colonies by the mother country, she was the first to perceive its blighting and degrading influences, her wise men were the first to denounce it, and, after the British power was overthrown at York Town, she should have been the first to abolish it. Fifty-seven years ago she was the Empire State; now, with half a dozen other slaveholding states thrown into the scale with her, she is far inferior to New York, which, at the time Cornwallis surrendered his sword to Washington, was less than half her equal. Had she obeyed the counsels of the good, the great and the wise men of our nation—especially of her own incomparable sons, the extendible element of slavery would have been promptly arrested, and the virgin soil of nine Southern States, Kentucky, Tennessee, Louisiana, Mississippi, Alabama, Missouri, Arkansas, Florida, and Texas, would have been saved from its horrid pollutions. Confined to the original states in which it existed, the institution would soon have been disposed of by legislative enactments, and long before the present day, by a gradual process that could have shocked no interest and alarmed no prejudice, we should have rid ourselves not only of African slavery, which is an abomination and a curse, but also of the negroes themselves, who, in our judgement, whether viewed in relation to their actual characteristics and condition, or through the strong antipathies of the whites, are, to say the least, an undesirable population.

This, then, is the ground of our expostulation with Virginia: that, in stubborn disregard of the advice and friendly warnings of Washington, Jefferson, Madison, Henry, and a host of other distinguished patriots who sprang from her soil—patriots whose voices shall be heard before we finish our task — and in utter violation of every principle of justice and humanity, *she still persists* in fostering an institution which is so manifestly detrimental to her vital interests. Every Virginian, whether living or dead, whose name is an honor to his country, has placed on record his abhorrence of slavery, and in doing so, has borne testimony to the blight and degradation that everywhere follow in its course. One of the best abolition speeches we have ever read was delivered in the Virginia House of Delegates, January 20th, 1832, by Charles James Faulkner, who still lives, and who has, we understand, generously emancipated several of his slaves, and sent them to Liberia. Here follows an extract from his speech; let Southern politicians read it attentively, and imbibe a moiety of the spirit of patriotism which it breathes:

"Sir, I am gratified to perceive that no gentleman has yet risen in this Hall, the avowed advocate of slavery. *The day has gone by when such a voice could be listened to with patience, or even with forbearance.* I even regret, Sir, that we should find those amongst us who enter the lists of discussion as its *apologists*, except alone upon the ground of uncontrollable necessity. And yet, who could have listened to the very eloquent remarks of the gentleman from Brunswick, without being forced to conclude that he at least considered slavery, however *not to be defended upon principle*, yet as being divested of much of its enormity, as you approach it in practice.

"Sir, if there be one who concurs with that gentleman in the harmless character of this institution, let me request him to compare the condition of the slaveholding portion of this commonwealth —*barren, desolate, and seared as it were by the avenging hand of Heaven*—with the descriptions which we have of this country from those who first broke its virgin soil. To what is this change ascribable? *Alone to the withering and blasting effects of slavery.* If this does not satisfy him, let me request him to extend his travels to the *Northern States of this Union,* and beg him to contrast the happiness and contentment which prevail throughout that country, the busy and cheerful sound of industry, the rapid and swelling growth of their population, their means and institutions of education, their skill and proficiency in the useful arts, their enterprise and public spirit, the monuments of their commercial and manufacturing industry; and, above all, their devoted attachment to the government from which they derive their protection, *with the derision, discontent, indolence, and poverty of the Southern country.* To what, Sir, is all this ascribable? *To that vice in the organization of society, by which one-half of its inhabitants are arrayed in interest and feeling against the other half*—to that unfortunate state of society in which freemen regard labor as disgraceful, and slaves shrink from it as a burden tyrannically imposed upon them — to that condition of things in which half a million of your population can feel no sympathy with the society in the prosperity of which they are forbidden to participate, and no attachment to a government at whose hands they receive nothing but injustice.

"If this should not be sufficient, and the curious and incredulous inquirer should suggest that the contrast which has been adverted to, and which is so manifest, might be traced to a difference of climate, or other causes distinct from slavery itself, permit me to refer him to the two States of Kentucky and Ohio. No difference of soil, no diversity of climate, no diversity in the original settlement of those two States, can account for the remarkable disproportion in their natural advancement. Separated by a river alone, *they seem to have been purposely and providentially designed to exhibit in their future histories the difference which necessarily results from a country free from, and a country afflicted with, the curse of slavery.*

"Vain and idle is every effort to strangle this inquiry. As well might you attempt to chain the ocean, or stay the avenging thunderbolts of Heaven, as to drive the people from any inquiry which may result in their better condition. This is too deep, too engrossing a subject of consideration. It addresses itself too strongly to our interests, to our passions, and to our feelings. I shall advocate no scheme that does not respect the right of property, *so far as it is entitled to be respected,* with a just regard to the safety and resources of the State. I would approach the subject as one of great magnitude and delicacy, as one whose varied and momentous consequences demand the calmest and most deliberate investigation. But still, Sir, I would approach it — aye, delicate as it may be, encompassed as it may be with difficulties and hazards, I would still approach it. The people demand it. Their security requires it. In the language of the wise and prophetic Jefferson, 'You must approach it — you must bear it — you must adopt some plan of emancipation, or worse will follow.'"

Mr. Curtis, in a speech in the Virginia Legislature in 1832, said:

"There is a malaria in the atmosphere of these regions, which the new comer shuns, as being deleterious to his views and habits. See the wide-spreading ruin which the avarice of our ancestral government has produced in the South, as witnessed in a sparse population of freemen, deserted habitations, and fields without culture! Strange to tell, even the wolf, driven back long since by the approach of man, now returns, after the lapse of a hundred years, to howl over the desolations of slavery."

Mr. Moore, also a member of the Legislature of Virginia, in speaking of the evils of slavery, said:

"The first I shall mention is the irresistible tendency which it has to undermine and destroy everything like virtue and morality in the community. If we look back through the long course of time which has elapsed since the creation to the present moment, we shall scarcely be able to point out a people whose situation was not, in many respects, preferable to our own, and that of the other States, in which negro slavery exists.

"In that part of the State below tide-water, the whole face of the country wears an appearance of almost utter desolation, distressing to the beholder. The very spot on which our ancestors landed, a little more than two hundred years ago, appears to be on the eye of again becoming the haunt of wild beasts."

Mr. Rives, of Campbell county, said:

"On the multiplied and desolating evils of slavery, he was not disposed to say much. The curse and deteriorating consequence were within the observation and experience of the members of the House and the people of Virginia, and it did not seem to him that there could be two opinions about it."

Mr. Powell said:

"I can scarcely persuade myself that there is a solitary gentleman in this House who will not readily admit that slavery is an evil, and that its removal, if practicable, is a consummation most devoutly to be wished. I have not heard, nor do I expect to hear, a voice raised in this Hall to the contrary."

In the language of another, "we might multiply extracts almost indefinitely from Virginia authorities—testifying to the blight and degradation that have overtaken the Old Dominion, in every department of her affairs. Her commerce gone, her agriculture decaying, her land falling in value, her mining and manufactures nothing, her schools dying out,—she presents, according to the testimony of her own sons, the saddest of all pictures—that of a sinking and dying State." Every year leaves her in a worse condition than it found her; and as it is with Virginia, so it is with the entire South. In the terse language of Governor Wise, "all have grown poor together." The black god of slavery, which the South has worshipped for two hundred and thirty-seven years, is but a devil in disguise; and if we would save ourselves from being engulfed in utter ruin we must repudiate this foul god, for a purer deity, and abandon his altars for a holier shrine. No time is to be lost; his fanatical adorers, the despotic adversaries of human liberty, are concocting schemes for the enslavement of all the laboring classes' irrespective of race or color. The issue is before us; we cannot evade it; we must meet it with firmness, and with unflinching valor.

What it was that paralyzed the tongues of all those members of the Virginia Legislature, who, at the session of 1831-32, distinguished themselves by advocating a system of emancipation, is a mystery that has never yet been solved. Whether any or all of them shared a division of spoils with a certain newspaper editor, we have no means of knowing; but if all accounts be true, there was consummated in Richmond, in the latter part of the year 1832, one of the blackest schemes of bribery and corruption that was ever perpetrated in this or any other country. We are assured, however, that one thing is certain, and it is this: that the negro population of Virginia was very considerably and suddenly decreased by forcible emigration—that a large gang was driven further South, sold, and the proceeds divided among certain renegades and traitors, who, Judas-like, had agreed to serve the devil for a price.

We would fain avoid all personalities and uncomplimentary allusions to the dead, but when men, from love of lucre, from mere selfish motives, or from sheer turpitude of heart, inflict great injuries and outrages on the public, their villainy ought to be exposed, so that others may be deterred from following in their footsteps. As a general rule, man's moral nature is, we believe, so strong that it invariably prompts him to eschew vice and practice virtue—in other words, to do right; but this rule, like all others, has its exceptions, as might be most strikingly illustrated in the character of a particular man, and some half-dozen or more of his pro-slavery coadjutors. From whose hands did this man receive fifty thousand dollars —improperly, if not illegally, taken from the public funds in Washington? When did he receive it?—and for what purpose?—and who was the arch-demagogue through whose agency the transfer was made? He was an oligarchical member of the Cabinet under Mr.

Polk's administration in 1845, — and the money was *used*, — and who can doubt *intended?* — for the express purpose of establishing another negro-driving journal to support the tottering fortunes of slavery. From the second volume of a valuable political work, "by a Senator of thirty years," we make the following pertinent extract:

"The *Globe* was sold, and was paid for, and how? becomes a question of public concern to answer; for it was paid for out of public money — those same $50,000 which were removed to the village bank in the interior of Pennsylvania by a Treasury order on the fourth of November, 1844. Three annual installments made the payment, and the Treasury did not reclaim the money for these three years; and, though traveling through tortuous channels, the sharp-sighted Mr. Rives traced the money back to its starting point from that deposit. Besides, Mr. Cameron, who had control of the village bank, admitted before a committee of Congress, that he had furnished money for the payments — an admission which the obliging Committee, on request, left out of their report. Mr. Robert J. Walker was Secretary of the Treasury during these three years, and the convictions was absolute, among the close observers of the course of things, that he was the prime contriver and zealous manager of the arrangements which displaced Mr. Blair and installed Mr. Ritchie."

Thus, if we are to believe Mr. Benton, in his "Thirty Year's View," and we are disposed to regard him as good authority, the Washington *Union* was brought into existence under the peculiar auspices of the ostensible editor of the Richmond *Enquirer;* and the two papers, fathered by the same individual, have gone hand in hand for the last dozen or thirteen years, the shameless advocates and defenders of human bondage. To suppose that either has been sustained by fairer means than it was commenced with, would be wasting imagination on a great improbability. Both have uniformly and pertinaciously opposed every laudable enterprise that the white non-slaveholder has projected; indeed, so unmitigated has been their hostility to all manual pursuits in which their stupid and vulgar

slaves can not be employed to advantage—and if there is any occupation under the sun in which they can be employed to good advantage, we known not what it is — that it is an extremely difficult
matter to find a respectable merchant, mechanic, manufacturer, or
business man of any calling whatever, within the bounds of their
circulation.

We have been credibly informed by a gentleman from Powhattan
county in Virginia, that in the year 1836 or '37, or about that time,
the Hon. Abbott Lawrence, of Boston, backed by his brother Amos
and other millionaires of New England, went down to Richmond
with the sole view of reconnoitering the manufacturing facilities of
that place — fully determined, if pleased with the water-power, to
erect a large number of cotton-mills and machine-shops. He had
been in the capital of Virginia only a day or two before he discovered, much to his gratification, that nature had shaped everything
to his liking; and as he was a business man who transacted business
in a business-like manner, he lost no time in making preliminary
arrangements for the consummation of his noble purpose. His
mission was one of peace and promise; others were to share the
benefits of his laudable and concerted scheme; thousands of poor
boys and girls in Virginia, instead of growing up in extreme poverty
and ignorance, or of having to emigrate to the free States of the
West, were to have avenues of profitable employment opened to
them at home; thus they would be enabled to earn an honest and
reputable living to establish and sustain free schools, free libraries,
free lectures, and free presses, to become useful and exemplary
members of society, and to die fit candidates for heaven. The mag-
nanimous New Englander was in ecstasies with the prospect that
opened before him. Individually, so far as mere money was concerned, he was perfectly independent; his industry and economy in
early life had secured to him the ownership and control of an ample
fortune. With the aid of eleven other men, each equal to himself, he
could have bought the whole city of Richmond — negroes and all—
though it is not to be presumed that he would have disgraced his

name by becoming a trader in human flesh. But he was not selfish; unlike the arrogant and illiberal slaveholder, he did not regard himself as the centre around whom everybody else should revolve. On the contrary, he was a genuine philanthropist. While, with a shrewdness that will command the admiration of every practical business man, he engaged in nothing that did not swell the dimensions of his own purse, he was yet always solicitous to invest his capital in a manner calculated to promote the interest of those around him. Nor was he satisfied with simply furnishing the means whereby his less fortunate neighbors were to become prosperous, intelligent and contented. With his generous heart and sagacious mind, he delighted to aid them in making a judicious application of his wealth to their own use. Moreover, as a member of society, he felt that the community had some reasonable claims upon him, and he made it obligatory on himself constantly to devise plans and exert his personal efforts for the public good. Such was the character of the distinguished manufacturer who honored Richmond with his presence nineteen or twenty years ago; such was the character of the men whom he represented, and such were the grand designs which they sought to accomplish.

To the enterprising and moneyed descendant of the Pilgrim Fathers it was a matter of no little astonishment, that the immense water-power of Richmond had been so long neglected. He expressed his surprise to a number of Virginians and was at a loss to know why they had not, long prior to the period of his visit amongst them, availed themselves of the powerful element that is eternally gushing and foaming over the falls of James River. Innocent man! He was utterly unconscious of the fact that he was "interfering with the beloved institutions of the South," and little was he prepared to withstand the terrible denunciations that were immediately showered on his head through the columns of the Richmond *Enquirer.* Few words will suffice to tell the sequel. That negro-worshipping sheet, whose hireling policy, for the last four and twenty years, has been to support the worthless black slave and his tyrannical master at the expense of the free white laborer, wrote down the enterprise! and the noble son of New England, abused, insulted and disgusted, quietly returned to Massachusetts, and there employed his capital in building up the cities of Lowell and Lawrence, either of which, in all those elements of material and social prosperity that make up the greatness of States, is already far in advance of the most important of all the seedy and squalid 'niggervilles' in the Old Dominion. Such is an inkling of the infamous means that have been resorted to, from time to time, for the purpose of upholding and perpetuating in America the accursed institution of slavery.

Having in view all the foregoing facts, we were not in the least surprised when, while walking through Hollywood Cemetery, in the western suburbs of Richmond, not long since, our companion, a Virginian of the true school, directed our attention to a monument of some pretentions, and exclaimed, "There lie the remains of a man upon whose monument should be inscribed in everlasting prominence the finger of scorn pointing downward." The reader scarcely needs to be told that we were standing at the tomb of ———, who in the opinion of our friend, had, by concentrating within himself the views and purposes of all the evil spirits in Virginia, greatly retarded the abolition of slavery; so greatly, indeed, as, thereby, to throw the State at least fifty years behind her free competitors of the North, of the East, and of the West. It is to be hoped that Virginia may never give birth to another man whose evil influence will so justly entitle him to the reprobation of posterity.

How any rational man in this or any other country, with the astounding contrasts between Freedom and Slavery ever looming in his view, can offer an apology for the existing statism of the South, is to us a most inexplicable mystery. Indeed, we cannot conceive it possible that the conscience of any man, who is really sane, would permit him to become the victim of such an egregious and diabolical absurdity. Therefore, at this period of our history, with the light of the past, the reality of the present, and the prospect of the future, all so prominent and so palpable, we infer that every person who sets up an unequivocal defence of the institution of slavery, must, of necessity, be either a fool, a knave, or a madman.

It is much to be regretted that the slavocrats look at but one side of the question. Of all the fanatics in the country, they have, of late, become the most unreasonable and ridiculous. Let them deliberately view the subject of slavery in all its aspects and bearings, and if they are possessed of honest hearts and convincible minds, they will readily perceive the grossness of their past errors, renounce their allegiance to a cause so unjust and disgraceful, and at once enroll themselves among the hosts of Freedom and the friends of universal Liberty. There are thirty-one States in the Union; let them drop California, or any other new free State, and then institute fifteen comparisons, first comparing New York with Virginia, Pennsylvania with Carolina, Massachusetts with Georgia, and so on, until they have exhausted the catalogue. Then, for once, let them be bold enough to listen to the admonitions of their own souls, and if they do not soon start to their feet *demanding* the abolition of slavery, it will only be because they have reasons for suppressing their inmost sentiments. Whether we compare the old free States with the old slave States, or the new free States with the new slave States, the difference, unmistakable and astounding, is substantially the same. All the free States are alike, and all the slave States are alike. In the former, wealth, intelligence, power, progress, and prosperity, are the prominent characteristics; in the latter, poverty, ignorance, imbecility, inertia, and extravagance, are the distinguishing features. To be convinced, it is only necessary for us to open our eyes and look at facts — to examine the *statistics* of the country, to free ourselves from obstinacy and prejudice, and to unbar our minds to convictions of truth. Let figures be the umpire. Close attention to the preceding and subsequent tables is all we ask; so soon as they shall be duly considered and understood, the primary object of this work will have been accomplished.

Not content with eating out the vitals of the South, slavery, true to the character which it has acquired for insatiety and rapine, is beginning to make rapid encroachments on new territory; and as a basis for a few remarks on the blasting influence which it is shedding over the broad and fertile domains of the West, which in accordance with the views and resolutions offered by the immortal Jefferson, should have been irrevocably dedicated to freedom, we beg leave to call the attention of the reader to another presentation of the philosophy of free and slave labor. The *North American and United States Gazette* states:

"We have but to compare the States, possessing equal natural advantages, in which the two kinds of labor are employed, in order to decide with entire confidence as to which kind is the more profitable. At the origin of the government, Virginia, with a much larger extent of territory than New York, contained a population of seven hundred and fifty thousand, and sent ten representatives to Congress; while New York contained a population of three hundred and forty thousand, and sent six representatives to Congress. Behold how the figures are reversed. The population of New York is three and a half millions, represented by thirty-three members in Congress; while the population of Virginia is but little more than one and a half millions, represented by thirteen members in Congress. It is the vital sap of free labor that makes the one tree so thrifty and vigorous, so capable of bearing with all ease the fruit of such a population. And it is slave labor which strikes a decadence through the other, drying up many of its branches with a fearful sterility, and rendering the rest but scantily fruitful; really incapable of sustaining more. Look at Ohio, teeming with inhabitants, its soil loaded with every kind of agricultural wealth, its people engaged in every kind of freedom's diversified employments, abounding with numberless happy homes, and with all the trophies of civilization, and it exhibits the magic effect of free labor, waking a wilderness into life and beauty; while Kentucky, with equal or superior natural advantages, nature's very garden in this Western world, which commenced its career at a much earlier date, and was in a measure populous when Ohio was but a slumbering forest, but which in all the elements of progress, is now left far, very far, behind its young rival, shows how slave labor hinders the development of wealth among a people, and brings a blight on their prosperity. The one is a grand and beautiful poem in honor of free labor. The other is an humble confession to the world of the inferiority of slave labor."

Equally significant is the testimony of Daniel R. Goodloe, of North Carolina, who says:

"The history of the United States shows, that while the slave States increase in population less rapidly than the free, there is a tendency in slave society to diffusion, greater than is exhibited by free society. In fact, diffusion, or extension of area, is one of the necessities of slavery; the prevention of which is regarded as directly and immediately menacing to the existence of the institutor. This arises from the almost exclusive application of slave labor to the one occupation of agriculture, and the difficulty, if not impossibility, of diversifying employments. Free society, on the contrary, has indefinite resources of development within a restricted area. It will far excel slave society in the cultivation of the ground — first, on account of the superior intelligence of the laborers; and secondly, in consequence of the greater and more various demands upon the earth's products, where commerce, manufactures, and the arts, abound. Then, these arts of life, by bringing men together in cities and towns, and employing them in the manufacture or transportation of the raw materials of the farmer, give rise to an indefinite increase of wealth and population. The confinement of a free people within narrow limits seems only to develop new resources of wealth, comfort and happiness; while slave society, pent up, withers and dies. It must continually be fed by new fields and forests, to be wasted and wilted under the poisonous tread of the slave."

Were we simply a freesoiler, or anything else less than a thorough and uncompromising abolitionist, we should certainly tax our ability to the utmost to get up a cogent argument against the extension of slavery over any part of our domain where it does not now exist; but as our principles are hostile to the institution even where it does exist, and, therefore, by implication and in fact, more hostile still to its introduction into new territory, we forbear the preparation of any special remarks on this particular subject.

With regard to the unnational and demoralizing institution of slavery, we believe the majority of Northern people are too scrupulous. They seem to think that it is enough for them to be mere freesoilers, to keep in check the diffusive element of slavery, and to prevent it from crossing over the bounds within which it is now regulated by municipal law. Remiss in their *national* duties, as we contend, they make no positive attack upon the institution in the Southern States. Only a short while since, one of their ablest journals—the *North American and United States Gazette*, published in Philadelphia—made use of the following language:

"With slavery in the States, we make no pretense of having anything politically to do. For better or for worse, the system belongs solely to the people of those States; and is separated by an impassable gulf of State sovereignty from any legal intervention of ours. We cannot vote it down any more than we can vote down the institution of caste in Hindostan, or abolish polygamy in the Sultan's dominions. Thus, precluded from all political action in reference to it, prevented from touching one stone of the edifice, not the slightest responsibility attaches to us as citizens for its continued existence. But on the question of extending slavery over the free Territories of the United States, it is our right, it is our imperative duty to think, to feel, to speak and to vote. We cannot interfere to cover the shadows of slavery with the sunshine of freedom, but we can interfere to prevent the sunshine of freedom from being eclipsed by the shadows of slavery. We can interpose to stay the progress of that institution, which aims to drive free labor from its own heritage. Kansas should be divided up into countless homes for the ownership of men who have a right to the fruit of their own labors Free labor would make it bud and blossom like the rose; would cover it with beauty, and draw from it boundless wealth; would throng it with population; would make States, nations, empires out of it, prosperous, powerful, intelligent and free, illustrating on a wide theatre the beneficent ends of Providence in the formation of our government, to advance and elevate the millions of our race, and, like the heart in the body, from its central position, sending out on every side, far and near, the vital influences of freedom and civilization. May that region, therefore, be secured to free labor."

Now we fully and heartily indorse every line of the latter part of this extract; but, with all due deference to our sage contemporary, we do most emphatically dissent from the sentiments embodied in the first part. Permit us to ask — have the people of the North no interest in the United States as a *nation,* and do they not see that slavery is a great injury and disgrace to the *whole country?* Did they not, in "the days that tried men's souls," strike as hard blows to secure the independence of Georgia as they did in defending the liberties of Massachusetts, and is it not notoriously true that the Toryism of South Carolina prolonged the war two years at least? Is it not, moreover, equally true that the oligarchs of South Carolina have been unmitigated pests and bores to the General Government ever since it was organized, and that the free and conscientious people of the North are virtually excluded from her soil, in consequence of slavery? It is a well-known and incontestible fact, that the Northern States furnished about two-thirds of all the American troops engaged in the Revolutionary War; and, though they were neither more nor less brave or patriotic than their fellow-soldiers of the South, yet, inasmuch as the independence of our country was mainly secured by virtue of their numerical strength, we think they ought to consider it not only their right but their *duty* to make a firm and decisive effort to save the States which they fought to free, from falling under the yoke of a worse tyranny than that which overshadowed them under the reign of King George the Third. Freemen of the North! we earnestly entreat you to think of these things. Hitherto, as mere freesoilers, you have approached but half-way to the line of your duty; now, for your own sakes and for ours, and for the purpose of perpetuating this glorious Republic, which your fathers and our fathers founded in streams of blood, we ask you, in all seriousness, to organize yourselves as *one man* under the banners of Liberty, and to aid us in *exterminating* slavery, which is the only thing that militates against our complete aggrandizement as a nation.

In this extraordinary crisis of affairs, no man can be a true patriot without first becoming an abolitionist. (A freesoiler is only a tadpole in an advanced state of transformation; an abolitionist is the full and perfectly developed frog.) And here, perhaps, we may be pardoned for the digression necessary to show the exact definition of the terms *abolish, abolition* and *abolitionist*. We have looked in vain for an explanation of the signification of these words in any Southern publication; for no dictionary has ever yet been published in the South, nor is there the least probability that one ever will be published within her borders, until slavery is *abolished;* but, thanks to Heaven, a portion of this continent is what our Revolutionary Fathers and the Fathers of the Constitution fought and labored and prayed to make it — a land of freedom, of power, of progress, of prosperity, of intelligence, of religion, of literature, of commerce, of science, of arts, of agriculture, of manufactures, of ingenuity, of enterprise, of wealth, of renown, of goodness, and of grandeur. From that glorious part of our confederacy — from the North, whence, on account of slavery in the South, we are under the humiliating necessity of procuring almost everything that is useful or ornamental, from primers to Bibles, from wafers to printing-presses, from ladles to locomotives, and from portfolios to portraits and pianos—comes to us a huge volume bearing the honored name of Webster—Noah Webster, who, after thirty-five years of unremitting toil, completed a work which is, we believe, throughout Great Britain and the United States, justly regarded as the standard vocabulary of the English language—and in it the terms *abolish, abolition,* and *abolitionist,* are defined as follows:

"Abolish, *v. t.* To make void; to annul; to abrogate; applied chiefly and appropriately to establish laws, contracts, rites, customs and institutions; as to *abolish* laws by a repeal, actual or virtual. To destroy or put an end to; as to *abolish* idols."

"Abolition, *n.* The act of abolishing; or the state of being abolished; an annulling; abrogation; utter destruction; as the *abolition* of laws, decrees, or ordinances, rites, customs, &c. The putting an end to slavery; emancipation."

"Abolitionist, *n.* A person who favors abolition, or the immediate emancipation of slaves."

There, gentlemen of the South, you have the definitions of the transitive verb *abolish* and its two derivative nouns, *abolition* and *abolitionist;* can you, with the keenest possible penetration of vision, detect in either of these words even a tittle of the opprobrium which the oligarchs, in their wily and inhuman efforts to enslave all working classes irrespective of race or color, have endeavored to attach to them? We know you cannot; abolition is but another name for patriotism, and its other special synonyms are generosity, magnanimity, reason, prudence, wisdom, religion, progress, justice, and humanity.

And here, by the way, we may as well explain whom we refer to when we speak of gentlemen of the South. We say, therefore, that, deeply impressed with the conviction that slavery is a great social and political evil, a *sin and a crime,* in the fullest sense, whenever we speak of gentlemen of the South, or of gentlemen anywhere, or at whatever time, or in whatever connection we may speak of gentlemen, we seldom allude to slaveholders, for the simple reason that, with few exceptions, we cannot conscientiously recognize *them* as gentlemen. It is only in those rare instances where the crime is mitigated by circumstances over which the slaveholder has had no control, or where he himself, convinced of the impropriety, the folly and the wickedness of the institution, is anxious to abolish it, that we can sincerely apply to him the sacred appellation in question—an appellation which we would no sooner think of applying to a *pro-slavery* slaveholder, or any other pro-slavery man, than we would think of applying it to a border-ruffian, a thief or a murderer. Let it be understood, however, that the rare instances of which we speak are less rare than many persons may suppose. We are personally acquainted with several slaveholders in North Carolina, South Carolina, Maryland and Virginia, who have unreservedly assured us that they were disgusted with the institution, and some of them went so far as to say they would be glad to acquiesce in the provision of a statute which would make it obligatory on them all to manumit their slaves, without the smallest shadow or substance of compensation. These, we believe, are the sentiments of all the respectable and patriotic slaveholders, who have eyes to see, and see—ears to hear, and hear; who, perceiving the impoverishing and degrading effects of slavery, are unwilling to entail it on their children, and who, on account of their undeviating adherence to truth and justice, are, like the more intelligent non-slaveholders, worthy of being regarded as gentlemen in every sense of the term. Such slaveholders were Washington, Jefferson, Madison, and other illustrious Virginians, who, in the language of the great chief himself, declared it among their *"first wishes* to see some plan adopted by which slavery, in this country, may be abolished by law." The words embraced within this quotation were used by Washington, in a letter to John F. Mercer, dated September 9th, 1786—a letter from which we shall quote more freely hereafter; and we think his emphatic use of the participle *abolished,* at that early day, is proof positive that the glorious "Father of his Country" is entitled to the first place in the calendar of primitive American abolitionists.

It is against slavery on the whole, and against slaveholders as a body, that we wage an exterminating war. Those persons who, under the infamous slave-laws of the South—laws which have been correctly spoken of as a "disgrace to civilization," and which must be annulled simultaneously with the abolition of slavery—have had the vile institution entailed on them contrary to their wills, are virtually on our side. We may, therefore, very properly strike them off from the black list of three hundred and forty-seven thousand slaveholders, who, as a body, have shocked the civilized world with their barbarous conduct, and from whose conceited and presumptuous ranks are selected the officers who do all the legislation, town, county, state and national, for (against) five millions of poor outraged whites, and three millions of enslaved negroes.

Non-slaveholders of the South, farmers, mechanics and workingmen, we take this occasion to assure you that the slaveholders, the arrogant demagogues whom you have elected to offices of honor and profit, have tricked you, trifled with you, and used you as mere tools for the consummation of their wicked designs. They have purposely kept you in ignorance, and have, by moulding your passions and prejudices to suit themselves, induced you to act in direct opposition to your dearest rights and interests. By a system of the grossest subterfuge and misrepresentation, and in order to avert, for a season, the vengeance that will most assuredly overtake them before long, they have taught you to hate the abolitionists, who are your best and only true friends. Now, as one of your own number, we appeal to you to join us in our patriotic endeavors to rescue the generous soil of the South from the usurped and desolating control of these political vampires. Once and forever, at least so far as this country is concerned, the infernal question of slavery must be disposed of; a speedy and perfect abolishment of the whole institution is the true policy of the South — and this is the policy which we propose to pursue. Will you aid us, will you assist us, will you be freemen, or will you be slaves? These are questions of vital importance; weigh them well in your minds; come to a prudent and firm decision, and hold yourselves in readiness to act in accordance therewith. You must either be for us or against us—anti-slavery or pro-slavery; it is impossible for you to occupy a neutral ground; it is as certain as fate itself, that if you do not voluntarily oppose the usurpations and outrages of the slavocrats, they will force you into involuntary compliance with their infamous measures. Consider well the aggressive, fraudulent and despotic power which they have exercised in the affairs of Kansas; and remember that, if, by adhering to erroneous principles of neutrality or non-resistance, you allow them to force the curse of slavery on that vast and fertile field, the broad area of all the surrounding States and Territories — the whole nation, in fact — will soon fall a prey to their diabolical intrigues and machinations. Thus, if you are not vigilant, will they take advantage of your neutrality, and make you and others the victims of their inhuman despotism. Do not reserve the strength of your arms until you shall have been rendered powerless to strike; the present is the proper time for action; under all the circumstances, apathy or indifference is a crime. First ascertain, as nearly as you can, the precise nature and extent of your duty, and then, without a moment's delay, perform it in good faith. To facilitate you in determining what considerations of right, justice and humanity require at your hands, is one of the primary objects of this work; and we shall certainly fail in our desire if we do not accomplish our task in a manner acceptable to God and advantageous to man.

But we are carrying this chapter beyond all ordinary bounds; and yet, there are many important particulars in which we have drawn no comparison between the free and the slave States. The more weighty remarks which we intended to offer in relation to the new States of the West and Southwest, free and slave, shall appear in the succeeding chapter. With regard to agriculture, and all the multifarious interests of husbandry, we deem it quite unnecessary to say more. Cotton has been shorn of its magic power, and is no longer King; *dried grass,* commonly called hay, is, it seems, the rightful heir to the throne. Commerce, Manufactures, Literature, and other important subjects, shall be considered as we progress.

Chapter 2

How Slavery Can Be Abolished

PRELIMINARY TO OUR ELUCIDATION of what we conceive to be the most discreet, fair and feasible plan for the abolition of slavery, we propose to offer a few additional reasons why it should be abolished. Among the thousand and one arguments that present themselves in support of our position—which, before we part with the reader, we shall endeavor to define so clearly, that it shall be regarded as ultra only by those who imperfectly understand it—is the influence which slavery invariably exercises in depressing the value of real estate; and as this is a matter in which the non-slaveholders of the South, of the West, and of the Southwest, are most deeply interested, we shall discuss it in a sort of preamble of some length.

The oligarchs say we cannot abolish slavery without infringing on the right of property. Again we tell them we do not recognize property in man; but even if we did, and if we were to inventory the negroes at quadruple, the value of their last assessment, still, impelled by a sense of duty to others, and as a matter of simple justice to ourselves, we, the non-slaveholders of the South, would be fully warranted in emancipating all the slaves at once, and that, too, without any compensation whatever to those who claim to be their absolute masters and owners We will explain. In 1850, the average value per acre, of land in the Northern States was $28,07; in the Northwestern $11,39; in the Southern $5,34; and in the Southwestern $6,26. Now, in consequence of numerous natural advantages, among which may be enumerated the greater mildness of climate, richness of soil, deposits of precious metals, abundance and spaciousness of harbors, and super-excellence of water-power, we contend that, had it not been for slavery, the average value of land in all the Southern and Southwestern States, would have been *at least* equal to the average value of the same in the Northern States. We conclude, therefore, and we think the conclusion is founded on principles of equity, that you, the slaveholders, are indebted to us, the non-slaveholders, in the sum of $22,73, which is the difference between $28,07 and $5,34, on every acre of Southern soil in our possession. This claim we bring against you, because slavery, which has inured exclusively to your own benefit, if, indeed, it has been beneficial at all, has shed a blighting influence over our lands, thereby keeping them out of market, and damaging every acre to the amount specified. Sirs! are you ready to settle the account? Let us see how much it is.

There are in the fifteen slave States, 346,048 slaveholders, and 544,926,720 acres of land. Now the object is to ascertain how many acres are owned by slaveholders, and now many by non-slaveholders. Suppose we estimate five hundred acres as the average landed property of each slaveholder; will that be fair? We think it will, taking into consideration the fact that 174,503 of the whole number of slaveholders hold less than five slaves each—68,820 holding only one each. According to this hypothesis, the slaveholders own 173,024,000 acres, and the non-slaveholders the balance, with the exception of about 40,000,000 of acres, which belong to the General Government. The case may be stated thus:

	Area of the Slave States (acres)	544,926,720
Estimates	Acres owned by slaveholders	173,024,000
Estimates	Acres owned by the government	40,000,000 -
		213,024,000
Estimates	Acres owned by non-slaveholders	331,902,720

Now, the total value of three hundred and thirty-one million nine hundred and two thousand seven hundred and twenty acres, at twenty-two dollars and seventy-three cents per acre, is *seven billion five hundred and forty-four million one hundred and forty-eight thousand eight hundred and twenty-five dollars;* and this is our account against you, the slave-holders, on a single score. Considering how this villainous institution has retarded the development of our commercial and manufacturing interests, how it has stifled the aspirations of inventive genius; and, above all, how it has barred from us the fruits of literature and religion — concernments too sacred to be estimated in a pecuniary point of view — might we not, with perfect justice and propriety, duplicate the amount, and still be accounted modest in our demands? Fully advised, however, of your indigent circumstances, we feel it would be utterly useless to call on you for the whole amount that is due us; we shall, therefore, in your behalf, make another draft on the fund of non-slaveholding generosity, and let the account, meagre as it is, stand as above. Though we have given you all the offices, and you have given us none of the benefits of legislation; though we have fought the battles of the South, while you were either lolling in your piazzas, or playing the tory, and endeavoring to filch from us our birthright of freedom; though you have absorbed the wealth of our communities in sending your own children to Northern seminaries and colleges, or in employing Yankee teachers to officiate exclusively in your own families, and have refused to us the limited privilege of common schools; though you have scorned to patronize our mechanics and industrial enterprises, and have passed to the North for every article of apparel, utility, and adornment; and though you have maltreated, outraged and defrauded us in every relation of life, civil, social, and political, yet we are willing to forgive and *forget* you, if you will but do us justice on a single count. Of you, the introducers, aiders and abettors of slavery, we demand indemnification for the damage our lands have sustained on account thereof; the amount of that damage is $7,544,148,825; and now, Sirs, we are ready to receive the money, and if it is perfectly convenient to you, we would be glad to have you pay it in specie! It will not avail you, Sirs, to parley or prevaricate. We must have a settlement. Our claim is just and overdue. We have already indulged you too long. Your criminal extravagance has almost ruined us. We are determined that you shall no longer play the profligate, and fair sumptuously every day at our expense. How do you propose to settle? Do you offer us your negroes in part payment? We do not want your negroes. We would not have all of them, nor any number of them, even as a gift. We hold ourselves above the disreputable and iniquitous practices of buying, selling, and owning slaves. What we demand is damages in money, or other absolute property, as an equivalent for the pecuniary losses we have suffered at your hands. You value your negroes at sixteen hundred millions of dollars, and propose to sell them to us for that sum; we should consider ourselves badly cheated, and disgraced for all time, here and hereafter, if we were to take them off your hands at sixteen farthings! We tell you emphatically, we are firmly resolved never to degrade ourselves by becoming the mercenary purchasers or proprietors of human beings. Except for the purpose of liberating them, we would not give a handkerchief or a tooth-pick for all the slaves in the world. But, in order to show how brazenly absurd are the howls and groans which you invariably set up for compensation, whenever we speak of the abolition of slavery, we will suppose your negroes are worth all you ask for them, and that we are bound to secure to you every cent of the sum before they can become free — in which case, our accounts would stand thus:

Non-slaveholder's account against Slaveholders	$7,544,148,825
Slaveholder's account against Non-slaveholders	1,600,000,000
Balance due Non-slaveholders	$5,944,148,825

Now, Sirs, we ask you in all seriousness, Is it not true that you have filched from us nearly five times the amount of the assessed value of your slaves? Why, then, do you still clamor for more? Is it your purpose to make the game perpetual? Think you that we will ever continue to bow at the wave of your wand, that we will bring humanity into everlasting disgrace by licking the hand that smites us, and that with us there is no point beyond which forbearance ceases to be a virtue? Sirs, if these be your thoughts, you are laboring under a most fatal delusion. Slavery has polluted and impoverished your lands; freedom will restore them to their virgin purity, and add from twenty to thirty dollars to the value of every acre. Correctly speaking, emancipation will cost you nothing; the moment you abolish slavery, that very moment will the putative value of the slave become actual value in the soil. Though there are ten millions of people in the South, and though you, the slaveholders, are only three hundred and forty-seven thousand in number, you have within a fraction of one-third of all the territory belonging to the fifteen slave States. You have a landed estate of 173,024,000 acres, the present average market value of which is only $5,34 per acre; emancipate your slaves on Wednesday morning, and on the Thursday following the value of your lands, and ours too, will have increased to an average of at least $28,07 per acre. Let us see, therefore, even in this one particular, whether the abolition of slavery will not be a real pecuniary advantage to you. The present total market value of all your landed property, at $5,34 per acre, is only $923,248,160! With the beauty and sunlight of freedom beaming on the same estate, it would be worth, at $28,07 per acre, $4,856,873,680! The former sum, deducted from the latter, leaves a balance of $3,933,535,520, and to the full extent of this amount will *your* lands be increased in value whenever you abolish slavery; that is, provided you abolish it before it completely "dries up all the organs of increase." Here is a more manifest and distinct statement of the case:

Estimated value of slaveholders' lands
after slavery shall have been abolished $4,856,783,680

Present value of slaveholders' lands   923,248,160

Probable aggregate enhancement
of value $3,933,535,520

Now, Sirs, this last sum is considerably more than twice as great as the estimated value of your negroes; and those of you, if any there be, who are yet heirs to sane minds and honest hearts, must, it seems to us, admit that the bright prospect which freedom presents for a wonderful increase in the value of real estate, ours as well as yours, to say nothing of the thousand other kindred considerations, ought to be quite sufficient to induce all the Southern States, in their sovereign capacities, to abolish slavery at the earliest practical period. You yourselves, instead of losing anything by the emancipation of your negroes — even though we suppose them to be worth every dime of $1,600,000,000—would, in this one particular, the increased value of land, realize a *net profit* of over *twenty three hundred millions of dollars!* Here are the exact figures:

Net increment of value which it is estimated
will accrue to slaveholders' lands in consequence of the abolition of slavery $3,933,535,520

Putative value of the slaves $1,600,000,000

Slaveholders' estimated net profits of
emancipation $2,333,535,520

What is the import of these figures? They are full of meaning. They proclaim themselves the financial intercessors for freedom, and, with that open-hearted liberality which is so characteristic of the sacred cause in whose behalf they plead, they propose to pay you upward of three thousand nine hundred millions of dollars for the very "property" which you, in all the reckless extravagance of your inhuman avarice, could not find a heart to price at more than one thousand six hundred millions.

In other words, your own lands, groaning and languishing under the monstrous burden of slavery, announce their willingness to pay you all you ask for the negroes, and offer you, besides, a bonus of more than twenty-three hundred millions of dollars, if you will but convert those lands into free soil! *Our* lands, also, cry aloud to be spared from the further pollutions and desolations of slavery; and now, Sirs, we want to know explicitly whether, or not, it is your intention to heed these lamentations of the ground? We want to know whether you are men or devils — whether you are entirely selfish and cruelly dishonest, or whether you have any respect for the rights of others.

We, the non-slaveholders of the South, have many very important interests at stake — interests which, heretofore, you have steadily despised and trampled under foot, but which, henceforth, we shall foster and defend in utter defiance of all the unhallowed influences which it is possible for you, or any other class of slaveholders or slave-breeders to bring against us. Not the least among these interests is our landed property, which, to command a decent price, only needs to be disencumbered of slavery.

In his present condition, we believe man exercises one of the noblest virtues with which heaven has endowed him, when, without taking any undue advantage of his fellowmen, and with a firm, unwavering purpose to confine his expenditures to the legitimate pursuits and pleasures of life, he covets money and strives to accumulate it. Entertaining this view, and having no disposition to make an improper use of money, we are free to confess that we have a greater penchant for twenty-eight dollars than for five; for ninety than for fifteen; for a thousand than for one hundred. South of Mason and Dixon's line we, the non-slaveholders, have 331,902,720 acres of land, the present average market value of which, as previously stated, is only $5,34 per acre; by abolishing slavery we expect to enhance the value to an average of at least $28,07 per acre, and thus realize an average net increase of wealth of more than *seventy-five hundred millions of dollars.* The hope of realizing smaller sums has frequently induced men to perpetrate acts of injustice; we can see no reason why the certainty of becoming immensely rich in real estate, or other property, should make us falter in the performance of a *sacred duty.*

As illustrative of our theme, a bit of personal history may not be out of place in this connection.

Only a few months have elapsed since we sold to an elder brother an interest we held in an old homestead which was willed to us many years ago by our dear departed father. The tract of land, containing two hundred acres, or thereabouts, is situated two and a half miles west of Mocksville, the capital of Davie county, North Carolina, and is very nearly equally divided by Bear Creek, a small tributary of the South Yadkin. More than one-third of this tract — on which we have plowed, and hoed, and harrowed, many a long summer without ever suffering from the effects of *coup de soleil* — is under cultivation; the remaining portion is a well timbered forest, in which, without being very particular, we counted, while hunting through it not long since, sixty-three different kinds of indigenous trees — to say nothing of either coppice, shrubs or plants — among which the hickory, oak, ash, beech, birch, and black walnut, were most abundant. No turpentine or rosin is produced in our part of the State; but there are, on the place of which we speak, several species of the genus Pinus, by the light of whose flammable knots, as radiated on the contents of some half-dozen old books, which, by hook or by crook, had found their way into the neighborhood, we have been enabled to turn the long winter evenings to our advantage, and have thus *partially* escaped from the prison-grounds of those loathsome dungeons of illiteracy in which it has been the constant policy of the oligarchy to keep the masses, the non-slaveholding whites and the negroes, forever confined. The fertility of the soil may be inferred from the quality and variety of its natural productions; the meadow and the bottom, comprising, perhaps, an area of forty acres, are hardly surpassed by the best lands in the valley of the Yadkin. A thorough examination of the orchard will disclose the fact that considerable attention has been paid to the selection of fruits; the buildings are tolerable; the water is good. Altogether, to be frank, and nothing more, it is, for its size, one of the most desirable farms in the county, and will, at any time, command the maximum price of land in Western Carolina. Our brother, anxious to become the sole proprietor, readily agreed to give us the highest market price, which we shall publish.

While reading the Baltimore *Sun*, the morning after we had made the sale, our attention was allured to a paragraph headed "Sales of Real Estate," from which, among other significant items, we learned that a tract of land containing exactly two hundred acres, and occupying a portion of one of the rural districts in the southeastern part of Pennsylvania, near the Maryland line, had been sold the week before, at *one hundred and five dollars and fifty cents* per acre. Judging from the succinct account given in the *Sun*, we are of the opinion that, with regard to fertility of soil, the Pennsylvania tract always has been, is now, and perhaps always will be, rather inferior to the one under special consideration. One is of the same size as the other; both are used for agricultural purposes; in all probability the only *essential* difference between them is this: one is blessed with the pure air of freedom, the other is cursed with the malaria of slavery. For our interest in the old homestead we received a nominal sum, amounting to an average of precisely *five dollars and sixty cents* per acre. No one but our brother, who was keen for the purchase, would have given us quite so much.

And, now, let us ask, what does this narrative teach? We shall use few words in explanation; there is an extensive void, but it can be better filled with reflection. The aggregate value of the one tract is $21,100; that of the other is only $1,120; the difference is $19,980. We contend, therefore, in view of all the circumstances detailed, that the advocates and retainers of slavery, have, to all intents and purposes, defrauded our family out of this last-mentioned sum. In like manner, and on the same basis of deduction, we contend that almost every non-slaveholder, who either is or has been the owner of real estate in the South, would, in a court of strict justice, be entitled to damages—the amount in all cases to be determined with reference to the quality of the land in question. We say this because, in violation of every principle of expediency, justice, and humanity, and in direct opposition to our solemn protests, slavery was foisted upon us, and has been thus far perpetuated, by and through the diabolical intrigues of the oligarchs, and by them alone; and furthermore, because the very best agricultural lands in the Northern States being worth from one hundred to one hundred and seventy-five dollars per acre, there is no possible reason, except slavery, why the more fertile and congenial soil of the South should not be worth at least as much. If, on this principle, we could ascertain, in the matter of real estate, the total indebtedness of the slaveholders to the non-slaveholders, we should doubtless find the sum quite equivalent to the amount estimated on a preceding page — $7,544,148,825.

We have recently conversed with two gentlemen who, to save themselves from the poverty and disgrace of slavery, left North Carolina six or seven years ago, and who are now residing in the territory of Minnesota, where they have accumulated handsome fortunes.

One of them had traveled extensively in Kentucky, Missouri, Ohio, Indiana, and other adjoining States; and, according to his account, and we know him to be a man of veracity, it is almost impossible for persons at a distance, to form a proper conception of the magnitude of the difference between the current value of lands in the Free and the Slave States of the West. On one occasion, embarking at Wheeling, he sailed down the Ohio; Virginia and Kentucky on the one side, Ohio and Indiana on the other. He stopped at several places along the river, first on the right bank, then on the left, and so on, until he arrived at Evansville; continuing his trip, he sailed down to Cairo, thence up the Mississippi to the mouth of the Des Moines; having tarried at different points along the route, sometimes in Missouri, sometimes in Illinois. Wherever he landed on free soil, he found it from one to two hundred per cent more valuable than the slave soil on the opposite bank. If, for instance, the maximum price of land was eight dollars in Kentucky, the minimum price was sixteen in Ohio; if it was seven dollars in Missouri, it was fourteen in Illinois. Furthermore, he assured us, that, so far as he could learn, two years ago, when he traveled through the States of which we speak, the range of prices of agricultural lands, in Kentucky, was from three to eight dollars per acre; in Ohio, from sixteen to forty; in Missouri, from two to seven; in Illinois, from fourteen to thirty; in Arkansas, from one to four; in Iowa, from six to fifteen.

In all the old slave States, as is well known, there are vast bodies of land that can be bought for the merest trifle. We know an enterprising capitalist in Philadelphia, who owns in his individual name, in the State of Virginia, *one hundred and thirty thousand acres,* for which he paid only *thirty-seven and a half cents* per acre! Some years ago, in certain parts of North Carolina, several large tracts were purchased at the rate of *twenty-five cents* per acre!

Hiram Berdan, the distinguished inventor, who has frequently seen freedom and slavery side by side, and who is, therefore, well qualified to form an opinion of their relative influence upon society, says:

"Many comparisons might be drawn between the free and the slave States, either of which should be sufficient to satisfy any man that slavery is not only ruinous to free labor and enterprise, but injurious to morals, and blighting to the soil where it exists. The comparison between the States of Michigan and Arkansas, which were admitted into the Union at the same time, will fairly illustrate the difference and value of free and slave labor, as well as the difference of moral and intellectual progress in a free and in a slave State.

In 1836 these young Stars were admitted into the constellation of the Union. Michigan, with one-half the extent of territory of Arkansas, challenged her sister State for a twenty years' race, and named as her rider, 'Neither slavery, nor involuntary servitude, unless for the punishment of crime, shall ever be tolerated in this State.' Arkansas accepted the challenge, and named as her rider, 'The General Assembly shall have no power to pass laws for the emancipation of slaves without the consent of the owners.' Thus mounted, these two States, the one free and the other slave, started together twenty years ago, and now, having arrived at the end of the proposed race, let us review and mark the progress of each. Michigan comes out in 1856 with three times the population of slave Arkansas, with five times the assessed value of farms, farming implements and machinery, and with eight times the number of public schools."

In the foregoing part of our work, we have drawn comparisons between the old free States and the old slave States, and between the new free States and the new slave States; had we sufficient time and space, we might with the most significant results, change this method of comparison, by contrasting the new free States with the old slave States. Can the slavocrats compare Ohio with Virginia, Illinois with Georgia, or Indiana with South Carolina, without experiencing the agony of inexpressible shame? If they can, then indeed has slavery debased them to a lower deep than we care to contemplate. Herewith we present a brief contrast, as drawn by a Maryland abolitionist, between the most important old slave State and the most important new free State:

"Virginia was a State, wealthy and prosperous, when Ohio was a wilderness belonging to her. She gave that territory away, and what is the result? Ohio supports a population of two million souls, and the mother contains but one and a half millions; yet Virginia is one-third larger than the Buckeye State. Virginia contains 61,000 square miles, Ohio but 40,000. The latter sustains 50 persons to the square mile, while Virginia gives employment to but 25 to the square mile. Notwithstanding Virginia's superiority in years and in soil—for she grows tobacco, as well as corn and wheat—notwithstanding her immense coal-fields, and her splendid Atlantic ports, Ohio, the infant State, had 21 representatives in Congress in 1850, while Virginia had but 13 — the latter having *commenced* in the Union with 10 Congressmen. Compare the progress of these States, and then say, what is it but Free Labor that has advanced Ohio? and to what, except slavery, can we attribute the non-progression of the Old Dominion?"

As a striking illustration of the selfish and debasing influences which slavery exercises over the hearts and minds of slaveholders themselves, we will here state the fact that, when we, the non-slave-holders, remonstrate against the continuance of such a manifest wrong and inhumanity — a system of usurpation and outrage so obviously detrimental to *our* interests—they fly into a terrible passion, exclaiming, among all sorts of horrible threats, which are not unfrequently executed, "It's none of your business!"—meaning to say thereby that their slaves do not annoy us, that slavery affects no one except the masters and their chattels personal, and that *we* should give ourselves no concern about it, whatever! To every man of common sense and honesty of purpose the preposterousness of this assumption is so evident, that any studied attempt to refute it would be a positive insult. Would it be none of our business, if they were to bring the small-pox into the neighborhood, and, with premeditated design, let "foul contagion spread?" Or, if they were to throw a pound of strychnine into a public spring, would that be none of our business? Were they to turn a pack of mad dogs loose on the community, would we be performing the part of good citizens by closing ourselves within doors for the space of nine days, saying nothing to anybody? Small-pox is a nuisance; strychnine is a nuisance; mad dogs are a nuisance; slavery is a nuisance; slave-holders are a nuisance, and so are slave-breeders; it is our business, no, it is our imperative duty, to abate nuisances; we propose, therefore, with the exception of strychnine, which is the least of all these nuisances, to exterminate this catalogue from beginning to end.

We mean precisely what our words express, when we say we believe thieves are, as a general rule, less amenable to the moral law than slaveholders; and here is the basis of our opinion: Ordinarily, thieves wait until we acquire a considerable amount of property, and then they steal a dispensable part of it; but they deprive no one of physical liberty, nor do they fetter the mind; slaveholders, on the contrary, by clinging to the most barbarous relic of the most barbarous age, bring disgrace on themselves, their neighbors, and their country, depreciate the value of their own and others' lands, degrade labor, discourage energy and progress, prevent non-slaveholders from accumulating wealth, curtail their natural rights and privileges, doom their children to ignorance, and all its attendant evils, rob the negroes of their freedom, throw a damper on every species of manual and intellectual enterprise, that is not projected under their own roofs and for their own advantage, and, by other means equally at variance with the principles of justice, though but an insignificant fractional part of the population, they constitute themselves the sole arbiters and legislators for the entire South. Not merely so; the thief rarely steals from more than one man out of an hundred; the slaveholder defrauds ninety and nine, and the hundredth does not escape him. Again, thieves steal trifles from rich men; slaveholders oppress poor men, and enact laws for the perpetuation of their poverty. Thieves practice deceit on the wise; slaveholders take advantage of the ignorant.

We contend, moreover, that slaveholders are more criminal than common murderers. According to their own infamous statutes, if the slave raises his hand to ward off an unmerited blow, they are permitted to take his life with impunity. We are personally acquainted with three ruffians who have become actual murderers under circumstances of this nature. One of them killed two negroes on one occasion; the other two have murdered but one each. Neither of them has ever been subjected to even the preliminaries of a trial; not one of them has ever been arrested; their own private explanations of the homicides exculpated them from all manner of blame in the premises. They had done nothing wrong in the eyes of the community. The negroes made an effort to shield themselves from the tortures of a merciless flagellation, and were shot dead on the spot. Their murderers still live, and are treated as honorable members of society! No matter how many slaves or free negroes may witness the perpetration of these atrocious homicides, not one of them is ever allowed to lift up his voice in behalf of his murdered brother. In the South, negroes, whether bond or free, are never, under any circumstances, permitted to utter a syllable under oath, except for or against persons of their own color; their testimony against white persons is of no more consequence than the idle zephyr of the summer.

We shall now introduce four tables of valuable and interesting statistics, to which philosophic and discriminating readers will doubtless have frequent occasions to refer. Tables 22 and 23 will show the area of the several States, in square miles and in acres, and the number of inhabitants to the square mile in each State; also the grand total, or the average, of every statistical column; tables 24 and 25 will exhibit the total number of inhabitants residing in each State, according to the census of 1850, the number of whites, the number of free colored, and the number of slaves. The recapitulations of these tables will be followed by a complete list of the number of slaveholders in the United States, showing the exact number in each Southern State, and in the District of Columbia. Most warmly do we commend all these statistics to the *studious* attention of the reader. Their language is more eloquent than any possible combination of Roman vowels and consonants. We have spared no pains in arranging them so as to express at a single glance the great truths of which they are composed; and we doubt not that the plan we have adopted will meet with general approbation. Numerically considered, it will be perceived that the slaveholders are, in reality, a very insignificant class. Of them, however, we shall have more to say hereafter.

Table No. XXII.
Area of the Free States

	Square Miles	Acres	Inhabitants to square mile
California	155,980	99,827,200	1
Connecticut	4,674	2,991,360	79
Illinois	55,405	35,359,200	15
Indiana	33,809	21,637,760	29
Iowa	50,914	32,584,960	4
Maine	31,766	20,330,240	18
Massachusetts	7,800	4,992,000	128
Michigan	56,243	35,995,520	7
New Hampshire	9,280	5,939,200	34
New Jersey	8,320	5,324,800	59
New York	47,000	30,080,000	66
Ohio	39,964	26,576,960	50
Pennsylvania	46,000	29,440,000	50
Rhode Island	1,306	835,840	113
Vermont	10,212	6,535,680	31
Wisconsin	53,924	34,511,360	6
TOTAL	612,597	392,062,082	2,191
Corrected		*392,962,080*	

Table No. XXIII.
Area of the Slave States

	Square Miles	Acres	Inhabitants to square mile
Alabama	50,722	32,027,490	15
Arkansas	52,198	33,406,720	4
Delaware	2,120	1,356,800	43
Florida	59,268	37,931,520	1
Georgia	58,000	37,120,000	16
Kentucky	37,680	24,115,200	26
Louisiana	41,255	26,403,200	13
Maryland	11,124	7,119,360	52
Mississippi	47,156	30,179,840	13
Missouri	67,380	43,123,200	10
North Carolina	50,704	32,450,560	17
South Carolina	29,385	18,805,400	23
Tennessee	45,600	29,184,000	22
Texas	237,504	152,002,560	1
Virginia	61,352	39,165,280	23
TOTAL	851,448	544,926,720	11
Corrected		*544,391,130*	

Table No. XXIV.
Population of the Free States — 1850

	Whites	Free Colored	Total
California	91,635	962	92,597
Connecticut	363,099	7,693	370,792
Illinois	846,034	5,436	851,470
Indiana	977,154	11,262	988,416
Iowa	191,881	333	192,214
Maine	581,813	1,356	583,169
Massachusetts	985,450	9,064	994,514
Michigan	395,071	2,583	397,654
New Hampshire	317,456	520	317,976
New Jersey	465,509	23,810	489,555
New York	3,048,325	49,069	3,097,394
Ohio	1,955,050	25,279	1,980,329
Pennsylvania	2,258,160	53,626	2,311,786
Rhode Island	143,875	3,670	147,545
Vermont	313,402	718	314,120
Wisconsin	304,756	635	305,391
TOTAL	13,233,670	196,116	13,434,922
Corrected	*13,238,670*	*196,016*	

Table No. XXV.

Population of the Slave States — 1850

	Whites	Free Colored	Slaves	Total
Alabama	426,514	2,265	342,844	771,623
Arkansas	162,189	608	47,100	209,897
Delaware	71,169	18,073	2,290	91,532
Florida	47,203	932	89,310	87,445
Georgia	521,572	2,931	381,622	906,185
Kentucky	761,413	10,011	210,981	982,405
Louisiana	255,491	17,462	244,809	517,762
Maryland	417,943	74,723	90,368	583,034
Mississippi	295,718	930	309,878	606,326
Missouri	592,004	2,618	87,422	682,044
North Carolina	553,028	27,463	288,548	869,039
South Carolina	274,563	8,960	384,984	668,507
Tennessee	756,836	6,422	239,459	1,002,717
Texas	154,034	397	58,161	212,592
Virginia	894,800	54,333	472,528	1,421,661
TOTAL	6,184,477	228,128	3,250,304	9,612,769
Corrected		*228,138*	*3,200,364*	*9,612,979*

Recapitulation — Area

	Square Miles	Acres
Area of the Slave States	851,448	544,926,720
Area of the Free States	612,597	392,062,082
Balances in favor of Slave States	238,851	152,864,638

Recapitulation — Population — 1850

	Whites	Total
Population of the Free States	13,233,670	13,434,922
Population of the Slave States	6,184,477	9,612,976
Balances in favor of the Free States	7,049,193	3,821,946

Free Colored and Slave — 1850

Free Negroes in the Slave States	228,138
Free Negroes in the Free States	196,116
Excess of Free Negroes in the Slave States	32,022
Slaves in the Slave States	3,200,364
Free Negroes in the Slave States	228,138
Aggregate Negro Population of the Slave	3,428,502

The Territories and the District of Columbia		
	Area in Square Miles	Population
Indian Territory	71,127	
Kansas Territory	114,798	
Minnesota Territory	166,025	6,077
Nebraska Territory	335,882	
N. Mexico Territory	207,007	61,547
Oregon Territory	185,030	13,294
Utah Territory	269,170	11,380
Washington Territory	123,022	
Columbia, Dist. of	60	*51,687
Aggregate of Area and Population	1,472,121	143,985

* Of the 51,687 inhabitants in the District of Columbia, in 1850, 10,057 were Free Colored, and 3,687 were slaves.

Number of Slaveholders in the United States — 1850

Alabama	29,295
Arkansas	5,999
Columbia, District of	1,477
Delaware	809
Florida	3,520
Georgia	38,456
Kentucky	38,385
Louisiana	20,670
Maryland	16,040
Mississippi	23,116
Missouri	19,185
North Carolina	28,303
South Carolina	25,596
Tennessee	33,864
Texas	7,747
Virginia	55,063
Total Number of Slaveholders	347,525

Classification of the Slaveholders — 1850

Holders of 1 slave	68,820
Holders of 1 and under 5	105,683
Holders of 5 and under 10	80,765
Holders of 10 and under 20	54,595
Holders of 20 and under 50	29,733
Holders of 50 and under 100	6,196
Holders of 100 and under 200	1,479
Holders of 200 and under 300	187
Holders of 300 and under 500	56
Holders of 500 and under 1,000	9
Holders of 1,000 and over	2
Aggregate Number of Slaveholders	347,525

It thus appears that there are in the United States, three hundred and forty-seven thousand five hundred and twenty-five slavehold-ers. But this appearance is deceptive. The actual number is certainly less than two hundred thousand. Professor De Bow, the Superinten-dent of the Census, informs us that "the number includes slave-hirers," and furthermore, that "where the party owns slaves in different counties, or in different States, he will be entered more than once." Now every Southerner, who has any practical knowl-edge of affairs, must know, and does know, that every New Year's day, like almost every other day, is desecrated in the South, by publicly hiring out slaves to large numbers of non-slaveholders. The slave-owners, who are the exclusive manufacturers of public senti-ment, have popularized the dictum that white servants, decency, virtue, and justice, are unfashionable; and there are, we are sorry to say, nearly one hundred and sixty thousand non-slaveholding sycophants, who have subscribed to this false philosophy, and who are giving constant encouragement to the infamous practices of slaveholding and slave-breeding, by hiring at least one slave every year.

In the Southern States, as in all other slave countries, there are three odious classes of mankind; the slaves themselves, who are cowards; the slaveholders, who are tyrants; and the non-slaveholding slave-hirers, who are lickspittles. Whether either class is really entitled to the regards of a gentleman is a matter of grave doubt. The slaves are pitiable; the slaveholders are detestable; the slave-hirers are contemptible.

With the statistics at our command, it is impossible for us to ascertain the exact numbers of slaveholders and non-slaveholding slave-hirers in the slave States; but we have data which will enable us to approach very near to the facts. The town from which we hail, Salisbury, the capital of Rowan county, North Carolina, contains about twenty-three hundred inhabitants, including three hundred and seventy-two slaves, fifty-one slaveholders, and forty-three non-slaveholding slave-hirers. Taking it for granted that this town furnishes a fair relative proportion of all the slaveholders, and non-slaveholding slave-hirers in the slave States, the whole number of the former, including those who have been "entered more than once," is one hundred and eighty-eight thousand five hundred and fifty-one; of the latter, one hundred and fifty-eight thousand nine hundred and seventy-four; and, now, estimating that there are in Maryland, Virginia, and other grain-growing States, an aggregate of two thousand slave-owners, who have cotton plantations *stocked* with negroes in the far South, and who have been "entered more than once," we find, as the result of our calculations, that the total number of actual slaveholders in the Union, is precisely one hundred and eighty-six thousand five hundred and fifty-one — as follows:

Number of actual slaveholders in the United States	186,551
Number "entered more than once"	2,000
Number of non-slaveholding slave-hirers	158,974
Aggregate number, according to De Bow	347,525

The greater number of non-slaveholding slave-hirers, are a kind of third-rate aristocrats — persons who formerly owned slaves, but whom slavery, as is its custom, has dragged down to poverty, leaving them, in their false and shiftless pride, to eke out a miserable existence over the hapless chattels personal of other men.

So it seems that the total number of actual slave-owners, including their entire crew of cringing lickspittles, against whom we have to contend, is but three hundred and forty-seven thousand five hundred and twenty-five. Against this army for the defense and propagation of slavery, we think it will be an easy matter — independent of the negroes, who, in nine cases out of ten, would be delighted with an opportunity to cut their masters' throats, and without accepting of a single recruit from either of the free States, England, France or Germany—to muster one at least three times as large, and far more respectable for its utter extinction. We hope, however, and believe, that the matter in dispute may be adjusted without arraying these armies against each other in hostile attitude. We desire peace, not war — justice, not blood. Give us fair-play, secure to us the right of discussion, the freedom of speech, and we will settle the difficulty at the ballot-box, not on the battle-ground —by force of reason, not by force of arms. But we are wedded to one purpose from which no earthly power can ever divorce us. We are determined to abolish slavery at all hazards—in defiance of all the opposition, of whatever nature, which it is possible for the slavocrats to bring against us. Of this they may take due notice, and govern themselves accordingly.

Before we proceed further, it may be necessary to call attention to the fact that, though the ostensible proprietorship of the slaves is vested in fewer individuals than we have usually counted in our calculations concerning them, the force and drift of our statistics remain unimpaired. In the main, all our figures are correct. The tables which we have prepared, especially, and the recapitulations of those tables, may be relied on with all the confidence that is due to American official integrity; for, as we have substantially remarked on a previous occasion, the particulars of which they are composed have been obtained from the returns of competent census agents, who, with Prof. De Bow as principal, were expressly employed to collect them. As for our minor labors in the science of numbers, we cheerfully submit them to the candid scrutiny of the impartial critic.

A majority of the slaveholders with whom we are acquainted— and we happen to know a few dozen more than we care to know— own, or pretend to own, at least fifteen negroes each; some of them are the masters of more than fifty each; and we have had the *honor*(!) of an introduction to one man who is represented as the owner of sixteen hundred! It is said that if all the lands of this latter worthy were in one tract, they might be formed into two counties of more than ordinary size; he owns plantations and woodlands in three cotton-growing States.

The quantity of land owned by the slaveholder is generally in proportion to the number of negroes at his "quarter;" the master of only one or two slaves, if engaged in agriculture, seldom owns less than three hundred acres; the holder of eight or ten slaves usually owns from a thousand to fifteen hundred acres; five thousand acres are not unfrequently found in the possession of the master of fifty slaves; while in Columbia, South Carolina, about twelve months ago, a certain noted slaveholder was pointed out to us, and reported as the owner of nearly two hundred thousand acres in the State of Mississippi. How the great mass of illiterate poor whites, a majority of whom are the indescribably wretched tenants of these slavocratic landsharks, are specially imposed upon and socially outlawed, we shall, if we have time and space, take occasion to explain in a subsequent chapter.

Thus far, in giving expression to our sincere and settled opinions, we have endeavored to show, in the first place, that slavery is a great moral, social, civil, and political evil — a dire enemy to true wealth and national greatness, and an atrocious crime against both God and man; and, in the second place, that it is a paramount duty which we owe to heaven, to the earth, to America, to humanity, to our posterity, to our consciences, and to our pockets, to adopt effectual and judicious measures for its immediate abolition. The questions now arise, How can the evil be averted? What are the most prudent and practical means that can be devised for the abolition of slavery? In the solution of these problems it becomes necessary to deal with a multiplicity of stubborn realities. And yet, we can see no reason why North Carolina, in her sovereign capacity, may not, with equal ease and success, do what forty-five other States of the world have done within the last forty-five years. Nor do we believe any good reason exists why Virginia should not perform as great a deed in 1859 as did New York in 1799. Massachusetts abolished slavery in 1780; would it not be a masterly stroke of policy in Tennessee, and every other slave State, to abolish it in or before 1860?

Not long since, a slavocrat, writing on this subject, said, apologetically, "we frankly admit that slavery is a monstrous evil; but what are we to do with an institution which has baffled the wisdom of our greatest statesmen?" Unfortunately for the South, since the days of Washington, Jefferson, Madison, and their illustrious compatriots, she has never had more than half a dozen statesmen, all told; of mere politicians, wire-pullers, and slave-driving demagogues, she has had enough, and to spare; but of statesmen, in the true sense of the term, she has had, and now has, but precious few—fewer just at this time, perhaps, than ever before. It is far from a matter of surprise to us that slavery has, for such a long period, baffled the "wisdom" of the oligarchy; but our surprise is destined to culminate in amazement, if the wisdom of the non-slaveholders does not soon baffle slavery.

From the eleventh year previous to the close of the eighteenth century down to the present moment, slaveholders and slave-breeders, who, to speak naked truth, are, as a general thing, unfit to occupy any honorable station in life, have, by chicanery and usurpation, wielded all the official power of the South; and, excepting the patriotic services of the noble abolitionists above-mentioned, the sole aim and drift of their legislation has been to aggrandize themselves, to strengthen slavery, and to keep the poor whites, the constitutional majority, bowed down in the deepest depths of degradation. We propose to subvert this entire system of oligarchal despotism. We think there should be *some* legislation for decent white men, not alone for negroes and slaveholders. Slavery lies at the root of all the shame, poverty, ignorance, tyranny and imbecility of the South; slavery must be thoroughly eradicated; let this be done, and a glorious future will await us.

The statesmen who are to abolish slavery in Kentucky, must be mainly and independently constituted by the non-slaveholders of

Kentucky; so in every other slave State. Past experience has taught us the sheer folly of ever expecting voluntary justice from the slaveholders. Their illicit intercourse with "the mother of harlots" has been kept up so long, and their whole natures have, in consequence, become so depraved, that there is scarcely a spark of honor or magnanimity to be found amongst them. As well might one expect to hear highwaymen clamoring for a universal interdict against traveling, as to expect slaveholders to pass laws for the abolition of slavery. Under all the circumstances, it is the duty of the non-slaveholders to mark out an independent course for themselves, to steer entirely clear of the oligarchy, and to utterly contemn and ignore the many vile instruments of power, animate and inanimate, which have been so freely and so effectually used for their enslavement. Now is the time for them to assert their rights and liberties; never before was there such an appropriate period to strike for Freedom in the South.

Had it not been for the better sense, the purer patriotism, and the more practical justice of the non-slaveholders, the Middle States and New England would still be groaning and groveling under the ponderous burden of slavery; New York would never have risen above the dishonorable level of Virginia; Pennsylvania, trampled beneath the iron-heel of the black code, would have remained the unprogressive parallel of Georgia; Massachusetts would have continued till the present time, and Heaven only knows how much longer, the contemptible coequal of South Carolina.

Succeeded by the happiest moral effects and the grandest physical results, we have seen slavery crushed beneath the wisdom of the non-slaveholding statesmen of the North; followed by corresponding influences and achievements, many of us who have not yet passed the meridian of life, are destined to see it equally crushed beneath the wisdom of the non-slaveholding Statesmen of the South. With righteous indignation, we enter our disclaimer against the base yet baseless admission that Louisiana and Texas are incapable of producing as great statesmen as Rhode Island and Connecticut. What has been done for New Jersey by the statesmen of New Jersey, can be done for North Carolina by the statesmen of North Carolina; the wisdom of the former State has abolished slavery; as sure as the earth revolves on its axis, the wisdom of the latter will not do less.

That our plan for the abolition of slavery, is the best that can be devised, we have not the vanity to contend; but that it is a good one, and will do to act upon until a better shall have been suggested, we do firmly and conscientiously believe. Though but little skilled in the delicate art of surgery, we have pretty thoroughly probed slavery, the frightful tumor on the body politic, and have, we think, ascertained the precise remedies requisite for a speedy and perfect cure. Possibly the less ardent friends of freedom may object to our prescription, on the ground that some of its ingredients are too griping, and that it will cost the patient a deal of most excruciating pain. But let them remember that the patient is exceedingly refractory, that the case is a desperate one, and that drastic remedies are indispensably necessary. When they shall have invented milder yet equally efficacious ones, it will be time enough to discontinue the use of ours — then no one will be readier than we to discard the infallible strong recipe for the infallible mild. Not at the persecution of a few thousand slaveholders, but at the restitution of natural rights and prerogatives to several millions of non-slaveholders, do we aim.

Inscribed on the banner, which we herewith unfurl to the world, with the full and fixed determination to stand by it or die by it, unless one of more virtuous efficacy shall be presented, are the mottoes which, in substance, embody the principles, as we conceive, that should govern us in our patriotic warfare against the most subtle and insidious foe that ever menaced the inalienable rights and liberties and dearest interests of America:

1st. Thorough Organization and Independent Political Action on the part of the Non-Slaveholding whites of the South.

2nd. Ineligibility of Slaveholders — Never another vote to the

Trafficker in Human Flesh.

3rd. No Cooperation with Slaveholders in Politics—No Fellowship with them in Religion—No Affiliation with them in Society.

4th. No Patronage to Slaveholding Merchants—No Guestship in Slave-waiting Hotels — No Fees to Slaveholding Lawyers — No Employment of Slaveholding Physicians — No Audience to Slaveholding Parsons.

5th. No Recognition of Pro-slavery Men, except as Ruffians, Outlaws, and Criminals.

6th. Abrupt Discontinuance of Subscription to Pro-slavery Newspapers.

7th. The Greatest Possible Encouragement to Free White Labor.

8th. No more Hiring of Slaves by Non-slaveholders.

9th. Immediate Death to Slavery, or if not immediate, unqualified Proscription of its Advocates during the Period of its Existence.

10th. A Tax of Sixty Dollars on every Slaveholder for each and every Negro in his Possession at the present time, or at any intermediate time between now and the 4th of July, 1863—said Money to be Applied to the transportation of the Blacks to Liberia, to their Colonization in Central or South America, or to their Comfortable Settlement within the Boundaries of the United States.

11th. An additional Tax of Forty Dollars per annum to be levied annually, on every Slaveholder for each and every Negro found in his possession after the 4th of July, 1863—said Money to be paid into the hands of the Negroes so held in Slavery, or, in cases of death, to their next of kin, and to be used by them at their own option

This, then, is the outline of our scheme for the abolition of slavery in the Southern States. Let it be acted upon with due promptitude, and, as certain as truth is mightier than error, fifteen years will not elapse before every foot of territory, from the mouth of the Delaware to the emboguing of the Rio Grande, will glitter with the jewels of freedom. Some time during this year, next, or the year following, let there be a general convention of non-slaveholders from every slave State in the Union, to deliberate on the momentous issues now pending. First, let them adopt measures for holding in restraint the diabolical excesses of the oligarchy; secondly, in order to cast off the thraldom which the infamous slave-power has fastened upon them, and, as the first step necessary to be taken to regain the inalienable rights and liberties with which they were invested by Nature, but of which they have been divested by the accursed dealers in human flesh, let them devise ways and means for the complete annihilation of slavery; thirdly, let them put forth an equitable and comprehensive platform, fully defining their position, and inviting the active sympathy and cooperation of the millions of down-trodden non-slaveholders throughout the Southern and Southwestern States. Let all these things be done, not too hastily, but with calmness, deliberation, prudence, and circumspection; if need be, let the delegates to the convention continue in session one or two weeks; only let their labors be wisely and thoroughly performed; let them, on Wednesday morning, present to the poor whites of the South, a well-digested scheme for the reclamation of their ancient rights and prerogatives, and, on the Thursday following, slavery in the United States will be worth absolutely less than nothing; for then, besides being so vile and precarious that nobody will want it, it will be a lasting reproach to those in whose hands it is lodged.

Were it not that other phases of the subject admonish us to be economical of space, we could suggest more than a dozen different plans, either of which, if scrupulously carried out, would lead to a wholesome, speedy, and perfect termination of slavery. Under all the circumstances, however, it might be difficult for us — perhaps it would not be the easiest thing in the world for any body else — to suggest a better plan than the one above. Let it, or one embodying its principal features, be adopted forthwith, and the last wail of slavery will soon be heard, growing fainter and fainter, till it dies utterly away, to be succeeded by the jubilant shouts of emancipated millions.

Henceforth, let it be distinctly understood that ownership in slaves constitutes ineligibility—that it is a crime, as we verily believe it is, to vote for a slavocrat for any office whatever. Indeed, it is our honest conviction that all the pro-slavery slaveholders, who are alone responsible for the continuance of the baneful institution among us, deserve to be at once reduced to a parallel with the basest criminals that lie fettered within the cells of our public prisons. Beyond the power of computation is the extent of the moral, social, civil, and political evils which they have brought, and are still bringing, on the country. Were it possible that the whole number could be gathered together and transformed into four equal gangs of licensed robbers, ruffians, thieves, and murderers, society, we feel assured, would suffer less from their atrocities then than it does now. Let the wholesome public sentiment of the non-slaveholders be vigilant and persevering in bringing them down to their proper level. Long since, and in the most unjust and cruel manner, have they socially outlawed the non-slaveholders; now security against further oppression, and indemnity for past grievances, make it incumbent on the non-slaveholders to cast them into the identical pit that they dug for their betters—thus teaching them how to catch a Tartar!

At the very moment we write, as has been the case ever since the United States have had a distinct national existence, and as will always continue to be the case, unless right triumphs over wrong, all the civil, political, and other offices, within the gift of the South, are filled with negro-nursed incumbents from the ranks of that execrable band of misanthropes—three hundred and forty-seven thousand in number—who, for the most part, obtain their living by breeding, buying and selling slaves. The magistrates in the villages, the constables in the districts, the commissioners of the towns, the mayors of the cities, the sheriffs of the counties, the judges of the various courts, the members of the legislatures, the governors of the States, the representatives and senators in Congress—are all slaveholders. Nor does the catalogue of their usurpations end here.

Through the most heart-sickening arrogance and bribery, they have obtained control of the General Government, and all the consuls, ambassadors, envoys extraordinary and ministers plenipotentiary, who are chosen from the South, and commissioned to foreign countries, are selected with special reference to the purity of their proslavery antecedents. If credentials have ever been issued to a single non-slaveholder of the South, we are ignorant of both the fact and the hearsay; indeed, it would be very strange if this much abused class of persons were permitted to hold important offices abroad, when they are not allowed to hold unimportant ones at home.

And, then, there is the Presidency of the United States, which office has been held *forty-eight* years by slaveholders from the South, and only *twenty* years by non-slaveholders from the North. Nor is this the full record of oligarchal obtrusion. On an average, the offices of Secretary of State, Secretary of the Treasury, Secretary of the Interior, Secretary of the Navy, Secretary of War, Postmaster-General and Attorney-General, have been under the control of slave-drivers nearly two-thirds of the time. The Chief Justices and the Associate Justices of the Supreme Court of the United States, the Presidents pro tem. of the Senate, and the Speakers of the House of Representatives, have, in a large majority of instances, been slave-breeders from the Southern side of the Potomac. Five slaveholding Presidents have been reëlected to the chief magistracy of the Republic, while no non-slaveholder has ever held the office more than a single term. Thus we see plainly that even the non-slaveholders of the North, to whose freedom, energy, enterprise, intelligence, wealth, population, power, progress, and prosperity, our country is almost exclusively indebted for its high position among the nations of the earth, have been arrogantly denied a due participation in the honors of federal office. When "the sum of all villainies" shall have ceased to exist, then the rights of the non slaveholders of the North, of the South, of the East, and of the West, will be duly recognized and respected; not before.

With all our heart, we hope and believe it is the full and fixed determination of a majority of the more intelligent and patriotic citizens of this Republic, that the Presidential chair shall never again be filled by a slavocrat. Safely may we conclude that the doom of the oligarchy is already sealed with respect to that important and dignified station; it now behooves us to resolve, with equal firmness and effect, that, after a certain period during the next decade of years, no slaveholder shall occupy any position in the Cabinet, that no slave-breeder shall be sent as a diplomatist to any foreign country, that no slave-driver shall be permitted to bring further disgrace on either the Senate or the House of Representatives, that the chief justices, associate justices, and judges of the several courts, the governors of the States, the members of the legislatures, and all the minor functionaries of the land, shall be free from the heinous crime of ownership in man.

For the last sixty-eight years, slaveholders have been the sole and constant representatives of the South, and what have they accomplished? It requires but little time and few words, to tell the story of their indiscreet and unhallowed performances. In fact, with what we have already said, gestures alone would suffice to answer the inquiry. We can make neither a more truthful nor emphatic reply than to point to our thinly inhabited States, to our fields despoiled of their virgin soil, to the despicable price of lands to our unvisited cities and towns, to our vacant harbors and idle water-power, to the dreary absence of shipping and manufactories, to our unpensioned soldiers of the revolution, to the millions of living monuments of ignorance, to the poverty of the whites, and to the wretchedness of the blacks.

Either directly or indirectly, are slave-driving demagogues, who have ostentatiously set up pretensions to statesmanship, responsible for every dishonorable weakness and inequality that exists between the North and the South. Let them shirk the responsibility if they can; but it is morally impossible for them to do so. We know how ready they have always been to cite the numerical strength of the

North, as a valid excuse for their inability to procure appropriations from the General Government, for purposes of internal improvement, for the establishment of lines of ocean steamers to South American and European ports, and for the accomplishment of other objects. Before that apology ever escapes from their lips again, let them remember that the numerical weakness of the South is wholly attributable to their own villainous statism. Had the Southern States, in accordance with the principles enunciated in the Declaration of Independence, abolished slavery at the same time the Northern States abolished it, there would have been, long since, and most assuredly at this moment, a larger, wealthier, wiser, and more powerful population, south of Mason and Dixon's line, than there now is north of it. This fact being so well established that no reasonable man denies it, it is evident that the oligarchy will have to devise another subterfuge for even temporary relief.

Until slavery and slaveholders cease to be the only favored objects of legislation in the South, the North will continue to maintain the ascendency in every important particular. With those loathsome objects out of the way, it would not take the non-slaveholders of the South more than a quarter of a century to bring her up, in all respects, to a glorious equality with the North; nor would it take them much longer to surpass the latter, which is the most vigorous and honorable rival that they have in the world. Three quarters of a century hence, if slavery is abolished within the next ten years, as it ought to be, the South will, we believe, be as much greater than the North, as the North is now greater than the South. Three quarters of a century hence, if the South retains slavery, which God forbid! she will be to the North much the same that Poland is to Russia, that Cuba is to Spain, or that Ireland is to England.

What we want and must have, as the only sure means of attaining to a position worthy of Sovereign States in this eminently progressive and utilitarian age, is an energetic, intelligent, enterprising, virtuous, and unshackled population; an untrammeled press, and the Freedom of Speech. For ourselves, as white people, and for the negroes and other persons of whatever color or condition, we demand all the rights, interests and prerogatives, that are guarantied to corresponding classes of mankind in the North, in England, in France, in Germany, or in any other civilized and enlightened country. Any proposition that may be offered conceding less than this demand, will be promptly and disdainfully rejected.

Speaking of the non-slaveholders of the South, George M. Weston, a zealous co-laborer in the cause of Freedom, says:

"The non-slaveholding whites of the South, being not less than seven-tenths of the whole number of whites, would seem to be entitled to some enquiry into their actual condition; and especially, as they have no real political weight or consideration in the country, and little opportunity to speak for themselves. I have been for twenty years a reader of Southern newspapers, and a reader and hearer of Congressional debates; but, in all that time, I do not recollect ever to have seen or heard these non-slaveholding whites referred to by Southern 'gentlemen,' as constituting any part of what they call 'the South.' When the rights of the South, or its wrongs, or its policy, or its interests, or its institutions, are spoken of, reference is always intended to the rights, wrongs, policy, interests, and institutions of the three hundred and forty-seven thousand slaveholders. Nobody gets into Congress from the South but by their direction; nobody speaks at Washington for any Southern interest except theirs. Yet there is, at the South, quite another interest than theirs; embracing from two to three times as many white people; and, as we shall presently see, entitled to the deepest sympathy and commiseration, in view of the material, intellectual, and moral privations to which it has been subjected, the degradation to which it has already been reduced, and the still more fearful degradation with which it is threatened by the inevitable operation of existing causes and influences."

The following extract, from a paper on "Domestic Manufactures in the South and West," published by M. Tarver, of Missouri, may be appropriately introduced in this connection:

"The non-slaveholders possess, generally, but very small means, and the land which they possess is almost universally poor, and so sterile that a scanty subsistence is all that can be derived from its cultivation; and the more fertile soil, being in the possession of the slaveholders, must ever remain out of the power of those who have none. This state of things is a great drawback, and bears heavily upon and depresses the moral energies of the poorer classes. The acquisition of a respectable position in the scale of wealth appears so difficult, that they decline the hopeless pursuit, and many of them settle down into habits of idleness, and become the almost passive subjects of all its consequences. And I lament to say that I have observed of late years, that an evident deterioration is taking place in this part of the population, the younger portion of it being less educated, less industrious, and in every point of view less respectable than their ancestors."

Equally worthy of attention is the testimony of Gov. Hammond, of South Carolina, who says:

"According to the best calculation, which, in the absence of statistic facts, can be made, it is believed, that of the three hundred thousand white inhabitants of South Carolina, there are not less than fifty thousand whose industry, such as it is, and compensated as it is, is not, in the present condition of things, and does not promise to be hereafter, adequate to procure them, honestly, such a support as every white person is, and feels himself entitled to. And this, next to emigration, is, perhaps, the heaviest of the weights that press upon the springs of our prosperity. Most of these now follow agricultural pursuits, in feeble, yet injurious competition with slave labor. Some, perhaps, not more from inclination, than from the want of due encouragement, can scarcely be said to work at all. They obtain a precarious subsistence, by occasional jobs, by hunting, by fishing, sometimes by plundering fields or folds, and too often by what is, in its effects, far worse—trading with slaves, and seducing them to plunder for their benefit."

Conjoined with the sundry plain straightforward facts which have issued from our own pen, these extracts show conclusively that immediate and independent political action on the part of the non-slaveholding whites of the South, is, with them, a matter, not only of positive duty, but also of the utmost importance. As yet, it is in their power to rescue the South from the gulf of shame and guilt, into which slavery has plunged her; but if they do not soon arouse themselves from their apathy, this power will be wrenched from them, and then, unable to resist the strong arm of the oppressor, they will be completely degraded to a social and political level with the negroes, whose condition of servitude will, in the meantime, become far more abject and forlorn than it is now.

In addition to the reasons which we have already assigned why no slavocrat should, in the future, be elected to any office whatever, there are others that deserve to be carefully considered. Among these may be mentioned the illbreeding and the ruffianism of slaveholding officials. Tedious indeed would be the task to enumerate all the homicides, duels, assaults and batteries, and other crimes, of which they are the authors in the course of a single year. To the general reader their career at the seat of government is well known; there, on frequent occasions, choking with rage at seeing their wretched sophistries scattered to the winds by the sound, logical reasoning of the champions of Freedom, they have over-stepped the bounds of common decency, vacated the chair of honorable controversy, and, in the most brutal and cowardly manner, assailed their unarmed opponents with bludgeons, bowie knives and pistols. Compared with some of their barbarisms at home, however, their frenzied onslaughts at the national Capital have been but the simplest breaches of civil deportment; and it is only for the purpose of avoiding personalities that we now refrain from divulging a few instances of the unparalleled atrocities which they have perpetrated in legislative halls South of the Potomac. Nor is it alone in the national and State legislatures that they substitute brute force for genteel behavior and acuteness of intellect. Neither court-houses nor public streets, hotels nor private dwellings, rum-holes nor law-offices, are held sacred from their murderous conflicts. About certain silly abstractions that no practical business man ever allows to occupy his time or attention, they are eternally wrangling; and thus it is that hostile encounters, duels, homicides, and other demonstrations of personal violence, have become so popular in all slaveholding communities. A few years of entire freedom from the cares and perplexities of public life, would, we have no doubt, greatly improve both their manners and their morals; and we suggest that it is a Christian duty, which devolves on the non-slaveholders of the South, to disrobe them of the mantle of office, which they have so long worn with disgrace to themselves, injustice to their constituents, and ruin to their country.

But what shall we say of such men as Botts, Stuart, and Macfarland of Virginia; of Raynor, Morehead, Miller, Stanly, Graves, and Graham of North Carolina; of Davis and Hoffman of Maryland; of Blair and Benton of Missouri; of the Marshalls of Kentucky; and of Etheridge of Tennessee? All these gentlemen, and many others of the same school, entertain, we believe, sentiments similar to those that were entertained by the Fathers of the Republic—that slavery is a great moral, social, civil, and political evil, to be got rid of at the earliest practical period—and if they do, in order to secure our votes, it is only necessary for them to "have the courage of their opinions," to renounce slavery, and to come out frankly, fairly and squarely, in favor of freedom. To neither of these patriotic sons of the South, nor to anyone of the class to which they belong, would we give any offence whatever. In our strictures on the criminality of pro-slavery demagogues we have had heretofore, and shall have hereafter, no sort of reference to any respectable slaveholder—by which we mean, any slaveholder who admits the injustice and inhumanity of slavery, and who is not averse to the discussion of measures for its speedy and total extinction.

Such slaveholders are virtually on our side, that is, on the side of the non-slaveholding whites, with whom they may very properly be classified. On this point, once for all, we desire to be distinctly understood; for it would be manifestly unjust not to discriminate between the anti-slavery proprietor who owns slaves by the law of entailment, and the pro-slavery proprietor who engages in the traffic and becomes an aider and abettor of the institution from sheer turpitude of heart; hence the propriety of this special disclaimer.

If we have a correct understanding of the positions which they assumed, some of the gentlemen whose names are written above, gave, during the last presidential campaign, ample evidence of their unswerving devotion to the interests of the great majority of the people, the non-slaveholding whites; and it is our unbiassed opinion that a more positive truth is no where recorded in Holy Writ, than Kenneth Raynor uttered, when he said, in substance, that the greatest good that could happen to this country would be the complete overthrow of slave-driving democracy, *alias* the nigger party, which has for its head and front the Ritchies and Wises of Virginia, and for its caudal termination the Butlers and Quattlebums of South Carolina.

And this, by the way, is a fit occasion to call attention to the fact, that slave-driving Democrats have been the perpetrators of almost every brutal outrage that ever disgraced our halls of legislation. Of countless instances of assault and battery, affrays, and fatal encounters, that have occurred in the court-houses, capitols, and other public buildings in the Southern States, we feel safe in saying that the aggressor, in at least nine cases out of ten, has been a negro-nursed adherent of modern, miscalled democracy. So, too, the challenger to almost every duel has been an abandoned wretch, who, on many occasions during infancy, sucked in the corrupt milk of slavery from the breasts of his father's sable concubines, and who has never been known to become weary of boasting of a fact that invariably impressed itself on the minds of his auditors or observers, the very first moment they laid their eyes upon him, namely, that *he* was a member of the Democratic party. Brute violence, however, can hardly be said to be the worst characteristic of

the slave-driving Democrat; his ignorance and squalidity are prover-
bial; his senseless enthusiasm is disgusting.

Peculiarly illustrative of the material of which sham democracy
is composed was the vote polled at the Five Points precinct, in the
city of New York, on the 4th of November, 1856, when James Buchanan was chosen President by a *minority* of the people. We will
produce the figures:

Five Points Precinct,
New York City, 1856

Votes cast for James Buchanan	574
Votes cast for John C. Fremont	16
Votes cast for Millard Fillmore	9

It will be recollected that Col. Fremont's majority over Buchanan,
in the State of New York, was between seventy-eight and seventy-
nine thousand, and that he ran ahead of the Fillmore ticket to the
number of nearly one hundred and fifty-one thousand. We have not
the shadow of a doubt that he is perfectly satisfied with Mr. Buchanan's triumph at the Five Points, which, with the exception of
the slave-pens in Southern cities, is, perhaps, the most vile and
heart-sickening locality in the United States.

One of the most noticeable and commendable features of the last
general election is this: almost every State, whose inhabitants have
enjoyed the advantages of free soil, free labor, free speech, free
presses, and free schools, and who have, in consequence, become
great in numbers, in virtue, in wealth, and in wisdom, voted for
Fremont, the Republican candidate, who was pledged to use his
influence for the extension of like advantages to other parts of the
country. On the other hand, with a single honorable exception, all
the States which "have got to hating everything with the prefix Free,
from free negroes down and up through the whole catalogue—free

farms, free labor, free society, free will, free thinking, free children, and free schools," and which have exposed their citizens to all the perils of numerical weakness, absolute ignorance, and hopeless poverty, voted for Buchanan, the Democratic candidate, who, in reply to the overtures of his slave-driving partisans, had signified his willingness to pursue a policy that would perpetuate and disseminate, without limit, the multitudinous evils of human bondage.

Led on by a huckstering politician, whose chief vocation, at all times, is the rallying of ragamuffins, shoulder-strikers, and liquor-house vagabonds, into the ranks of his party, and who, it is well known, receives from the agents of the slave power, regular installments of money for this infamous purpose, a Democratic procession, exceedingly motley and unrefined, marched through the streets of one of the great cities of the North, little less than a fortnight previous to the election of Mr. Buchanan to the Presidency; and the occasion gave rise, on the following day, to a communication in one of the morning papers, from which we make the following pertinent extract:

"While the Democratic procession was passing through the streets of this city, a few days since, I could not but think how significant the exultation of that ignorant multitude was of the ferocious triumphs which would be displayed if ever false Democracy should succeed in throwing the whole power of the country into the hands of the Slave Oligarchy. It is melancholy to think that every individual in that multitude, ignorant and depraved though he may be, foreign perhaps in his birth, and utterly unacquainted with the principles upon which the welfare of the country depends, and hostile it may be to those principles, if he does understand them, is equal in the power which he may exercise by his vote to the most intelligent and upright man in the community.

"Of this, indeed, it is useless to complain. We enjoy our freedom with the contingency of its loss by the acts of a numerical majority. It behooves all men, therefore, who have a regard to the common good, to look carefully at the influences which may pervert the popular mind; and this, I think, can only be done by guarding against the corruption of individual character. A man who has nothing but political business to attend to—I mean the management of elections — ought to be shunned by all honest men. If it were possible, he should have the mark of Cain put upon him, that he might be known as a plotter against the welfare of his country."

That less than *three* per cent of those who voted for Col. Fremont, that only about *five* per cent of those who gave their suffrages to Mr. Fillmore, and that more than *eighteen* per cent of those who supported Mr. Buchanan, were persons over one and twenty years of age who could not read and write, are estimates which we have no doubt are not far from the truth, and which, in the absence of reliable statistics, we venture to give, hoping, by their publicity, to draw closer attention to the fact, that the illiterate foreigners of the North, and the unlettered natives of the South, were cordially united in their suicidal adherence to the Nigger party.

With few exceptions, all the intelligent non-slaveholders of the South, in concert with the more respectable slaveholders, voted for Mr. Fillmore; indeed, certain rigidly patriotic persons of the former class, whose hearts were so entirely with the gallant Fremont that they refused to vote at all — simply because they did not dare to express their preference for him—form the exceptions to which we allude.

Though the Whig, Democratic, and Know-Nothing newspapers, in all the States, free and slave, denounced Col. Fremont as an intolerant Catholic, it is now generally conceded that he was no-where supported by the friends of Pope Pius IX. The votes polled at the Five Points precinct, which is almost exclusively inhabited by Irish Catholics, show how powerfully the Jesuitical influence was brought to bear against him. At that delectable locality, as we have already shown, the timid Sage of Wheatland received five hundred and seventy-four votes; whereas the dauntless Finder of Empire received only sixteen.

There is, indeed, no lack of evidence to show that the Democratic party of today is simply and unreservedly a sectional Nigger party. On the 15th of December, 1856, but a few weeks subsequent to the appearance of a scandalous message from an infamous governor of South Carolina, recommending the reöpening of the African slave trade, Emerson Etheridge of Tennessee — honor to his name! — submitted, in the House of Representatives, the following timely resolution:

"Resolved, That this House regard all suggestions or propositions of every kind, by whomsoever made, for a revival of the slave trade, as shocking to the moral sentiments of the enlightened portion of mankind, and that any act on the part of Congress, legislating for, conniving at, or legalizing that horrid and inhuman traffic, would justly subject the United States to the reproach and execration of all civilized and Christian people throughout the world."

Who voted *for* this resolution? and who voted *against* it? Let the yeas and nays answer; they are on record, and he who takes the trouble to examine them will find that the resolution encountered no opposition worth mentioning, except from members of the Democratic party. Scrutinize the yeas and nays on any other motion or resolution affecting the question of slavery, and the fact that a majority of the members of this party have uniformly voted for the retention and extension of the "sum of all villanies," will at once be apparent.

For many years the slave-driving Democrats of the South have labored most strenuously, both by day and by night—we regret to say how unsuccessfully—to point out abolition proclivities in the Whig and Know-Nothing parties, the latter of which is now buried, and deservedly, so deep in the depths of the dead, that it is quite preposterous to suppose it will ever see the light of resurrection.

For its truckling concessions to the slave power, the Whig party merited defeat, and defeated it was, and that, too, in the most decisive and overwhelming manner. But there is yet in this party much vitality, and if its friends will reorganize, detach themselves from the burden of slavery, espouse the cause of the white man, and hoist the fair flag of freedom, the time may come, at a day by no means remote, when their hearts will exult in triumph over the ruins of miscalled Democracy.

It is not too late, however, for the Democratic party to secure to itself a pure renown and an almost certain perpetuation of its power. Let it at once discard the worship of slavery, and do earnest battle for the principles of freedom, and it will live victoriously to a period far in the future. On the other hand, if it does not soon repudiate the fatal heresies which it has incorporated into its creed, its doom will be inevitable. Until the black flag entirely disappears from its array, we warn the non-slaveholders of the South to repulse and keep it at a distance, as they would the emblazoned skull and cross-bones that flout them from the flag of the pirate.

With regard to the sophistical reasoning which teaches that abolitionists, before abolishing slavery, should compensate the slaveholders for all or any number of the negroes in their possession, we have, perhaps, said quite enough; but wishing to brace our arguments, in every important particular, with unequivocal testimony from men whom we are accustomed to regard as models of political sagacity and integrity—from Southern men as far as possible—we herewith present an extract from a speech delivered in the Virginia House of Delegates, January 20, 1832, by Charles James Faulkner, whose sentiments, as then and there expressed, can hardly fail to find a response in the heart of every intelligent, upright man:

"But, Sir, it is said that society having conferred this property on the slaveholder, it cannot *now* take it from him without an adequate compensation, by which is meant full value. I may be singular in the opinion, but I defy the legal research of the House to point me to a principle recognized by the law, even in the ordinary course of its adjudications, where the community pays for property which is removed or destroyed because it is a nuisance, and found injurious to that society. There is, I humbly apprehend, no such principle. There is no obligation upon society to continue your right one moment after it becomes injurious to the best interests of society; nor to compensate you for the loss of that, the deprivation of which is demanded by the safety of the State, and in which general benefit you participate as members of the community. Sir, there is to my mind a manifest distinction between condemning private property to be applied to some beneficial public purpose, and condemning or removing private property which is ascertained to be a positive wrong to society. It is a distinction which pervades the whole genius of the law; and is founded upon the idea, that any man who holds property injurious to the peace of that society of which he is a member, thereby violates the condition upon the observance of which his right to the property is alone guarantied. For property of the first class condemned, there ought to be compensation; but for property of the latter class, none can be demanded upon principle, none accorded as matter of right.

"It is conceded that, at this precise moment of our legislation, slaves are injurious to the interests and threaten the subversion and ruin of this Commonwealth. Their present number, their increasing number, all admonish us of this. In different terms, and in more measured language, the same fact has been conceded by all who have yet addressed this House. 'Something must be done,' emphatically exclaimed the gentleman from Dinwiddie; and I thought I could perceive a response to that declaration, in the countenance of a large majority of this body. And why must something be done? Because if not, says the gentleman from Campbell, the throats of all the *white* people of Virginia will be cut. No, says the gentleman from Dinwiddie—'The whites cannot be conquered—the throats of the *blacks* will be cut.' It is a trifling difference, to be sure, Sir, and matters not to the argument. For the fact is conceded, that one race or the other must be exterminated.

"Sir, such being the actual condition of this Commonwealth, I ask if we would not be justified *now*, supposing all considerations of policy and humanity concurred, without even a moment's delay, in staving off this appalling and overwhelming calamity? Sir, if this immense negro population were now in arms, gathering into black and formidable masses of attack, would that man be listened to, who spoke about property, who asked you not to direct your artillery to such or such a point, for you would destroy some of *his* property? Sir, to the eye of the Statesman, as to the eye of Omniscience, dangers pressing, and dangers that must *necessarily* press, are alike present. With a single glance he embraces Virginia now, with the elements of destruction reposing quietly upon her bosom, and Virginia is lighted from one extremity to the other with the torch of servile insurrection and massacre. It is not sufficient for him that the match is not yet applied. It is enough that the magazine is open, and the match will shortly be applied.

"Sir, it is true in national as it is in private contracts, that loss and injury to one party may constitute as fair a consideration as gain to the other. Does the slaveholder, while he is enjoying his slaves, reflect upon the deep injury and incalculable loss which the possession of that property inflicts upon the true interests of the country? Slavery, it is admitted, is an evil—it is an institution which presses heavily against the best interests of the State. It banishes free white labor, it exterminates the mechanic, the artisan, the manufacturer. It deprives them of occupation. It deprives them of bread. It converts the energy of a community into indolence, its power into imbecility, its efficiency into weakness. Sir, being thus injurious, have we not a right to demand its extermination? shall society suffer, that the slaveholder may continue to gather his *crop* of human flesh? What is his mere pecuniary claim, compared with the great interests of the common weal? Must the country languish, droop, die, that the slaveholder may flourish? Shall all interests be subservient to one—all rights subordinate to those of the slaveholder? Has not the mechanic, have not the middle classes their rights—rights incompatible with the existence of slavery?

"Sir, so great and overshadowing are the evils of slavery—so sensibly are they felt by those who have traced the causes of our national decline—so perceptible is the poisonous operation of its principles in the diversified interests of this Commonwealth, that all, whose minds are not warped by prejudice or interest, must admit that the disease has now assumed that mortal tendency, as to justify the application of any remedy which, under the great law of State necessity, we might consider advisable."

From the abstract of our plan for the abolition of slavery, it will be perceived that, so far from allowing slaveholders any compensation for their slaves, we are, and we think justly, in favor of imposing on them a tax of sixty dollars for each and every negro now in their possession, as also for each and every one that shall be born to them between now and the 4th of July, 1863; after which time, we propose that they shall be taxed forty dollars per annum, annually, for every person by them held in slavery, without regard to age, sex, color, or condition — the money, in both instances, to be used for the sole advantage of the slaves. As an addendum to this proposition, we would say that, in our opinion, if slavery is not totally abolished by the year 1869, the annual tax ought to be increased from forty to one hundred dollars; and furthermore, that if the institution does not then almost immediately disappear under the onus of this increased taxation, the tax ought in the course of one or two years thereafter, to be augmented to such a degree as will, in harmony with other measures, prove an infallible deathblow to slavery on or before the 4th of July, 1876.

At once let the good and true men of this country, the patriot sons of the patriot fathers, determine that the sun which rises to celebrate the centennial anniversary of our national independence, shall not set on the head of any slave within the limits of our Republic. Will not the non-slaveholders of the North, of the South, of the East, and of the West, heartily, unanimously sanction this proposition? Will it not be cheerfully indorsed by many of the slaveholders themselves? Will any *respectable* man enter a protest against it? On the 4th of July, 1876 — sooner, if we can — let us make good, at least so far as we are concerned, the Declaration of Independence, which was proclaimed in Philadelphia on the 4th of July, 1776 — that "all men are endowed by their Creator with certain inalienable rights;

that among these, are life, liberty, and the pursuit of happiness; that to secure these rights, governments are instituted among men, deriving their just powers from the consent of the governed; that whenever any form of government becomes destructive of these ends, it is the right of the people to alter or to abolish it, and to institute a new government, laying its foundation on such principles, and organizing its powers in such form, as to them shall seem most likely to effect their safety and happiness." In purging our land of the iniquity of negro slavery, we will only be carrying on the great work that was so successfully commenced by our noble sires of the Revolution; some future generation may possibly complete the work by annulling the last and least form of oppression.

To turn the slaves away from their present homes—away from all the property and means of support which their labor has mainly produced, would be unpardonably cruel—exceedingly unjust. Still more cruel and unjust would it be, however, to the non-slaveholding whites no less than to the negroes, to grant further toleration to the existence of slavery. In any event, come what will, transpire what may, the institution must be abolished. The evils, if any, which are to result from its abolition, cannot, by any manner of means, be half as great as the evils which are certain to overtake us in case of its continuance. The perpetuation of slavery is the climax of iniquity.

Two hundred and thirty-seven years have the negroes in America been held in inhuman bondage. During the whole of this long period they have toiled unceasingly from the gray of dawn till the dusk of eve, for their cruel task-masters, who have rewarded them with scanty allowances of the most inferior qualities of victuals and clothes, with heartless separations of the tenderest ties of kindred, with epithets, with scoldings, with execrations, and with the lash— and, not unfrequently, with the fatal bludgeon or the more deadly weapon. From the labor of their hands, and from the fruit of their loins, the human mongers of the South have become wealthy, insolent, corrupt, and tyrannical. In reason and in conscience the slaves might claim from their masters a much larger sum than we have proposed to allow them. If they were to demand an equal share of all the property, real and personal, which has been accumulated or produced through their efforts, Heaven, we believe, would recognize them as honest claimants.

Elsewhere we have shown, by just and liberal estimates, that, on the single score of damages to lands, the slaveholders are, at this moment, indebted to the non-slaveholding whites in the extraordinary sum of $7,544,148,825.

Considered in connection with the righteous claim of wages for services which the negroes might bring against their masters, these figures are the heralds of the significant fact that, if strict justice could be meted out to all parties in the South, the slaveholders would not only be stripped of every dollar, but they would become in law as they are in reality, the hopeless debtors of the myriads of unfortunate slaves, white and black, who are now cringing, and fawning, and festering around them. In this matter, however, so far has wrong triumphed over right, that the slaveholders — a mere handful of tyrants, whose manual exercises are wholly comprised in the use they make of instruments of torture, such as whips, clubs, bowie-knives and pistols — have, as the result of a series of acts of their own villainous legislation, become the sole and niggardly proprietors of almost every important item of Southern wealth; not only do they own all the slaves — none of whom any really respectable person cares to own — but they are also in possession of the more valuable tracts of land and the appurtenances thereto belonging; while the non-slaveholding whites and the negroes, who compose at least nine-tenths of the entire population, and who are the actual producers of every article of merchandise, animal, vegetable, and mineral, that is sold from the South, are most wickedly despoiled of the fruits of their labors, and cast into the dismal abodes of extreme ignorance, destitution and misery.

For the services of the blacks from the 20th of August, 1620, up to the 4th of July, 1863 — an interval of precisely two hundred and forty-two years ten months and fourteen days — their masters, if unwilling, ought, in our judgment, to be compelled to grant them their freedom, and to pay each and every one of them at least sixty dollars cash in hand. The aggregate sum thus raised would amount to about two hundred and forty-five millions of dollars, which is less than the total market value of two entire crops of cotton—one-half of which sum would be amply sufficient to land every negro in this country on the coast of Liberia, whither, if we had the power, we would ship them all within the next six months. As a means of protection against the exigencies which might arise from a sudden transition from their present homes in America to their future homes in Africa, and for the purpose of enabling them there to take the initiatory step in the walks of civilized life, the remainder of the sum—say about one hundred and twenty-two millions of dollars— might, very properly, be equally distributed amongst them after their arrival in the land of their fathers.

Dr. James Hall, the Secretary of the Maryland Colonization Society, informs us that the average cost of sending negroes to Liberia does not exceed thirty dollars each; and it is his opinion that arrangements might be made on an extensive plan for conveying them thither at an average expense of not more than twenty-five dollars each.

The American colonization movement, as now systematized and conducted, is simply an American humane farce. At present the slaves are increasing in this country at the rate of nearly one hundred thousand per annum; within the last ten years, as will appear below, the American Colonization Society has sent to Liberia less than five thousand negroes.

Emigrants sent to Liberia by the American Colonization Society, during the ten years ending January 1st, 1857.

In 1847	39	Emigrants
In 1848	213	Emigrants
In 1849	474	Emigrants
In 1850	590	Emigrants
In 1851	279	Emigrants
In 1852	568	Emigrants
In 1853	583	Emigrants
In 1854	783	Emigrants
In 1855	207	Emigrants
In 1856	544	Emigrants
TOTAL	4280	Emigrants

The average of this total is precisely four hundred and twenty-eight, which may be said to be the number of negroes annually colonized by the society; while the yearly increase of slaves, as previously stated, is little less than one hundred thousand! Fiddle-sticks for such colonization! Once for all, within a reasonably short period, let us make the slaveholders do something like justice to their negroes by giving each and every one of them his freedom, and sixty dollars in current money; then let us charter all the ocean steamers, packets and clipper ships that can be had on liberal terms, and keep them constantly plying between the ports of America and Africa, until all slaves shall enjoy freedom in the land of their fathers. Under a well-devised and properly conducted system of operations, but a few years would be required to redeem the United States from the monstrous curse of negro slavery.

Some few years ago, when certain ethnographical oligarchs

proved to their own satisfaction that the negro was an inferior "type of mankind," they chuckled wonderfully, and avowed, in substance, that it was right for the stronger race to kidnap and enslave the weaker—that because Nature had been pleased to do a trifle more for the Caucasian race than for the African, the former, by virtue of its superiority, was perfectly justifiable in holding the latter in absolute and perpetual bondage! No system of logic could be more antagonistic to the spirit of true democracy. It is probable that the world does not contain two persons who are exactly alike in all respects; yet "*all* men are endowed by their Creator with certain *inalienable* rights, among which are life, *liberty*, and the pursuit of happiness."

All mankind may or may not be the descendants of Adam and Eve. In our own humble way of thinking, we are frank to confess, we do not believe in the unity of the races. This is a matter, how-ever, which has little or nothing to do with the great question at issue. Aside from any theory concerning the original parentage of the different races of men, facts, material and immaterial, palpable and impalpable — facts of the eyes and facts of the conscience — crowd around us on every hand, heaping proof upon proof, that slavery is a shame, a crime, and a curse — a great moral, social, civil, and political evil—an oppressive burden to the blacks, and an incalculable injury to the whites—a stumbling-block to the nation, an impediment to progress, a damper on all the nobler instincts, principles, aspirations and enterprises of man, and a dire enemy to every true interest.

Waving all other counts, we have, we think, shown to the satisfac-tion of every impartial reader, that, as elsewhere stated, on the single score of damages to lands, the slaveholders are, at this mo-ment, indebted to us, the non-slaveholding whites, in the enormous sum of nearly seventy-six hundred millions of dollars. What shall be done with this amount? It is just; shall payment be demanded? No; all the slaveholders in the country could not pay it; nor shall we ever ask them for even a moiety of the amount—no, not even for a dime, nor yet for a cent; we are willing to forfeit every farthing for the sake of freedom; for ourselves we ask no indemnification for the past: we only demand justice for the future.

But, Sirs, knights of bludgeons, chevaliers of bowie-knives and pistols, and lords of the lash, we are unwilling to allow you to swindle the slaves out of all the rights and claims to which, as human beings, they are most sacredly entitled. Not alone for ourself as an individual, but for others also—particularly for five or six millions of Southern non-slaveholding whites, whom your iniquitous statism has debarred from almost all the mental and material comforts of life—do we speak, when we say, you *must* emancipate your slaves, and pay each and every one of them at least sixty dollars cash in hand. By doing this, you will be restoring to them their natural rights, and remunerating them at the rate of less than twenty-six cents per annum for the long and cheerless period of their servitude, from the 20th of August, 1620, when, on James River, in Virginia, they became the unhappy slaves of heartless masters. Moreover, by doing this you will be performing but a simple act of justice to the non-slave holding whites, upon whom the institution of slavery has weighed scarcely less heavily than upon the negroes themselves. You will also be applying a saving balm to your own outraged hearts and consciences, and your children—yourselves in fact —freed from the accursed stain of slavery, will become respectable, useful, and honorable members of society.

And now, Sirs, we have thus laid down our ultimatum. What are you going to do about it? Something dreadful, as a matter of course! Perhaps you will dissolve the Union *again*. Do it, if you dare! Our motto, and we would have you to understand it, is *the abolition of slavery, and the perpetuation of the American Union*. If, by any means, you do succeed in your treasonable attempts to take the South out of the Union today, we will bring her back tomorrow— if she goes away with you, she will return without you.

Do not mistake the meaning of the last clause of the last sentence; we could elucidate it so thoroughly that no intelligent person could fail to comprehend it; but, for reasons which may hereafter appear, we forego the task.

Henceforth there are other interests to be consulted in the South, aside from the interests of negroes and slaveholders. A profound sense of duty incites us to make the greatest possible efforts for the abolition of slavery; an equally profound sense of duty calls for a continuation of those efforts until the very last foe to freedom shall have been utterly vanquished. To the summons of the righteous monitor within, we shall endeavor to prove faithful; no opportunity for inflicting a mortal wound in the side of slavery shall be permitted to pass us unimproved. Thus, terror-engenderers of the South, have we fully and frankly defined our position; we have no modifications to propose, no compromises to offer, nothing to retract. Frown, Sirs, fret, foam, prepare your weapons, threat, strike, shoot, stab, bring on civil war, dissolve the Union, no, annihilate the solar system if you will—do all this, more, less, better, worse, anything —do what you will, Sirs, you can neither foil nor intimidate us; our purpose is as firmly fixed as the eternal pillars of Heaven; we have determined to abolish slavery, and, so help us God, abolish it we will! Take this to bed with you tonight, Sirs, and think about it, dream over it, and let us know how you feel tomorrow morning.

Chapter 3

Southern Testimony
Against Slavery

IF IT PLEASE THE READER, let him forget all that we have written on
the subject of slavery; if it accord with his inclination, let him ignore
all that we may write hereafter. We seek not to give currency to our
peculiar opinions; our greatest ambition, in these pages, is to
popularize the sayings and admonitions of wiser and better men.
Miracles, we believe, are no longer wrought in this bedeviled world;
but if, by any conceivable or possible supernatural event, the great
Founders of the Republic, Washington, Jefferson, Henry, and
others, could be reinvested with corporeal life, and returned to the
South, there is scarcely a slaveholder between the Potomac and the
mouth of the Mississippi, that would not burn to pounce upon them
with bludgeons, bowie-knives and pistols! Yes, without adding
another word, Washington would be *mobbed* for what he has
already said. Were Jefferson now employed as a professor in a
Southern college, he would be dismissed and driven from the State,
perhaps murdered before he reached the border. If Patrick Henry
were a bookseller in Alabama, though it might be demonstrated
beyond the shadow of a doubt that he had never bought, sold,
received, or presented, any kind of literature except Bibles and
Testaments, he would first be subjected to the ignominy of a coat
of tar and feathers, and then limited to the option of unceremonious
expatriation or death. How seemingly impossible are these statements, and yet how true! Where do we stand? What is our faith? Are
we a flock without a shepherd? a people without a prophet? a nation
without a government?

Has the past, with all its glittering monuments of genius and
patriotism, furnished no beacon by which we may direct our foot-

steps in the future? If we but prove true to ourselves, and worthy of our ancestry, we have nothing to fear; our Revolutionary sires have devised and bequeathed to us an almost perfect national policy. Let us cherish, and defend, and build upon, the fundamental principles of that polity, and we shall most assuredly reap the golden fruits of unparalleled power, virtue and prosperity. Heaven forbid that a desperate faction of slaveholding criminals should succeed in their infamous endeavors to quench the spirit of liberty, which our forefathers infused into those two sacred charts of our political faith, the Declaration of Independence, and the Constitution of the United States. Oligarchal politicians are alone responsible for the continuance of African slavery in the South. For purposes of self-aggrandizement, they have kept learning and civilization from the people; they have wilfully misinterpreted the national compacts, and have outraged their own consciences by declaring to their illiterate constituents, that the Founders of the Republic were not abolitionists. When the dark clouds of slavery, error and ignorance shall have passed away,—and we believe the time is near at hand when they are to be dissipated,—the freemen of the South, like those of other sections, will learn the glorious truth, that inflexible opposition to Human Bondage has formed one of the distinguishing characteristics of every really good or great man that our country has produced.

The principles, aims and objects that actuated the framers of the Constitution, are most graphically and eloquently set forth, in the following extract from a speech recently delivered by the Hon. A. H. Cragin, of New Hampshire, in the House of Representatives:

"When our forefathers reared the magnificent structure of a free Republic in this Western land, they laid its foundations broad and deep in the eternal principles of right. Its materials were all quarried from the mountain of truth; and, as it rose majestically before an astonished world, it rejoiced the hearts and hopes of mankind. Tyrants only cursed the workmen and their workmanship. Its architecture was new. It had no model in Grecian or Roman history. It seemed a paragon, let down from Heaven to inspire the hopes of men, and to demonstrate the favor of God to the people of a new world. The builders recognized the rights of human nature as universal. Liberty, the great first right of man, they claimed for 'all men,' and claimed it from 'God himself.' Upon this foundation they erected the temple, and dedicated it to Liberty, Humanity, Justice, and Equality. Washington was crowned its patron saint."

"The work completed was the noblest effort of human wisdom. But it was not perfect. It had one blemish—a little spot—the black stain of slavery. The workmen—the friends of freedom everywhere—deplored this. They labored long and prayerfully to remove this deformity. They applied all the skill of their art; but they labored in vain. Self-interest was too strong for patriotism and love of liberty. The work stood still, and for a time it was doubtful whether the experiment would succeed. The blot must remain, or the whole must fail. The workmen revarnished their work, to conceal and cover up the stain. Slavery was recognized, but not sanctioned. The word slave or slavery must not mar the Constitution. So great an inconsistency must not be proclaimed to the world."

"All agreed, at that time, that the anomaly should not increase, and all concurred in the hope and belief that the blemish would gradually disappear. Those noble men looked forward to the time when slavery would be abolished in this land of ours. They believed that the principles of liberty were so dear to the people, that they would not long deny to others what they claimed for themselves. They never dreamed that slavery would be extended, but firmly believed it would be wholly blotted out. *I challenge any man to show me a single patriot of the Revolution who was in favor of slavery, or who advocated its extension.* So universal was the sentiment of liberty then, that no man, North or South, could be found to justify it. Some palliated the evil, and desired that it might be gradually extinguished; but none contemplated it as a permanent institution."

"Liberty was then the national goddess, worshiped by all the people. They sang of liberty, they harangued for liberty, they prayed for liberty, and they sacrificed for liberty. Slavery was then hateful. It was denounced by all. The British king was condemned for foisting it upon the Colonies. Southern men were foremost in entering their protest against it. It was then everywhere regarded as an evil, and a crime against humanity."

The fact is too palpable to be disguised, that slavery and slaveholders have always been a clog and a dead-weight upon the government—a disgrace and a curse to humanity. The slaveholding Tories of the South, particularly of South Carolina, in their atrocious hostility to freedom, prolonged the arduous war of the Revolution from two to three years; and since the termination of that momentous struggle, in which, thank Heaven, they were most signally defeated, it has been their constant aim and effort to subvert the dear-bought liberties which were achieved by the non-slaveholding patriots.

Non-slaveholders of the South! up to the present period, neither as a body, nor as individuals, have you ever had an independent existence; but, if true to yourselves and to the memory of your fathers, you, in equal copartnership with the non-slaveholders of the North, will soon become the honored rulers and proprietors of the most powerful, prosperous, virtuous, free, and peaceful nation, on which the sun has ever shone. Already has the time arrived for you to decide upon what basis you will erect your political superstructure. Upon whom will you depend for an equitable and judicious form of constitutional government? Whom will you designate as models for your future statesmen? Your choice lies between the dead and the living—between the Washingtons, the Jeffersons and the Madisons of the past, and the Quattlebums, the Quitmans and the Butlers of the present. We have chosen; choose ye, remembering that freedom or slavery is to be the issue of your option.

As the result of much reading and research, and at the expenditure of no inconsiderable amount of time, labor and money, we now proceed to make known the anti-slavery sentiments of those noble abolitionists, the Fathers of the Republic, whose liberal measures of public policy have been so criminally perverted by the treacherous advocates of slavery.

Let us listen, in the first place, to the voice of him who was "first in war, first in peace, and first in the hearts of his countrymen," to:

THE VOICE OF WASHINGTON

In a letter to John F. Mercer, dated September 9th, 1786, General Washington says:

"I never mean, unless some particular circumstances should compel me to it, to possess another slave by purchase, it being among my *first wishes* to see some plan adopted by which slavery, in this country, may be abolished by law."

In a letter to Robert Morris, dated Mount Vernon, April 12, 1786, he says:

"I can only say that there is not a man living who wishes more sincerely than I do to see a plan adopted for the abolition of it. But there is only one proper and effectual mode by which it can be accomplished, and that is by legislative authority; and this, as far as my suffrage will go, shall never be wanting."

He says, in a letter

"To the Marquis De Lafayette—April 5th, 1783:

The scheme, my dear Marquis, which you propose as a precedent, to encourage the emancipation of the black people in this country from the state of bondage in which they are held, is a striking evidence of the benevolence of your heart. I shall be happy to join you in so laudable a work; but will defer going into a detail of the business till I have the pleasure of seeing you."

In another letter to Lafayette, he says:

"The benevolence of your heart, my dear Marquis, is so conspicuous on all occasions, that I never wonder at any fresh proofs of it; but your late purchase of an estate in the Colony of Cayenne, with the view of emancipating the slaves on it, is a generous and noble proof of your humanity. Would to God a like spirit might diffuse itself generally into the minds of the people of this country."

In a letter to Sir John Sinclair, he further said:

"There are in Pennsylvania laws for the gradual abolition of slavery, which neither Virginia nor Maryland have at present, but which nothing is more certain than they must have, and at a period *not remote.*"

From his last will and testament we make the following extract:

"Upon the decease of my wife, it is my will and desire that all the slaves which I hold in my own right shall receive their freedom. To emancipate them during her life would, though earnestly wished by me, be attended with such insuperable difficulties, on account of their intermixture by marriage with the dower negroes, as to excite the most painful sensation, if not disagreeable consequences, from the latter, while both descriptions are in the occupancy of the same proprietor, it not being in my power, under the tenure by which the dower negroes are held, to manumit them."

It is said that, "when Mrs. Washington learned, from the will of her deceased husband, that the only obstacle to the immediate perfection of this provision was her right of dower, she at once gave it up, and the slaves were made free." A man might possibly concentrate within himself more real virtue and influence than ever Washington possessed, and yet he would not be too good for such a wife.

From the Father of his Country, we now turn to the author of the Declaration of Independence. We will listen to:

THE VOICE OF JEFFERSON

On the 39th and 40th pages of his Notes on Virginia, Jefferson says:

"There must doubtless be an unhappy influence on the manners of our people, produced by the existence of slavery among us. The whole commerce between master and slave is a perpetual exercise of the most boisterous passions—the most unremitting despotism on the one part, and degrading submissions on the other. Our children see this, and learn to imitate it; for man is an imitative animal. This quality is the germ of all education in him. From his cradle to his grave, he is learning to do what he sees others do. If a parent could find no motive, either in his philanthropy or his self-love, for restraining the intemperance of passion towards his slave, it should always be a sufficient one that his child is present. But generally it is not sufficient. The parent storms, the child looks on, catches the lineaments of wrath, puts on the same airs in the circle of smaller slaves, gives a loose rein to the worst of passions; and, thus nursed, educated, and daily exercised in tyranny, cannot but be stamped by it with odious peculiarities. The man must be a prodigy who can retain his manners and morals undepraved by such circumstances. And with what execration should the Statesman be loaded, who, permitting one half the citizens thus to trample on the rights of the other, transforms those into despots and these into enemies, destroys the morals of the one part, and the *amor patriae* of the other; for if a slave can have a country in this world, it must be any other in preference to that in which he is born to live and labor for another; in which he must look up the faculties of his nature, contribute, as far as depends on his individual endeavors, to the evanishment of the human race, or entail his own miserable condition on the endless generations proceeding from him. With the morals of the people, their industry also is destroyed; for, in a warm climate, no man will labor for himself who can make another labor for him. This is so true, that of the proprietors of slaves a very small proportion, indeed, are ever seen to labor. And can the liberties of a nation be thought secure, when we have removed their only firm basis — a conviction in the minds of the people that these liberties are of the gift of God? that they are not to be violated but with his wrath? Indeed, I tremble for my country when I reflect that God is just; that his justice cannot sleep forever; that considering numbers, nature, and natural means only, a revolution of the wheel of fortune, an exchange of situation is among possible events; that it may become probable by supernatural interference! The Almighty has no attribute which can take side with us in such a contest."

While Virginia was yet a Colony, in 1774, she held a Convention to appoint delegates to attend the first general Congress, which was to assemble, and did assemble, in Philadelphia, in September of the same year. Before that Convention, Mr. Jefferson made an exposition of the rights of British America, in which he said:

"The abolition of domestic slavery is the greatest object of desire in these Colonies, where it was unhappily introduced in their infant State. But previous to the enfranchisement of the slaves, it is necessary to exclude further importations from Africa. Yet our repeated attempts to effect this by prohibitions, and by imposing duties which might amount to prohibition, have been hitherto defeated by his Majesty's negative; thus preferring the immediate advantage of a few African corsairs to the lasting interests of the American States, and the rights of human nature, deeply wounded by this infamous practice."

In the original draft of the Declaration of Independence, of which it is well known he was the author, we find this charge against the King of Great Britain:

"He has waged cruel war against human nature itself, violating its most sacred rights of life and liberty, in the persons of a distant people who never offended him, captivating and carrying them into slavery in another hemisphere, or to incur miserable death in their transportation thither. This piratical warfare, the opprobrium of infidel powers, is the warfare of the Christian King of Great Britain. Determined to keep a market where men should be bought and sold, he has at length prostituted his negative for suppressing any legislative attempt to prohibit and restrain this execrable commerce."

Hear him further; he says:

"We hold these truths to be self-evident, that all men are created equal; that they are endowed by their Creator with certain unalienable rights; that among these are life, liberty, and the pursuit of happiness; that to secure these rights, governments are instituted among men, deriving their just powers from the consent of the governed."

Under date of August 7th, 1785, in a letter to Dr. Price of London, he says:

"Northward of the Chesapeake you may find, here and there, an opponent of your doctrine, as you may find, here and there, a robber and murderer; but in no great number. Emancipation is put into such a train, that in a few years there will be no slaves northward of Maryland. In Maryland I do not find such a disposition to begin the redress of this enormity, as in Virginia. This is the next State to which we may turn our eyes for the interesting spectacle of justice in conflict with avarice and oppression; a conflict wherein the sacred side is gaining daily recruits from the influx into office of young men grown up, and growing up. These have sucked in the principles of liberty, as it were, with their mother's milk; and it is to them I look with anxiety to turn the fate of the question."

In another letter, written to a friend in 1814, he made use of the following emphatic language:

"Your favor of July 31st was duly received, and read with peculiar pleasure. The sentiments do honor to the head and heart of the writer. Mine on the subject of the slavery of negroes have long since been in the possession of the public, and time has only served to give them stronger root. The love of justice and the love of country plead equally the cause of these people, and it is a reproach to us that they should have pleaded it so long in vain."

Again, he says:

"What an incomprehensible machine is man! who can endure toil, famine, stripes, imprisonment, and death itself, in vindication of his own liberty; and the next moment be deaf to all those motives whose power supported him through his trial, and inflict on his fellow man a bondage, one hour of which is fraught with more misery than ages of that which he rose in rebellion to oppose."

Throughout the South, at the present day, especially among slaveholders, negroes are almost invariably spoken of as "goods and chattels," "property," "human cattle." In our first quotation from Jefferson's works, we have seen that he spoke of the blacks as *citizens.* We shall now hear him speak of them as *brethren.* He says:

"We must wait with patience the workings of an overruling Providence, and hope that that is preparing the deliverance of these our brethren. When the measure of their tears shall be full, when their groans shall have involved Heaven itself in darkness, doubtless a God of justice will awaken to their distress. Nothing is more certainly written in the Book of Fate, than that this people shall be free."

In a letter to James Heaton, on this same subject, dated May 20, 1826, only six weeks before his death, he says:

"My sentiments have been forty years before the public. Had I repeated them forty times, they would have only become the more stale and threadbare. Although I shall not live to see them consummated, they will not die with me."

From the Father of the Declaration of Independence, we now turn to the Father of the Constitution. We will listen to:

THE VOICE OF MADISON

Advocating the abolition of the slave-trade, Mr. Madison said:

"The dictates of humanity, the principles of the people, the national safety and happiness, and prudent policy, require it of us. It is to be hoped, that by expressing a national disapprobation of the trade, we may *destroy* it, and save our country from reproaches, and our posterity from the imbecility ever attendant on a country filled with slaves."

Again, he says:

"It is wrong to admit into the Constitution the idea that there can be property in man."

In the 39th No. of "The Federalist," he says:

"The first question that offers itself is, whether the general form and aspect of the government be strictly Republican. It is evident that no other form would be reconcilable with the genius of the people of America, and with the fundamental principles of the Revolution, or with that honorable determination which animates every votary of freedom, to rest all our political experiments on the capacity of mankind for self-government."

In the Federal Convention, he said:

"And in the third place, where slavery exists, the Republican theory becomes still more fallacious."On another occasion, he says:

"We have seen the mere distinction of color made, in the most enlightened period of time, a ground of the most oppressive dominion ever exercised by man over man."

THE VOICE OF MONROE

In a speech in the Virginia Convention, Mr. Monroe said:

"We have found that this evil has preyed upon the very vitals of the Union, and has been prejudicial to all the States, in which it has existed."

THE VOICE OF HENRY

The eloquent Patrick Henry says, in a letter dated January 18, 1773:

"Is it not a little surprising that the professors of Christianity, whose chief excellence consists in softening the human heart, in cherishing and improving its finer feelings, should encourage a practice so totally repugnant to the first impressions of right and wrong? What adds to the wonder is, that this abominable practice has been introduced in the most enlightened ages. Times that seem to have pretensions to boast of high improvements in the arts and sciences, and refined morality, have brought into general use, and guarded by many laws, a species of violence and tyranny which our more rude and barbarous, but more honest ancestors detested. Is it not amazing that at a time when the rights of humanity are defined and understood with precision, in a country above all others fond of liberty—that in such an age and in such a country, we find men professing a religion the most mild, humane, gentle, and generous, adopting such a principle, as repugnant to humanity as it is inconsistent with the Bible, and destructive to liberty? Every thinking, honest man rejects it in speculation. How free in practice from conscientious motives! Would anyone believe that I am master of slaves of my own purchase? I am drawn along by the general inconvenience of living here without them. I will not, I cannot justify it. However culpable my conduct, I will so far pay my devoir to virtue as to own the excellence and rectitude of her precepts, and lament my want of conformity to them. I believe a time will come when an opportunity will be offered to abolish this lamentable evil. Everything we can do is to improve it, if it happens in our day; if not, let us transmit to our descendants, together with our slaves, a pity for their unhappy lot, and an abhorrence for slavery. If we cannot reduce this wished-for reformation to practice, let us treat the unhappy victims with lenity. It is the furthest advance we can make towards justice. It is a debt we owe to the purity of our religion, to show that it is at variance with that law which warrants slavery."

Again, this great orator says:

"It would rejoice my very soul, that every one of my fellow-beings was emancipated. We ought to lament and deplore the necessity of holding our fellow-men in bondage. Believe me; I shall honor the Quakers for their noble efforts to abolish slavery."

THE VOICE OF RANDOLPH

That eccentric genius, John Randolph, of Roanoke, in a letter to William Gibbons, in 1820, says:

"With unfeigned respect and regard, and as sincere a deprecation on the extension of slavery and its horrors, as any other man, be him whom he may, I am your friend, in the literal sense of that much abused word. I say much abused, because it is applied to the leagues of vice and avarice and ambition, instead of good will toward man from love of him who is the Prince of Peace."

While in Congress, he said:

"Sir, I envy neither the heart nor the head of that man from the North who rises here to defend slavery on principle."

It is well known that he emancipated all of his negroes. The following lines from his will are well worth perusing and preserving:

"I give to my slaves their freedom, to which my conscience tells me they are justly entitled. It has a long time been a matter of the deepest regret to me that the circumstances under which I inherited them, and the obstacles thrown in the way by the laws of the land, have prevented my emancipating them in my life-time, which it is my full intention to do in case I can accomplish it."

THOMAS M. RANDOLPH

In an address to the Virginia Legislature, in 1820, Gov. Randolph said:

"We have been far outstripped by States to whom nature has been far less bountiful. It is painful to consider what might have been, under other circumstances, the amount of general wealth in Virginia."

THOMAS JEFFERSON RANDOLPH

In 1832, Mr. Randolph, of Albemarle, in the Legislature of Virginia, used the following most graphic and emphatic language:

"I agree with gentlemen in the necessity of arming the State for internal defence. I will unite with them in any effort to restore confidence to the public mind, and to conduce to the sense of the safety of our wives and our children. Yet, Sir, I must ask upon whom is to fall the burden of this defence? Not upon the lordly masters of their hundred slaves, who will never turn out except to retire with their families when danger threatens. No, Sir; it is to fall upon the less wealthy class of our citizens, chiefly upon the non-slaveholder. I have known patrols turned out when there was not a slaveholder among them; and this is the practice of the country. I have slept in times of alarm quiet in bed, without having a thought of care, while these individuals, owning none of this property themselves, were patrolling under a compulsory process, for a pittance of seventy-five cents per twelve hours, the very curtilage of my house, and guarding that property which was alike dangerous to them and myself. After all, this is but an expedient. As this population becomes more numerous, it becomes less productive. Your guard must be increased, until finally its profits will not pay for the expense of its subjection. Slavery has the effect of lessening the free population of a country.

"The gentleman has spoken of the increase of the female slaves being a part of the profit. It is admitted; but no great evil can be averted, no good attained, without some inconvenience. It may be questioned how far it is desirable to foster and encourage this branch of profit. It is a practice, and an increasing practice, in parts of Virginia, to rear slaves for market. How can an honorable mind, a patriot, and a lover of his country, bear to see this Ancient Dominion, rendered illustrious by the noble devotion and patriotism of her sons in the cause of liberty, converted into one grand menagerie, where men are to be reared for the market, like oxen for the shambles? Is it better, is it not worse, than the slave trade—that trade which enlisted the labor of the good and wise of every creed, and every clime, to abolish it? The trader receives the slave, a stranger in language, aspect, and manners, from the merchant who has brought him from the interior. The ties of father, mother, husband, and child, have all been rent in twain; before he receives him, his soul has become callous. But here, Sir, individuals whom the master has known from infancy, whom he has seen sporting in the innocent gambols of childhood, who have been accustomed to look to him for protection, he tears from the mother's arms and sells into a strange country among strange people, subject to cruel taskmasters.

"He has attempted to justify slavery here, because it exists in Africa, and has stated that it exists all over the world. Upon the same principle, he could justify Mahometanism, with its plurality of wives, petty wars for plunder, robbery, and murder, or any other of the abominations and enormities of savage tribes. Does slavery exist in any part of civilized Europe? No, Sir, in no part of it."

PEYTON RANDOLPH

On the 20th of October, 1774, while Congress was in session in Philadelphia, Peyton Randolph, President, the following resolution, among others, was unanimously adopted:

"That we will neither import nor purchase any slave imported after the first day of December next; after which time we will wholly discontinue the slave-trade, and will neither be concerned in it ourselves, nor will we hire our vessels, nor sell our commodities or manufactures, to those who are concerned in it."

EDMUND RANDOLPH

The Constitution of the United States contains the following provision:

"No person held to service or labor in another State, under the laws thereof, escaping to another, shall, in consequence of any law or regulation therein, be discharged from such service or labor, but shall be delivered up on claim of the party to whom such service or labor may be due."

To the studious attention of those vandals who contend that the above provision requires the rendition of fugitive *slaves*, we respectfully commend the following resolution, which, it will be observed, was *unanimously* adopted:

"On motion of Mr. Randolph, the word '*servitude*' was struck out, and '*service*' unanimously inserted — the former being thought to express the condition of *slaves*, and the latter the obligation of *free* persons." — *Madison Papers, vol.* III., *p.* 1569.

Well done for the Randolphs!

THE VOICE OF CLAY

Henry Clay, whom everybody loved, and at the mention of whose name the American heart always throbs with emotions of grateful remembrance, said, in an address before the Kentucky Colonization Society, in 1829:

"It is believed that nowhere in the *farming* portion of the United States would slave-labor be generally employed, if the proprietor were not tempted to raise slaves by the high price of the Southern market, which keeps it up in his own."

In the United States Senate, in 1850, he used the following memorable words:

"I am extremely sorry to hear the Senator from Mississippi say that he requires, first the extension of the Missouri Compromise line to the Pacific, and also that he is not satisfied with that, but requires, if I understand him correctly, a positive provision for the admission of slavery South of that line. And now, Sir, coming from a slave State, as I do, I owe it to myself, I owe it to truth, I owe it to the subject to say that no earthly power could induce me to vote for a specific measure for the introduction of slavery where it had not before existed, either South or North of that line. Coming as I do from a slave State, it is my solemn, deliberate and well-matured determination that no power, no earthly power, shall compel me to vote for the positive introduction of slavery either South or North of that line. Sir, while you reproach, and justly too, our British ancestors for the introduction of this institution upon the continent of America, I am, for one, unwilling that the posterity of the present inhabitants of California and of New Mexico, shall reproach us for doing just what we reproach Great Britain for doing to us. If the citizens of those territories choose to establish slavery, and if they come here with Constitutions establishing slavery, I am for admitting them with such provisions in their Constitutions; but then it will be their own work, and not ours, and their posterity will have to reproach them, and not us, for forming Constitutions allowing the institution of slavery to exist among them. These are my views, Sir, and I choose to express them; and I care not how extensively or universally they are known."

Hear him further; he says:

"So long as God allows the vital current to flow through my veins, I will never, never, never, by word, or thought, by mind or will, aid in admitting one rood of free territory to the everlasting curse of human bondage."

A bumper to the memory of noble Harry of the West!

CASSIUS M. CLAY

Of the great number of good speeches made by members of the Republican party during the late Presidential campaign, it is, we believe, pretty generally admitted that the best one was made by Cassius M. Clay, of Kentucky, at the Tabernacle, in New York City, on the 24th of October, 1856. From the speech of that noble champion of freedom, then and there delivered, we make the following graphic extract:

"If there are no manufactures, there is no commerce. In vain do the slaveholders go to Knoxville, to Nashville, to Memphis and to Charleston, and resolve that they will have nothing to do with these abolition eighteen millions of Northern people; that they will build their own vessels, manufacture their own goods, ship their own products to foreign countries, and break down New York, Philadelphia and Boston! Again they resolve and re-resolve, and yet there is not a single ton more shipped and not a single article added to the wealth of the South. But, gentlemen, they never invite such men as I am to attend their Conventions. They know that I would tell them that slavery is the cause of their poverty, and that I will tell them that what they are aiming at is the dissolution of the Union — that they may be prepared to strike for that whenever the nation rises. They well know that by slave labor the very propositions which they make can never be realized; yet when we show these things, they cry out, 'Oh, Cotton is King!' But when we look at the statistics, we find that so far from Cotton being King, Grass is King. There are nine articles of staple productions which are larger than that of cotton in this country."

"I suppose it does not follow because slavery is endeavoring to modify the great dicta of our fathers, that cotton and free labor are incompatible. In the extreme South, at New Orleans, the laboring men—the stevedores and hackmen on the levee, where the heat is intensified by the proximity of the red brick buildings, are all white men, and they are in the full enjoyment of health. But how about cotton? I am informed by a friend of mine—himself a slaveholder, and therefore good authority—that in Northwestern Texas, among the German settlements, who, true to their national instincts, will not employ the labor of a slave—they produce more cotton to the acre, and of a better quality, and selling at prices from a cent to a cent and a half a pound higher than that produced by slave labor. This is an experiment that illustrates what I have always held, that whatever is right is expedient."

THE VOICE OF BENTON

In his "Thirty Years' View," Thomas H. Benton says:

"My opposition to the extension of slavery dates further back than 1844—forty years further back; and as this is a suitable time for a general declaration, and a sort of general conscience delivery, I will say that my opposition to it dates from 1804, when I was a student at law in the State of Tennessee, and studied the subject of African slavery in an American book—a Virginia book—Tucker's edition of Blackstone's Commentaries."

Again, in a speech delivered in St. Louis, on the 3rd of November, 1856, he says:

"I look at white people, and not at black ones; I look to the peace and reputation of the race to which I belong. I look to the peace of this land—the world's last hope for a free government on the earth. One of the occasions on which I saw Henry Clay rise higher than I thought I ever saw him before, was when in the debate on the admission of California, a dissolution was apprehended if slavery was not carried into this Territory, where it never was. Then Mr. Clay, rising, loomed colossally in the Senate of the United States, as he rose declaring that for no earthly purpose, no earthly object, could he carry slavery into places where it did not exist before. It was a great and proud day for Mr. Clay, towards the latter days of his life, and if an artist could have been there to catch his expression as he uttered that sentiment, with its reflex on his face, and his countenance beaming with firmness of purpose, it would have been a glorious moment in which to transmit him to posterity—his countenance all alive and luminous with the ideas that beat in his bosom. That was a proud day. I could have wished that I had spoken the same words. I speak them now, telling you they were his, and adopting them as my own."

THE VOICE OF MASON

Colonel Mason, a leading and distinguished member of the Convention that formed the Constitution, from Virginia, when the provision for prohibiting the importation of slaves was under consideration, said:

"The present question concerns not the importing States alone, but the whole Union. Slavery discourages arts and manufactures. The poor despise labor when performed by slaves. They prevent the emigration of whites who really enrich and strengthen a country. They produce the most pernicious effect on manners. Every master of slaves is born a petty tyrant. They bring the judgment of Heaven on a country. As nations cannot be rewarded or punished in the next world, they must be in this. By an inevitable chain of causes and effects, Providence punishes national sins by national calamities. He lamented that some of our Eastern brethren had, from a lust of gain, embarked in this nefarious traffic. As to the States being in possession of the right to import, this was the case with many other rights, now to be properly given up. He held it essential, in every point of view, that the General Government should have power to prevent the increase of slavery."

THE VOICE OF MCDOWELL

In 1832, Gov. McDowell used this language in the Virginia Legislature:

"Who that looks to this unhappy bondage of an unhappy people, in the midst of our society, and thinks of its incidents or issues, but weeps over it as a curse as great upon him who inflicts as upon him who suffers it?

"Sir, you may place the slave where you please—you may dry up, to your uttermost, the fountains of his feelings, the springs of his thought—you may close upon his mind every avenue of knowledge, and cloud it over with artificial night—you may yoke him to your labors, as the ox, which liveth only to work and worketh only to live —you may put him under any process which, without destroying his value as a slave, will debase and crush him as a rational being —you may do this, and the idea that he was born to be free will survive it all. It is allied to his hope of immortality—it is the etherial part of his nature which oppression cannot rend. It is a torch lit up in his soul by the hand of Deity, and never meant to be extinguished by the hand of man."

The Voice of Iredell

In the debates of the North Carolina Convention, Mr. Iredell, afterwards a Judge of the United States Supreme Court, said:

"When the entire abolition of slavery takes place, it will be an event which must be pleasing to every generous mind, and every friend of human nature."

The Voice of Pinkney

William Pinkney, of Maryland, in the House of Delegates in that State, in 1789, made several powerful arguments in favor of the abolition of slavery. Here follows a brief extract from one of his speeches:

"Iniquitous and most dishonorable to Maryland, is that dreary system of partial bondage which her laws have hitherto supported with a solicitude worthy of a better object, and her citizens by their practice, countenanced. Founded in a disgraceful traffic, to which the parent country lent its aid, from motives of interest, but which even she would have disdained to encourage, had England been the destined mart of such inhuman merchandise, its continuance is as shameful as its origin.

I have no hope that the stream of general liberty will forever flow unpolluted through the mire of partial bondage, or that they who have been habituated to lord it over others, will not, in time, become base enough to let others lord it over them. If they resist, it will be the struggle of pride and selfishness, not of principle."

THE VOICE OF LEIGH

In the Legislature of Virginia, in 1832, Mr. Leigh said:

"I thought, till very lately that it was known to every body that, during the Revolution, and for many years after, the abolition of slavery was a favorite topic with many of our ablest Statesmen, who entertained with respect all the schemes which wisdom or ingenuity could suggest for its accomplishment."

THE VOICE OF MARSHALL

Thomas Marshall, of Fauquier, said, in the Virginia Legislature, in 1832:

"Wherefore, then, object to slavery? Because it is ruinous to the whites—retards improvements, roots out an industrious population, banishes the yeomanry of the country—deprives the spinner, the weaver, the smith, the shoemaker, the carpenter, of employment and support."

THE VOICE OF BOLLING

Philip A. Bolling, of Buckingham, a member of the Legislature of Virginia in 1832, said:

"The time will come—and it may be sooner than many are willing to believe—when this oppressed and degraded race cannot be held as they now are—when a change will be effected, abhorrent, Mr. Speaker, to you, and to the feelings of every good man.

The wounded adder will recoil, and sting the foot that tramples upon it. The day is fast approaching, when those who oppose all action upon this subject, and, instead of aiding in devising some feasible plan for freeing their country from an acknowledged curse, cry '*impossible,*' to every plan suggested, will curse their perverseness, and lament their folly."

THE VOICE OF CHANDLER

Mr. Chandler, of Norfolk, member of the Virginia Legislature, in 1832, took occasion to say:

"It is admitted, by all who have addressed this House, that slavery is a curse, and an increasing one. That it has been destructive to the lives of our citizens, history, with unerring truth, will record. That its future increase will create commotion, cannot be doubted."

THE VOICE OF SUMMERS

Mr. Summers, of Kanawha, member of the Legislature of Virginia, in 1832, said:

"The evils of this system cannot be enumerated. It were unnecessary to attempt it. They glare upon us at every step. When the owner looks to his wasted estate, he knows and feels them."

THE VOICE OF PRESTON

In the Legislature of Virginia, in 1832, Mr. Preston said:

"Sir, Mr. Jefferson, whose hand drew the preamble to the Bill of Rights, has eloquently remarked that we had invoked for ourselves the benefit of a principle which we had denied to others. He saw and felt that slaves, as men, were embraced within this principle."

THE VOICE OF FREMONT

John Charles Fremont, one of the noblest sons of the South, says:

"I heartily concur in all movements which have for their object to repair the mischiefs arising from the violation of good faith in the repeal of the Missouri Compromise. I am opposed to slavery in the abstract, and upon principles sustained and made habitual by long settled convictions. I am inflexibly opposed to its extension on this continent beyond its present limits. The great body of non-slave-holding Freemen, including those of the South, upon whose welfare slavery is an oppression, will discover that the power of the General Government over the Public Lands may be beneficially exerted to advance their interests, and secure their independence; knowing this, their suffrages will not be wanting to maintain that authority in the Union, which is absolutely essential to the maintenance of their own liberties, and which has more than once indicated the purpose of disposing of the Public Lands in such a way as would make every settler upon them a freeholder."

THE VOICE OF BLAIR

In an Address to the Republicans of Maryland, in 1856, Francis P. Blair says:

"In every aspect in which slavery among us can be considered, it is pregnant with difficulty. Its continuance in the States in which it has taken root has resulted in the monopoly of the soil, to a great extent, in the hands of the slaveholders, and the entire control of all departments of the State Government; and yet a majority of people in the slave States are not slave-owners. This produces an anomaly in the principle of our free institutions, which threatens in time to bring into subjugation to slave-owners the great body of the free white population."

THE VOICE OF MAURY

Lieut. Maury, to whom has been awarded so much well-merited praise in the world of science, says:

"The fact must be obvious to the far-reaching minds of our Statesmen, that unless some means of relief be devised, some channel afforded, by which the South can, when the time comes, get rid of the excess of her slave population, she will be ultimately found with regard to this institution, in the predicament of the man with the wolf by the ears; too dangerous to hold on any longer, and equally dangerous to let go. To our mind, the event is as certain to happen as any event which depends on the contingencies of the future, viz.: that unless means be devised for gradually relieving the slave States from the undue pressure of this class upon them — unless some way be opened by which they may be rid of their surplus black population—the time will come—it may not be in the next nor in the succeeding generation—but, sooner or later, come it will, and come it must—when the two races will join in the death struggle for the mastery."

THE VOICE OF BIRNEY

James G. Birney, of Kentucky, under whom the Abolitionists first became a National Party, and for whom they voted for President in 1844, giving him 66,304 votes, says:

"We have so long practiced injustice, adding to it hypocrisy, in the treatment of the colored race, both negroes and Indians, that we begin to regard injustice as an element—a chief element—the chief element of our government. But no government which admits injustice as an element can be a harmonious one or a permanent one. Harmony is the antagonist of injustice, ever has been, and ever will be; that is, so long as injustice lasts, which cannot always be, for it is a lie, a semblance, therefore, perishable. True, from the imperfection of man, his ambition and selfishness, injustice often finds its way incidentally into the administration of public affairs, and maintains its footing a long time before it is cast out by the legitimate elements of government."

"Our slave States, especially the more southern of them, in which the number of slaves is greater, and in which, of course the sentiment of injustice is stronger than in the more northern ones, are to be placed on the list of decaying communities. To a philosophic observer, they seem to be falling back on the scale of civilization. Even at the present point of retrogression, the cause of civilization and human improvement would lose nothing by their annihilation."

THE VOICE OF DELAWARE

Strong anti-slavery sentiment had become popular in Delaware as early as 1785. With Maryland and Missouri, it may now be ranked as a semi-slave State. Mr. McLane, a member of Congress from this State in 1825, said:

"I shall not imitate the example of other gentlemen by making professions of my love of liberty and abhorrence of slavery, not, however, because I do not entertain them. I am an enemy to slavery."

THE VOICE OF MARYLAND

Slavery has little vitality in Maryland. Baltimore, the greatest city of the South—greatest because freest—has a population of more than two hundred thousand souls, and yet less than three thousand of these are slaves. In spite of all the unjust and oppressive statutes enacted by the oligarchy, the non-slaveholders, who with the exception of a small number of slaveholding emancipationists, may in truth be said to be the only class of respectable and patriotic citizens in the South, have wisely determined that their noble State shall be freed from the sin and the shame, the crime and the curse of slavery; and in accordance with this determination, long since formed, they are giving every possible encouragement to free white labor, thereby, very properly, rendering the labor of slaves both unprofitable and disgraceful. The formation of an Abolition Society in this State, in 1789, was the result of the influence of the masterly speeches delivered in the House of Delegates, by the Hon. William Pinkney, whose undying testimony we have already placed on record. Nearly seventy years ago, this eminent lawyer and Statesman declared to the people of America, that if they did not mark out the bounds of slavery, and adopt measures for its total extinction, it would finally "work a decay of the spirit of liberty in the free States." Further, he said that, "by the eternal principles of natural justice, no master in the State has a right to hold his slave in bondage a single hour." In 1787, Luther Martin, of this State, said:

"Slavery is inconsistent with the genius of republicanism, and has a tendency to destroy those principles on which it is supported, as it lessens the sense of the equal rights of mankind, and habituates us to tyranny and oppression."

THE VOICE OF VIRGINIA

After introducing the unreserved and immortal testimony of Washington, Jefferson, Madison, Henry, and the other great men of the Old Dominion, against the institution of slavery, it may to some, seem quite superfluous to back the cause of Freedom by arguments from other Virginia abolitionists; but this State, notwithstanding all her more modern manners and inhumanity, has been so prolific of just views and noble sentiments, that we deem it eminently fit and proper to blazon many of them to the world as the redeeming features of her history. An Abolition Society was formed in this State in 1791. In a memorial which the members of this Society presented to Congress, they pronounced slavery "not only an odious degradation, but an outrageous violation of one of the most essential rights of human nature, and utterly repugnant to the precepts of the Gospel." A Bill of Rights, unanimously agreed upon by the Virginia Convention of June 12, 1776, holds —

"That all men are, by nature, equally free and independent;

That Government is, or ought to be, instituted for the common benefit, protection, and security, of the People, Nation, or Community;

That elections of members to serve as representatives of the people in assembly ought to be free;

That all men having sufficient evidence of permanent common interest with, and attachment to, the community, have the right of suffrage, and cannot be taxed or deprived of their property, for public uses, without their own consent or that of their representatives so elected, nor bound by any law to which they have not in like manner assented, for the public good;

That the freedom of the Press is one of the greatest bulwarks of

Liberty, and can never be restrained but by despotic Governments;

That no free Government or the blessing of Liberty can be preserved to any people, but by a firm adherence to justice, moderation, temperance, frugality, and virtue, and by a frequent recurrence to fundamental principles."

The "Virginia Society for the Abolition of Slavery," organized in 1791, addressed Congress in these words:

"Your memorialists, fully aware that righteousness exalteth a nation, and that slavery is not only an odious degradation, but an outrageous violation of one of the most essential rights of human nature, and utterly repugnant to the precepts of the gospel, which breathes 'peace on earth and good will to men,' lament that a practice so inconsistent with true policy and the inalienable rights of men, should subsist in so enlightened an age, and among a people professing that all mankind are, by nature, equally entitled to freedom."

THE VOICE OF NORTH CAROLINA

If the question, *slavery* or *no slavery*, could be fairly presented for the decision of the legal voters of North Carolina at the next popular election, we believe at least two-thirds of them would deposit the *no slavery* ticket. Perhaps one-fourth of the slaveholders themselves would vote it, for the slaveholders in this State are more moderate, decent, sensible, and honorable, than the slaveholders in either of the adjoining States, or the States further South; and we know that many of them are heartily ashamed of the vile occupations of slaveholding and slave-breeding in which they are engaged, for we have the assurance from their own lips. As a matter of course, all the non-slave-holders, who are so greatly in the majority, would vote to suppress the degrading institution which has kept them so long in poverty and ignorance, with the exception of those who are complete automatons to the beck and call of their imperious lords and masters, the major-generals of the oligarchy.

How long shall it be before the citizens of North Carolina shall have the privilege of expressing, at the ballot-box, their true sentiments with regard to this vexed question? Why not decide it at the next general election? Sooner or later, it must and will be decided — decided correctly, too — and the sooner the better. The first Southern State that abolishes slavery will do herself an immortal honor. God grant that North Carolina may be that State, and soon! There is at least one plausible reason why this good old State should be the first to move in this important matter, and we will state it. On the 20th of May, 1775, just one year one month and fourteen days prior to the adoption of the Jeffersonian Declaration of Independence, by the Continental Congress in Philadelphia, July 4, 1776, the Mecklenburg Declaration of Independence, the authorship of which is generally attributed to Ephraim Brevard, was proclaimed in Charlotte, Mecklenburg county, North Carolina, and fully ratified in a second Convention of the people of said county, held on the 31st of the same month. And here, by the way, we may remark, that it is supposed Mr. Jefferson made use of this last-mentioned document as the basis of his draft of the indestructible title-deed of our liberties. There is certainly an identicalness of language between the two papers that is well calculated to strengthen this hypothesis. This, however, is a controversy about which we are but little concerned. For present purposes, it is, perhaps, enough for us to know, that on the 20th of May, 1775, when transatlantic tyranny and oppression could no longer be endured, North Carolina set her sister colonies a most valorous and praiseworthy example, and that they followed it. To her infamous slaveholding sisters of the South, it is now meet that she should set another noble example of decency, virtue, and independence. Let her at once inaugurate a policy of common justice and humanity — enact a system of equitable laws, having due regard to the rights and interests of all classes of persons, poor whites, negroes, and nabobs, and the surrounding States will before long applaud her measures, and adopt similar ones for the governance of themselves.

Another reason, and a cogent one, why North Carolina should aspire to become the first free State of the South is this: The first slave State that makes herself respectable by casting out "the mother of harlots," and by rendering enterprise and industry honorable, will immediately receive a large accession of most worthy citizens from other States in the Union, and thus lay a broad foundation of permanent political power and prosperity. Intelligent white farmers from the Middle and New England States will flock to our more congenial clime, eager to give thirty dollars per acre for the same lands that are now a drug in the market because nobody wants them at the rate of five dollars per acre; an immediate and powerful impetus will be given to commerce, manufactures, and all the industrial arts; science and literature will be revived, and every part of the State will reverberate with the triumphs of manual and intellectual labor.

At this present time, we of North Carolina are worth less than either of the four adjoining States; let us abolish slavery at the beginning of the next regular decade of years, and if our example is not speedily followed, we shall, on or before the first day of January, 1870, be enabled to purchase the whole of Virginia and South Carolina, including, perhaps, the greater part of Georgia. An exclusive lease of liberty for ten years would unquestionably make us the Empire State of the South. But we have no disposition to debar others from the enjoyment of liberty or any other inalienable right; we ask no special favors; what we demand for ourselves we are willing to concede to our neighbors. Hereby we make application for a lease of freedom for ten years; shall we have it? May God enable us to secure it, as we believe He will. We give fair notice, however, that if we get it for ten years, we shall, with the approbation of Heaven, keep it twenty—forty—a thousand—forever!

We transcribe the Mecklenburg Resolutions, which, it will be observed, acknowledge the "inherent and inalienable rights of man," and "declare ourselves a free and independent people, are, and of right ought to be, a sovereign and self-governing association, under the control of no power other than that of our God, and the general government of the Congress."

MECKLENBURG DECLARATION OF INDEPENDENCE

As proclaimed in the town of Charlotte, North Carolina, May 20th, 1775, and ratified by the County of Mecklenburg, in Convention, May 31st, 1775.

"I. *Resolved*—That whosoever, directly or indirectly, abetted, or in any way, form or manner, countenanced the unchartered and dangerous invasion of our rights as claimed by Great Britain, is an enemy to this country, to America, and to the inherent and inalienable rights of man.

"II. *Resolved*—That we the citizens of Mecklenburg County, do hereby dissolve the political bands which have connected us to the mother country, and hereby absolve ourselves from all allegiance to the British Crown, and abjure all political connection, contract or association with that nation, who have wantonly trampled on our rights and liberties, and inhumanly shed the blood of American patriots at Lexington.

"III. *Resolved*—That we do hereby declare ourselves a free and independent people, are, and of right ought to be, a sovereign and self-governing association, under the control of no power other than that of our God, and the general government of the Congress; to the maintenance of which independence, we solemnly pledge to each other our mutual cooperation, our lives, our fortunes, and our most sacred honor.

"IV. *Resolved*—That as we now acknowledge the existence and control of no law or legal officer, civil or military, within this county, we do hereby ordain and adopt, as a rule of life, all, each, and every of our former laws — wherein, nevertheless, the crown of Great Britain never can be considered as holding rights, privileges, immunities or authority therein."

Had it not been for slavery, which, with all its other blighting and degrading influences, stifles and subdues every noble impulse of the heart, this consecrated spot would long since have been marked by an enduring monument, whose grand proportions should bear witness that the virtues of a noble ancestry are gratefully remembered by an emulous and appreciative posterity. Yet, even as things are, we are not without genuine consolation. The star of hope and promise is beginning to beam brightly over the long-obscured horizon of the South; and we are firm in the belief, that freedom, wealth, and magnanimity, will soon do justice to the memory of those fearless patriots, whose fair fame has been suffered to moulder amidst the multifarious abominations of slavery, poverty, ignorance and grovelling selfishness.

Judge Iredell's testimony, which will be found on a preceding page, and to which we request the reader to recur, might have been appropriately introduced under our present heading.

In the Provincial Convention held in North Carolina, in August, 1774, in which there were sixty-nine delegates, representing nearly every county in the province, it was—

"*Resolved*—That we will not import any slave or slaves, or purchase any slave or slaves imported or brought into the Province by others, from any part of the world, after the first day of November next."

In Iredell's Statutes, revised by Martin, it is stated that,

'In North Carolina, no general law at all was passed, prior to the revolution, declaring who might be slaves."

That there is no *legal* slavery in the Southern States, and that slavery no where can be legalized, any more than theft, arson or murder can be legalized, has been virtually admitted by some of the most profound Southern jurists themselves; and we will here digress so far as to furnish the testimony of one or two eminent lawyers, not of North Carolina, upon this point.

In the debate in the United States Senate, in 1850, on the Fugitive Slave Bill, Mr. Mason, of Virginia, objected to Mr. Dayton's amendment, providing for a trial by jury, because, said he:

"A trial by jury necessarily carries with it a trial of the whole right, and a trial of the right to service will be gone into, according to all the forms of the Court, in determining upon any other fact. Then, again, it is proposed, as a part of the proof to be adduced at the hearing, after the fugitive has been re-captured, that evidence shall be brought by the claimant to show that slavery is established in the State from which the fugitive has absconded. Now this very thing, in a recent case in the city of New York, was required by one of the judges of that State, which case attracted the attention of the authorities of Maryland, and against which they protested. In that case the State judge went so far as to say that the only mode of proving it was by reference to the Statute book. Such proof is required in the Senator's amendment; and if he means by this that proof shall be brought that slavery is established by existing laws, it is impossible to comply with the requisition, for no such law can be produced, I apprehend, in any of the slave States. I am not aware that there is a single State in which the institution is established by positive law."

Judge Clarke of Mississippi, says:

"In this State the legislature have considered slaves as reasonable and accountable beings; and it would be a stigma upon the character of the State, and a reproach to the administration of justice, if the life of a slave could be taken with impunity, or if he could be murdered in cold blood, without subjecting the offender to the highest penalty known to the criminal jurisprudence of the country. Has the slave no rights, because he is deprived of his freedom? He is still a human being, and possesses all those rights of which he is not deprived by the positive provisions of the law. The right of the master exists not by force of the law of nature or nations, but by virtue only of the positive law of the State."

The Hon. Judge Ruffin, of North Carolina, says:

"Arguments drawn from the well-established principles, which confer and restrain the authority of the parent over the child, the tutor over the pupil, the master over the apprentice, have been pressed on us. The Court does not recognize their application; there is no likeness between the cases; they are in opposition to each other, and there is an impassable gulf between them. The difference is that which exists between freedom and slavery, and a greater cannot be imagined. In the one, the end in view is the happiness of the youth, born to equal rights with that governor on whom the duty devolves of training the young to usefulness, in a station which he is afterwards to assume among freemen. To such an end, and with such a subject, moral and intellectual instruction seem the natural means, and, for the most part, they are found to suffice. Moderate force is superadded only to make the others effectual. If that fail, it is better to leave the party to his own headstrong passions, and the ultimate correction of the law, than to allow it to be immoderately inflicted by a private person. With slavery it is far otherwise. The end is the profit of the master, his security, and the public safety; the subject, one doomed, in his own person and his posterity, to live without knowledge, and without the capacity to make anything his own, and to toil that another may reap the fruits. What moral considerations shall be addressed to such a being to convince him, what it is impossible but that the most stupid must feel and know can never be true, that he is thus to labor upon a principle of natural duty, or for the sake of his own personal happiness? Such services can only be expected from one who has no will of his own; who surrenders his will in implicit obedience to that of another. Such obedience is the consequence only of uncontrolled authority over the body. There is nothing else which can operate to produce the effect. The power of the master must be absolute to render the submission of the slave perfect. I most freely confess my sense of the harshness of this proposition. I feel it as deeply as any man can; and as a principle of moral right, every person in his retirement must repudiate it."

An esteemed friend, a physician, who was born and bred in Rowan county, North Carolina, and who now resides there, informs us that Judge Gaston, who was one of the half dozen Statesmen whom the South has produced since the days of the venerable fathers of the Republic, was an avowed abolitionist, and that he published an address to the people of North Carolina, delineating, in a masterly manner, the material, moral, and social disadvantages of slavery. Where is that address? Has it been suppressed by the oligarchy? The fact that slaveholders have, from time to time, made strenuous efforts to expunge the sentiments of freedom which now adorn the works of nobler men than the noble Gaston, may, perhaps, fully account for the oblivious state into which his patriotic address seems to have fallen.

THE VOICE OF SOUTH CAROLINA

Poor South Carolina! Folly is her nightcap; fanaticism is her daydream; fire-eating is her pastime. She has lost her better judgment; the dictates of reason and philosophy have no influence upon her actions. Like the wife who is pitiably infatuated with a drunken, worthless husband, she still clings, with unabated love, to the cause of her shame, her misery, and her degradation.

A Kentuckian has recently expressed his opinion of this State in the following language:

"South Carolina is bringing herself irrecoverably in the public contempt. It is impossible for any impartial lover of his country, for any just thinking man, to witness her senseless and quenchless malignancy against the Union without the most immeasurable disgust and scorn. She is one vast hot-bed of disunion. Her people think and talk of nothing else. She is a festering mass of treason."

In 1854, there were assessed for taxation in:

South Carolina

Acres of Land	17,289,359
Valued at	$22,836,374
Average value per acre	$1.32

At the same time there were in:

New Jersey

Acres of Land	5324800
Valued at	$153,161,619
Average value per acre	$28.76

We hope the Slavocrats will look, first on that picture, and then on this; from one or the other, or both, they may glean a ray or two of wisdom, which, if duly applied, will be of incalculable advantage to them and their posterity We trust, also, that the non-slaveholding whites will view, with discriminating minds, the different lights and shades of these two pictures; they are the parties most deeply interested; and it is to them we look for the glorious revolution that is to substitute Freedom for Slavery. They have the power to retrieve the fallen fortunes of South Carolina, to raise her up from the loathsome sink of iniquity into which slavery has plunged her, and to make her one of the most brilliant stars in the great constellation of States. While their minds are occupied with other considerations, let them not forget the difference between *twenty-eight dollars and seventy-six cents*, the value of land per acre in New Jersey, which is a second-rate free State, and *one dollar and thirty-two cents*, the value of land per acre in South Carolina, which is, *par excellence*, the model slave State. The difference between the two sums is twenty-seven dollars and forty-four cents, which would amount to precisely two thousand seven hundred and forty-four dollars on every hundred acres. To present the subject in another form, the South Carolina tract of land, containing two hundred acres, is worth now only two hundred and sixty-four dollars, and is depreciating every day. Let slavery be abolished, and in the course of a few years, the same tract will be worth five thousand seven hundred and fifty-two dollars, with an upward tendency. At this rate, the increment of value on the total area of the State will amount to more than three times as much as the present estimated value of the slaves!

South Carolina has not always been, nor will she always continue to be, on the wrong side. From Ramsay's History of the State, we learn that, in 1774, she—

"*Resolved*—That His Majesty's subjects in North America (without respect to color or other accidents) are entitled to all the inherent rights and liberties of his natural born subjects within the Kingdom of Great Britain; that it is their fundamental right, that no man should suffer in his person or property without a fair trial, and judgment given by his peers, or by the law of the land."

One of her early writers, under the *non de plume* of Philodemus, in a political pamphlet published in Charleston in 1784, declares that—

"Such is the fatal influence of slavery on the human mind, that it almost wholly effaces from it even the boasted characteristic of rationality."

This same writer, speaking of the particular interests of South Carolina, says:

"It has been too common with us to search the records of other nations, to find precedents that may give sanction to our own errors, and lead us unwarily into confusion and ruin. It is our business to consult their histories, not with a view to tread right or wrong in their steps, but in order to investigate the real sources of the mischiefs that have befallen them, and to endeavor to escape the rocks which they have all unfortunately split upon. It is paying ourselves but a poor compliment, to say that we are incapable of profiting by others, and that, with all the information which is to be derived from their fatal experience, it is in vain for us to attempt to excel them. If, with all the peculiar advantages of our present situation, we are incapable of surpassing our predecessors, we must be a degenerate race indeed, and quite unworthy of those singular bounties of Heaven, which we are so unskilled or undesirous to turn to our benefit."

A recent number of Frazer's Magazine contains a well-timed and well-written article from the pen of Wm. Henry Hurlbut, of this State; and from it we make the following extract:

"As all sagacious observers of the operation of the system of slavery have demonstrated, the profitable employment of slave labor is inconsistent with the development of agricultural science, and demands a continual supply of new and unexhausted soil. The slaveholder, investing his capital in the purchase of the laborers themselves, and not merely in soil and machines, paying his free laborers out of the profit, must depend for his continued and progressive prosperity upon the cheapness and facility with which he can transfer his slaves to fresh and fertile lands. An enormous additional item, namely, the price of slaves, being added to the cost of production, all other elements of that cost require to be proportionably smaller, or profits fail."

In an address delivered before the South Carolina Institute, in Charleston, Nov. 20th, 1856, Mr. B. F. Perry, of Greenville, truthfully says:

"It has been South Carolina's misfortune, in this utilitarian age, to have her greatest talents and most powerful energies directed to pursuits, which avail her nothing, in the way of wealth and prosperity. In the first settlement of a new country, agricultural industry necessarily absorbs all the time and occupation of its inhabitants. They must clear the forests and cultivate the earth, in order to make their bread. This is their first consideration. Then the mechanical arts, and manufactures, and commerce, must follow in the footsteps of agriculture, to insure either individual or national prosperity. No people can be highly prosperous without them. No people ever have been. Agriculture, alone, will not make or sustain a great people. The true policy of every people is to cultivate the earth, manufacture its products, and send them abroad, in exchange for those comforts and luxuries, and necessaries, which their own country and their own industry cannot give or make. The dependence of South Carolina on Europe and the Northern States for all the necessaries, comforts and luxuries, which the mechanic arts afford, has, in fact, drained her of her wealth, and made her positively poor, when compared with her sister States of the Confederacy. It is at once mortifying and alarming, to see and reflect on our own dependence in the mechanic arts and manufactures, on strangers and foreigners. In the Northern States their highest talents and energy have been diversified, and more profitably employed in developing the resources of the country, in making new inventions in the mechanic arts, and enriching the community with science and literature, commerce and manufactures."

THE VOICE OF GEORGIA

Of the States strictly Southern, Georgia is, perhaps, the most thrifty. This prosperous condition of the State is mainly ascribable to her hundred thousand free white laborers — more than eighty-three thousand of whom are engaged in agricultural pursuits. In few other slave States are the non-slaveholders so little under the domination of the oligarchy. At best, however, even in the most liberal slave States, the social position of the non-slaveholding whites is but one short step in advance of that of the negroes; and as there is, on the part of the oligarchy, a constantly increasing desire and effort to usurp greater power, the more we investigate the subject the more fully are we convinced that nothing but the speedy and utter annihilation of slavery from the entire nation, can save the masses of white people in the Southern States from ultimately falling to a political level with the blacks—both occupying the most abject and galling condition of servitude of which it is possible for the human mind to conceive.

Gen. Oglethorpe, under whose management the Colony of Georgia was settled, in 1733, was bitterly opposed to the institution of slavery. In a letter to Granville Sharp, dated Oct. 13th, 1776, he says:

"My friends and I settled the Colony of Georgia, and by charter were established trustees, to make laws, &c. We determined not to suffer slavery there. But the slave merchants and their adherents occasioned us not only much trouble, but at last got the then government to favor them. We would not suffer slavery, (which is against the Gospel, as well as the fundamental law of England,) to be authorized under our authority; we refused, as trustees, to make a law permitting such a horrid crime. The government, finding the trustees resolved firmly not to concur with what they believed unjust, took away the charter by which no law could be passed without our consent."

On the 12th of January, 1775, in indorsing the proceedings of the first American Congress, among other resolutions, "the Representatives of the extensive District of Darien, in the Colony of Georgia" adopted the following:

"5. To show the world that we are not influenced by any contracted or interested motives, but a general philanthropy for all mankind, of whatever climate, language, or complexion, we hereby declare our disapprobation and abhorrence of the unnatural practice of slavery in America, (however the uncultivated state of our country or other arguments may plead for it,) a practice founded in injustice and cruelty, and highly dangerous to our liberties, (as well as lives,) debasing part of our fellow creatures below men, and corrupting the virtue and morals of the rest; and is laying the basis of that liberty we contend for, (and which we pray the Almighty to continue to the latest posterity,) upon a very wrong foundation. We therefore resolve, at all times, to use our utmost endeavors for the manumission of our slaves in this Colony, upon the most safe and equitable footing for the masters and themselves."

The Hon. Mr. Reid, of this State, in a speech delivered in Congress, Feb. 1, 1820, says:

"I am not the panegyrist of slavery. It is an unnatural state, a dark cloud, which obscures half the lustre of our free institutions. For my own part, though surrounded by slavery from my cradle to the present moment, yet—

'I hate the touch of servile hands, I loathe the slaves who cringe around.'"

As an accompaniment to those lines, he might have uttered these:

"I would not have a slave to till my ground; To carry me, to fan me while I sleep And tremble when I wake, for all the wealth That sinews bought and sold have ever earned."

Thus have we presented a comprehensive summary of the most unequivocal and irrefragable testimony of the South against the iniquitous institution of human slavery. What more can we say? What more can we do? We might fill a folio volume with similar extracts; but we must forego the task; the remainder of our space must be occupied with other arguments. In the foregoing excerpts is revealed to us, in language too plain to be misunderstood, the important fact that every truly great and good man the South has ever produced, has, with hopeful confidence, looked forward to the time when this entire continent shall be redeemed from the crime of slavery. Our self-sacrificing forefathers have performed their part, and performed it well. They have laid us a foundation as enduring as the earth itself; in their dying moments they admonished us to carry out their designs in the upbuilding and completion of the superstructure. Let us obey their patriotic injunctions.

From each of the six original Southern States we have introduced the most ardent aspirations for liberty—the most positive condemnations of slavery. From each of the nine slave States which have been admitted into the Union since the organization of the General Government, we could introduce, from several of their wisest and best citizens, anti-slavery sentiments equally as strong and convincing as those that emanated from the great founders of our movement — Washington, Jefferson, Madison, Patrick Henry and the Randolphs. As we have already remarked, however, the limits of this chapter will not admit of the introduction of additional testimony from either of the old or of the new slave States.

The reader will not fail to observe that, in presenting these solid abolition doctrines of the South, we have been careful to make such quotations as triumphantly refute, in every particular, the more specious sophistries of the oligarchy.

The mention of the illustrious names above, reminds us of the fact, that the party newspapers, whose venal columns are eternally teeming with vituperation and slander, have long assured us that the Whig ship was to be steered by the Washington rudder, that the Democratic barque was to sail with the Jefferson compass, and that the Know-Nothing brig was to carry the Madison chart. Imposed upon by these monstrous falsehoods, we have, from time to time, been induced to engage passage on each of these corrupt and rickety old hulks; but, in every instance, we have been basely swamped in the sea of slavery, and are alone indebted for our lives to the kindness of Heaven and the art of swimming. Washington the founder of the Whig party! Jefferson the founder of the Democratic party! Voltaire the founder of Christianity! God forbid that man's heart should always continue to be the citadel of deception—that he should ever be to others the antipode of what he is to himself.

There is now in this country but one party that promises, in good faith, to put in practice the principles of Washington, Jefferson, Madison, and the other venerable Fathers of the Republic — the Republican party. To this party we pledge unswerving allegiance, so long as it shall continue to pursue the statism advocated by the great political prototypes above-mentioned, but no longer. We believe it is, as it ought to be, the desire, the determination, and the destiny of this party, to give the death-blow to slavery; should future developments prove the party at variance with this belief—a belief, by the bye, which it has recently inspired in the breasts of little less than one and a half millions of the most intelligent and patriotic voters in America—we shall shake off the dust of our feet against it, and join one that will, in a summary manner, extirpate the intolerable grievance.

Chapter 4

Northern Testimony

THE BEST EVIDENCE THAT CAN BE GIVEN of the enlightened patriotism and love of liberty in the Free States, is the fact that, at the Presidential election in 1856, they polled thirteen hundred thousand votes for the Republican candidate, John C. Fremont. This fact of itself seems to preclude the necessity of strengthening our cause with the individual testimony of even their greatest men. Having, however, adduced the most cogent and conclusive anti-slavery arguments from the Washingtons, the Jeffersons, the Madisons, the Randolphs, and the Clays of the South, we shall now proceed to enrich our pages with gems of Liberty from the Franklins, the Hamiltons, the Jays, the Adamses, and the Websters of the North. Too close attention cannot be paid to the words of wisdom which we have extracted from the works of these truly eminent and philosophic Statesmen. We will first listen to:

THE VOICE OF FRANKLIN

Dr. Franklin was the first president of "The Pennsylvania Society for promoting the Abolition of Slavery;" and it is now generally conceded that this was the first regularly organized American abolition Society — it having been formed as early as 1774, while we were yet subjects of the British government. In 1790, in the name and on behalf of this Society, Dr. Franklin, who was then within a few months of the close of his life, drafted a memorial "to the Senate and House of Representatives of the United States," in which he said:

"Your memorialists, particularly engaged in attending to the distresses arising from slavery, believe it to be their indispensable duty to present this subject to your notice. They have observed, with real satisfaction, that many important and salutary powers are vested in you, for 'promoting the welfare and securing the blessings of liberty to the people of the United States; and as they conceive that these blessings ought rightfully to be administered, without distinction of color, to all descriptions of people, so they indulge themselves in the pleasing expectation that nothing which can be done for the relief of the unhappy objects of their care, will be either omitted or delayed.

From a persuasion that equal liberty was originally the portion, and is still the birthright of all men, and influenced by the strong ties of humanity and the principles of their institution, your memorialists conceive themselves bound to use all justifiable endeavors to loosen the bonds of slavery, and promote a general enjoyment of the blessings of freedom. Under these impressions, they earnestly entreat your attention to the subject of slavery; that you will be pleased to countenance the restoration to liberty of those unhappy men, who, alone, in this land of freedom, are degraded into perpetual bondage, and who, amid the general joy of surrounding freemen, are groaning in servile subjection; that you will devise means for removing this inconsistency of character from the American people; that you will promote mercy and justice towards this distressed race; and that you will step to the very verge of the power vested in you for discouraging every species of traffic in the persons of our fellowmen."

On another occasion, he says:"Slavery is an atrocious debasement of human nature."

THE VOICE OF HAMILTON

Alexander Hamilton, the brilliant Statesman and financier, tells us that—

"The sacred rights of mankind are not to be rummaged for among old parchments or musty records. They are written as with a sunbeam, in the whole volume of human nature, by the hand of the

Divinity itself, and can never be erased or obscured by mortal power."

Again, in 1774, addressing himself to an American Tory, he says:

"The fundamental source of all your errors, sophisms, and false reasonings, is a total ignorance of the natural rights of mankind. Were you once to become acquainted with these, you could never entertain a thought, that all men are not, by nature, entitled to equal privileges. You would be convinced that natural liberty is the gift of the beneficent Creator to the whole human race; and that civil liberty is founded on that."

THE VOICE OF JAY

John Jay, first Chief Justice of the United States under the Constitution of 1789, in a letter to the Hon. Elias Boudinot, dated Nov. 17, 1819, says:

"Little can be added to what has been said and written on the subject of slavery. I concur in the opinion that it ought not to be introduced nor permitted in any of the new States, and that it ought to be gradually diminished and finally abolished in all of them.

"To me, the constitutional authority of the Congress to prohibit the migration and importation of slaves into any of the States, does not appear questionable.

"The first article of the Constitution specifies the legislative powers committed to the Congress. The 9th section of that article has these words: 'The *migration* or *importation* of such persons as any of the *now-existing* States shall think proper to admit, shall not be prohibited by the Congress prior to the year 1808, but a tax or duty may be imposed on such importation, not exceeding ten dollars for each person.'

"I understand the sense and meaning of this clause to be, that the power of the congress, although competent to prohibit such migration and importation, was to be exercised with respect to the *then* existing States, and them only, until the year 1808, but the Congress were at liberty to make such prohibitions as to any *new* State, which might in the *mean* time be established. And further, that from and after *that* period, they were authorized to make such prohibitions as to *all* the States, whether *new* or *old*.

"It will, I presume, be admitted, that slaves were the persons intended. The word slaves was avoided, probably on account of the existing toleration of slavery, and its discordancy with the principles of the Revolution, and from a consciousness of its being repugnant to the following positions in the Declaration of Independence: 'We hold these truths to be self-evident: that all men are created equal; that they are endowed by their Creator with certain inalienable rights; that among these are life, liberty, and the pursuit of happiness.' "

In a previous letter, written from Spain, whither he had been appointed as minister plenipotentiary, he says, speaking of the abolition of slavery:

"Till America comes into this measure, her prayers to Heaven will be impious. This is a strong expression, but it is just. I believe that God governs the world, and I believe it to be a maxim in His, as in our Courts, that those who ask for equity ought to do it."

WILLIAM JAY

The Hon. Wm. Jay, a noble son of Chief Justice John Jay, says:
"A crisis has arrived in which we must maintain our rights, or surrender them for ever. I speak not to abolitionists alone, but to all who value the liberty our fathers achieved. Do you ask what we have to do with slavery? Let our muzzled presses answer—let the mobs excited against us by the merchants and politicians answer—let the gag laws threatened by our governors and legislatures answer, let the conduct of the National Government answer."

THE VOICE OF ADAMS

From the Diary of John Quincy Adams, "the old man eloquent," we make the following extract:
"It is among the evils of slavery, that it taints the very sources of

moral principle. It establishes false estimates of virtue and vice; for what can be more false and more heartless than this doctrine, which makes the first and holiest rights of humanity to depend upon the color of the skin? It perverts human reason, and induces men endowed with logical powers to maintain that slavery is sanctioned by the Christian religion; that slaves are happy and contented in their condition; that between master and slave there are ties of mutual attachment and affection; that the virtues of the master are refined and exalted by the degradation of the slave, while at the same time they vent execrations upon the slave-trade, curse Britain for having given them slaves, burn at the stake negroes convicted of crimes, for the terror of the example, and writhe in agonies of fear at the very mention of human rights as applicable to men of color."

THE VOICE OF WEBSTER

In a speech which he delivered at Niblo's Garden, in the city of New York, on the 15th of March, 1847, Daniel Webster, the great Expounder of the Constitution, said:

"On the general question of slavery, a great part of the community is already strongly excited. The subject has not only attracted attention as a question of politics, but it has struck a far deeper one ahead. It has arrested the religious feeling of the country, it has taken strong hold on the consciences of men. He is a rash man, indeed, and little conversant with human nature, and especially has he an erroneous estimate of the character of the people of this country, who supposes that a feeling of this kind is to be trifled with or despised. It will assuredly cause itself to be respected. But to endeavor to coin it into silver, or retain its free expression, to seek to compress and confine it, warm as it is, and more heated as such endeavors would inevitably render it — should this be attempted, I know nothing, even in the Constitution or Union itself, which might not be endangered by the explosion which might follow."

When discussing the Oregon Bill in 1848, he said:

"I have made up my mind, for one, that under no circumstances will I consent to the further extension of the area of slavery in the United States, or to the further increase of slave representation in the House of Representatives."

Under date of February 15th, 1850, in a letter to the Rev. Mr. Furness, he says:

"From my earliest youth I have regarded slavery as a great moral and political evil. I think it unjust, repugnant to the natural equality of mankind, founded only in superior power; a standing and permanent conquest by the stronger over the weaker. All pretense of defending it on the ground of different races, I have ever condemned. I have even said that if the black race is weaker, that is a reason against, not for, its subjection and oppression. In a religious point of view I have ever regarded it, and even spoken of it, not as subject to any express denunciation, either in the Old Testament or the New, but as opposed to the whole spirit of the Gospel and to the teachings of Jesus Christ. The religion of Jesus Christ is a religion of kindness, justice, and brotherly love. But slavery is not kindly affectionate; it does not seek anothers, and not its own; it does not let the oppressed go free. It is, as I have said, but a continual act of oppression. But then, such is the influence of a habit of thinking among men, and such is the influence of what has been long established, that even minds, religious and tenderly conscientious, such as would be shocked by any single act of oppression, in any single exercise of violence and unjust power, are not always moved by the reflection that slavery is a continual and permanent violation of human rights."

While delivering a speech at Buffalo, in the State of New York, in the summer of 1851, only about twelve months prior to his decease, he made use of the following emphatic words:

"I never would consent, and never have consented, that there should be one foot of slave territory beyond what the old thirteen States had at the formation of the Union. Never, never."

NOAH WEBSTER

Noah Webster, the great American vocabulist, says:

"That freedom is the sacred right of every man, whatever be his color, who has not forfeited it by some violation of municipal law, is a truth established by God himself, in the very creation of human beings. No time, no circumstance, no human power or policy can change the nature of this truth, nor repeal the fundamental laws of society, by which every man's right to liberty is guarantied. The act of enslaving men is always a violation of those great primary laws of society, by which alone, the master himself holds every particle of his own freedom."

THE VOICE OF CLINTON

DeWitt Clinton, the father of the great system of internal improvements in the State of New York, speaking of despotism in Europe, and of slavery in America, asks:

"Have not prescription and precedent—patriarchal dominion— divine right of kings and masters, been alternately called in to sanction the slavery of nations? And would not all the despotisms of the ancient and modern world have vanished into air, if the natural equality of mankind had been properly understood and practiced? . . . This declares that the same measure of justice ought to be measured out to all men, without regard to adventitious inequalities, and the intellectual and physical disparities which proceed from inexplicable causes."

THE VOICE OF WARREN

Major General Joseph Warren, one of the truest patriots of the Revolution, and the first American officer of rank that fell in our contest with Great Britain, says:

"That personal freedom is the natural right of every man, and that property, or an exclusive right to dispose of what he has honestly acquired by his own labor, necessarily arises therefrom, are truths that common sense has placed beyond the reach of contradiction. And no man, or body of men, can, without being guilty of flagrant injustice, claim a right to dispose of the persons or acquisitions of any other man or body of men, unless it can be proved that such a right has arisen from some compact between the parties, in which it has been explicitly and freely granted."

Otis, Hancock, Ames, and others, should be heard, but for the want of space. Volumes upon volumes might be filled with extracts similar to the above, from the works of the deceased Statesmen and sages of the North, who, while living, proved themselves equal to the task of exterminating from their own States the matchless curse of human slavery. Such are the men who, though no longer with us in the flesh, "still live." A living principle—an immortal interest— have they, invested in every great and good work that distinguishes the free States. The railroads, the canals, the telegraphs, the factories, the fleets of merchant vessels, the magnificent cities, the scientific modes of agriculture, the unrivaled institutions of learning, and other striking evidences of progress and improvement at the North, are, either directly or indirectly, the offspring of their gigantic intellects. When, if ever, commerce, and manufactures, and agriculture, and great enterprises, and truth, and liberty, and justice, and magnanimity, shall have become obsolete terms, then their names may possibly be forgotten, but not tell then.

An army of brave and worthy successors—champions of Freedom now living, have the illustrious forefathers of the North, in the persons of Garrison, Greeley, Giddings, Goodell, Grow, and Gerrit Smith; in Seward, Sumner, Stowe, Raymond, Parker, and Phillips; in Beecher, Banks, Burlingame, Bryant, Hale, and Hildreth; in Emerson, Dayton, Thompson, Tappan, King and Cheever; in Whittier, Wilson, Wade, Wayland, Weed, and Burleigh. These are the men whom, in connection with their learned and eloquent compatriots, the Everetts, the Bancrofts, the Prescotts, the Chapins, the Longfellows, and the Danas, future historians, if faithful to their calling, will place on record as America's true statesmen, literati, preachers, philosophers, and philanthropists, of the present age.

In this connection, however, it may not be amiss to remark that the Homers, the Platos, the Bacons, the Newtons, the Shakspeares, the Miltons, the Blackstones, the Cuviers, the Humboldts, and the Macaulays of America, have not yet been produced; nor, in our humble judgment, will they be, until slavery shall have been overthrown and freedom established in the States of Virginia, Kentucky, and Tennessee. Upon the soil of those States, when free, or on other free soil crossed by about the same degrees of latitude, and not distant from the Appalachian chain of mountains, will, we believe, be nurtured into manhood, in the course of one or two centuries, perhaps, as great men as those mentioned above—greater, possibly, than any that have ever yet lived. Whence their ancestors may come, whether from Europe, from Asia, from Africa, from Oceanica, from North or South America, or from the islands of the sea, or whatever honorable vocation they may now be engaged in, matters nothing at all. For ought we know, their great-grandfathers are now humble artisans in Maine, or moneyed merchants in Massachusetts; illiterate poor whites in Mississippi, or slave-driving lordlings in South Carolina; frugal farmers in Michigan, or millionaires in Illinois; daring hunters in the Rocky Mountains, or metal-diggers in California; peasants in France, or princes in Germany—no matter where, or what, the scope of country above-mentioned is, in our opinion, destined to be the birth-place of their illustrious offspring —the great savants of the New World, concerning whom we should console ourselves with the hope that they are not buried deeply in the matrix of the future.

Chapter 5

Testimony of the Nations

TO THE TRUE FRIENDS OF FREEDOM throughout the world, it is a pleasing thought, and one which, by being communicated to others, is well calculated to universalize the principles of liberty, that the great heroes, statesmen, and sages, of all ages and nations, ancient and modern, who have ever had occasion to speak of the institution of human slavery, have entered their most unequivocal and positive protests against it. To say that they disapproved of the system would not be sufficiently expressive of the utter detestation with which they uniformly regarded it. That they abhorred it as the vilest invention that the devil has ever assisted bad men to concoct, is quite evident from the very tone and construction of their language.

Having, with much pleasure and profit, heard the testimony of America, through her representative men, we will now hear that of other nations, through their representative men—doubting not that we shall be more than remunerated for our time and trouble.

THE VOICE OF ENGLAND

In the case of James Somerset, a negro who had been kidnapped in Africa, transported to Virginia, there sold into slavery, thence carried to England, as a waiting-boy, and there induced to institute proceedings against his master for the recovery of his freedom, MANSFIELD says:

"The state of slavery is of such a nature that it is incapable of being introduced on any reasons, moral or political, but only by positive law, which preserves its force long after the reasons, occasion, and time itself whence it was created, is erased from the memory. It is so odious that nothing can be sufficient to support it but positive law. Whatever inconveniences, therefore, may follow from the decision, I cannot say this case is allowed or approved by the law of England, and therefore the black must be discharged."

LOCKE says:

"Slavery is so vile, so miserable a state of man, and so directly opposite to the generous temper and courage of our nation, that it is hard to be convinced that an Englishman, much less a gentleman, should plead for it."

Again, he says:

"Though the earth, and all inferior creatures be common to all men, yet every man has a property in his own person; this nobody has any right to but himself."

PITT says:

"It is injustice to permit slavery to remain for a single hour."

FOX says:

"With regard to a regulation of slavery, my detestation of its existence induces me to know no such thing as a regulation of robbery, and a restriction of murder. Personal freedom is a right of which he who deprives a fellow-creature is criminal in so depriving him, and he who withholds is no less criminal in withholding."

SHAKSPEARE says:

"A man is master of his liberty."

Again, he says:

"It is the curse of Kings, to be attended By slaves, that take their humors for a warrant To break within the bloody house of life, And, on the winking of authority, To understand a law; to know the meaning Of dangerous majesty, when, perchance, it frowns More upon humor than advised respect."

Again:

"Heaven will one day free us from this slavery."

Again:

"Liberty! Freedom! Tyranny is dead!—Run hence, proclaim, cry it about the streets; Some to the common pulpits, and cry out, Liberty, freedom, and enfranchisement"

COWPER says:

"Slaves cannot breathe in England; if their lungs Receive our air, that moment they are free. They touch our country and their shackles fall. That's noble, and bespeaks a nation proud and jealous of the blessing. Spread it then, and let it circulate through every vein. Of all your Empire, that where Britain's power Is felt, mankind may feel her mercy too!"

MILTON asks:

"Where is the beauty to see, like the sun-brilliant brow of a nation when free?"

Again, he says:

"If our fathers promised for themselves, to make themselves slaves, they could make no such promise for us."

Again: "Since, therefore, the law is chiefly right reason, if we are bound to obey a magistrate as a minister of God, by the very same reason and the very same law, we ought to resist a tyrant, and minister of the devil."

DR. JOHNSON says:

"No man is by nature the property of another. The rights of nature must be some way forfeited before they can justly be taken away."

DR. PRICE says:

"If you have a right to make another man a slave, he has a right to make you a slave."

BLACKSTONE says:

"If neither captivity nor contract can, by the plain law of nature and reason, reduce the parent to a state of slavery, much less can they reduce the offspring."

Again, he says:

"The primary aim of society is to protect individuals in the enjoyment of those absolute rights which were vested in them by the immutable laws of nature. Hence it follows that the first and primary end of human laws is to maintain those absolute rights of individuals."

Again:

"If any human law shall allow or require us to commit crime, we are bound to transgress that human law, or else we must offend both the natural and divine."

COKE says:

"What the Parliament doth, shall be holden for naught, whenever it shall enact that which is contrary to the rights of nature."

HAMPDEN says:

"The essence of all law is justice. What is not justice is not law; and what is not law, ought not to be obeyed."

HARRINGTON says:

"All men naturally, are equal; for though nature with a noble variety has made different features and lineaments of men, yet as to freedom, she has made every one alike, and given them the same desires."

FORTESCUE says:

"Those rights which God and nature have established, and which are therefore called natural rights, such as life and liberty, need not the aid of human laws to be more effectually invested in every man than they are; neither do they receive any additional strength when declared by the municipal laws to be inviolable. On the contrary, no human power has any authority to abridge or destroy them, unless the owner himself shall commit some act that amounts to a forfeiture."

Again, he says:

"The law, therefore, which supports slavery and opposes liberty, must necessarily be condemned as cruel, for every feeling of human nature advocates liberty. Slavery is introduced by human wickedness, but God advocates liberty, by the nature which he has given to man

BROUGHAM says:

"Tell me not of rights—talk not of the property of the planter in his slaves. I deny the right; I acknowledge not the property. In vain you tell me of laws that sanction such a claim. There is a law above all the enactments of human codes, the same throughout the world, the same in all times; it is the law written by the finger of God on the hearts of men; and by that law, unchangeable and eternal, while men despise fraud, and loathe rapine, and abhor blood, they shall reject with indignation the wild and guilty fantasy that man can hold property in man."

THE VOICE OF IRELAND

BURKE says:

"Slavery is a state so improper, so degrading, and so ruinous to the feelings and capacities of human nature, that it ought not to be suffered to exist."

CURRAN says:

"I speak in the spirit of British law, which makes liberty commensurate with and inseparable from British soil; which proclaims even to the stranger and the sojourner, the moment he sets his foot upon British earth, that the ground on which he treads is holy and consecrated by the genius of Universal Emancipation. No matter in what language his doom may have been pronounced; no matter what complexion, incompatible with freedom, an Indian or African sun may have burnt upon him; no matter in what disastrous battle his liberty may have been cloven down; no matter with what solemnities he may have been devoted upon the altar of slavery, the moment he touches the sacred soil of Britain, the altar and the god sink together in the dust; his soul walks abroad in her own majesty; and he stands redeemed, regenerated and disenthralled by the irresistible genius of Universal Emancipation."

The Dublin University Magazine for December, 1856, says:

"The United States must learn, from the example of Rome, that Christianity and the pagan institution of slavery cannot co-exist together. The Republic must take her side and choose her favorite child; for if she love the one, she must hate the other."

THE VOICE OF SCOTLAND

BEATTIE says:

"Slavery is inconsistent with the dearest and most essential rights of man's nature; it is detrimental to virtue and industry; it hardens the heart to those tender sympathies which form the most lovely part of human character; it involves the innocent in hopeless misery, in order to procure wealth and pleasure for the authors of that misery; it seeks to degrade into brutes beings whom the Lord of Heaven and Earth endowed with rational souls, and created for immortality; in short, it is utterly repugnant to every principle of reason, religion, humanity, and conscience. It is impossible for a considerate and unprejudiced mind, to think of slavery without horror."

MILLER says:

"The human mind revolts at a serious discussion of the subject of slavery. Every individual, whatever be his country or complexion, is entitled to freedom."

MACKNIGHT says:

"Men-stealers are inserted among the daring criminals against whom the law of God directed its awful curses. These were persons who kidnapped men to sell them for slaves; and this practice seems inseparable from the other iniquities and oppressions of slavery; nor can a slave dealer easily keep free from this criminality, if indeed the receiver is as bad as the thief."

THE VOICE OF FRANCE

LAFAYETTE says:

"I would never have drawn my sword in the cause of America, if I could have conceived that thereby I was founding a land of slavery."

Again, while in the prison of Magdeburg, he says:

"I know not what disposition has been made of my plantation at Cayenne; but I hope Madame de Lafayette will take care that the negroes who cultivate it shall preserve their liberty."

O. LAFAYETTE, grandson of General Lafayette, in a letter under the date of April 26th, 1851, says:

"This great question of the Abolition of Negro Slavery, which has my entire sympathy, appears to me to have established its importance throughout the world. At the present time, the States of the Peninsula, if I do not deceive myself, are the only European powers who still continue to possess slaves; and America, while continuing to uphold slavery, feels daily, more and more how heavily it weighs upon her destinies."

MONTESQUIEU asks:

"What civil law can restrain a slave from running away, since he is not a member of society?"

Again, he says:

"Slavery is contrary to the fundamental principles of all societies."

Again:

"In democracies, where they are all upon an equality, slavery is contrary to the principles of the Constitution."

Again:

"Nothing puts one nearer the condition of a brute than a ways to see freemen and not be free."

Again:

"Even the earth itself, which teems with profusion under the cultivating hand of the free born laborer, shrinks into barrenness from the contaminating sweat of a slave."

Louis X. issued the following edict:

"As all men are by nature free born, and as this Kingdom is called the Kingdom of Franks, (freemen) it shall be so in reality. It is therefore decreed that enfranchisement shall be granted throughout the whole Kingdom upon just and reasonable terms."

Buffon says:

"It is apparent that the unfortunate negroes are endowed with excellent hearts, and possess the seeds of every human virtue. I cannot write their history without lamenting their miserable condition." "Humanity revolts at those odious oppressions that result from avarice."

Rousseau says:

"The terms *slavery* and *right*, contradict and exclude each other."

Brissot says:

"Slavery, in all its forms, in all its degrees, is a violation of divine law, and a degradation of human nature."

THE VOICE OF GERMANY

Grotius says:

"Those are men-stealers who abduct, keep, sell or buy slaves or free men. To steal a man is the highest kind of theft."

Goethe says:

"Such busy multitudes I fain would see Stand upon free soil with a people free."

Luther says:

"Unjust violence is, by no means, the ordinance of God, and therefore can bind no one in conscience and right, to obey, whether the command comes from pope, emperor, king or master."

An able German writer of the present day, says, in a recent letter to his friends in this country:

"Consider that the cause of American liberty is the cause of universal liberty; its failure, a triumph of despotism everywhere. Remember that while American liberty is the great argument of European Democracy, American slavery is the greater argument of its despotism. Remember that all our actions should be governed by the golden rule, whether individual, social, or political; and no government, and, above all, no republican government, is safe in the hands of men that practically deny that rule. Will you support by your vote a system that recognizes property of man in man? A system which sanctions the sale of the child by its own father, regardless of the purpose of the buyer? What need is there to present to you the unmitigated wrong of slavery? It is the shame of our age that argument is needed against slavery.

"Liberty is no exclusive property; it is the property of mankind of all ages. She is immortal, though crushed, can never die; though banished, she will return; though fettered, she will yet be free."

THE VOICE OF ITALY

CICERO says:

"By the grand laws of nature, all men are born free, and this law is universally binding upon all men."

Again, he says: "Eternal justice is the basis of all human laws."

Again:

"Law is not something wrought out by man's ingenuity, nor is it a decree of the people, but it is something eternal, governing the world by the wisdom of its commands and prohibitions."

Again:

"Whatever is just is also the true law, nor can this true law be abrogated by any written enactments."

Again:

"If there be such a power in the decrees and commands of fools, that the nature of things is changed by their votes, why do they not decree that what is bad and pernicious shall be regarded as good and wholesome, or why, if the law can make wrong right, can it not make bad good?"

Again:

"Those who have made pernicious and unjust decrees, have made anything rather than laws."

Again:

"The law of all nations forbids one man to pursue his advantage at the expense of another."

LACTANTIUS says:

"Justice teaches men to know God and to love men, to love and assist one another, being all equally the children of God."

LEO X. says:

"Not only does the Christian religion, but nature herself cry out against the state of slavery."

THE VOICE OF GREECE

SOCRATES says:

"Slavery is a system of outrage and robbery."

ARISTOTLE says:

"It is neither for the good, nor is it just, seeing all men are by nature alike, and equal, that one should be lord and master over others."

POLYBIUS says:

'None but unprincipled and beastly men in society assume the mastery over their fellows, as it is among bulls, bears, and cocks."

PLATO says:

"Slavery is a system of the most complete injustice."

From each of the above, and from other nations, additional testimony is at hand; but, for reasons already assigned, we forbear to introduce it. Corroborative of the correctness of the position which we have assumed, even Persia has a voice, which may be easily recognized in the tones of her immortal Cyrus, who says:

"To fight, in order not to be made a slave, is noble."

No nation has more heartily or honorably repented of the crime of slavery than Great Britain—no nation, on the perception of its error, has ever acted with more prompt magnanimity to its outraged and unhappy bondsmen. Entered to her credit, many precious jewels of liberty remain in our possession, ready to be delivered when called for; of their value some idea may be formed, when we state that they are filigreed with such names as Wilberforce Buxton, Granville, Grattan, Camden, Clarkson, Sharp, Sheridan, Sidney, Martin, and Macaulay.

Virginia, the Carolinas, and other Southern States, which are provided with *republican (!)* forms of government, and which have abolished freedom, should learn, from the history of the monarchal governments of the Old World, if not from the example of the more liberal and enlightened portions of the New, how to abolish slavery.

The lesson is before them in a variety of exceedingly interesting forms, and, sooner or later, they must learn it, either voluntarily or by compulsion. Virginia, in particular, is a spoilt child, having been the pet of the General Government for the last sixty-eight years; and like most other spoilt children, she has become froward, peevish, perverse, sulky and irreverent—not caring to know her duties, and failing to perform even those which she does know. Her superiors perceive that the abolition of slavery would be a blessing to her; she is, however, either too ignorant to understand the truth, or else, as is the more probable, her false pride and obstinacy restrain her from acknowledging it. What is to be done? Shall ignorance, or prejudice, or obduracy, or willful meanness, triumph over knowledge, and liberality, and guilelessness, and laudable enterprise? No, never! Assured that Virginia and all the other slaveholding States are doing wrong every day, it is our duty to make them do right, if we have the power; and we believe we have the power now resident within their own borders. What are the opinions, generally, of the non-slaveholding whites? Let them speak.

Chapter 6

Testimony of the
Churches

IN QUEST OF ARGUMENTS AGAINST SLAVERY, we have perused the
works of several eminent Christian writers of different denominations, and we now proceed to lay before the reader the result of a
portion of our labor. As it is the special object of this chapter to
operate on, to correct and cleanse the consciences of slaveholding
professors of religion, we shall adduce testimony only from the five
churches to which they, in their satanic piety, mostly belong—the
Presbyterian, the Episcopal, the Baptist, the Methodist, and the
Roman Catholic—all of which, thank Heaven, are destined, at no
distant day, to become thoroughly abolitionized. With few exceptions, all the other Christian sects are, as they should be, avowedly
and inflexibly opposed to the inhuman institution of slavery. The
Congregational, the Quaker, the Lutheran, the Dutch and German
Reformed, the Unitarian, and the Universalist, especially, are all
honorable, able, and eloquent defenders of the natural rights of
man. We will begin by introducing a mass of:

PRESBYTERIAN TESTIMONY

The Rev. Albert Barnes, of Philadelphia, one of the most learned
Presbyterian preachers and commentators of the day, says:-

"There is a deep and growing conviction in the minds of the mass
of mankind, that slavery violates the great laws of our nature; that
it is contrary to the dictates of humanity; that it is essentially unjust,
oppressive, and cruel; that it invades the rights of liberty with which
the Author of our being has endowed all human beings; and that,
in all the forms in which it has ever existed, it has been impossible
to guard it from what its friends and advocates would call '*abuses*

of the system.' It is a violation of the first sentiments expressed in our Declaration of Independence, and on which our fathers founded the vindication of their own conduct in an appeal to arms. It is at war with all that a man claims for himself and for his own children; and it is opposed to all the struggles of mankind, in all ages, for freedom. The claims of humanity plead against it. The struggles for freedom everywhere in our world condemn it. The instinctive feeling in every man's own bosom in regard to himself is a condemnation of it. The noblest deeds of valor, and of patriotism in our own land, and in all lands where men have struggled for freedom, are a condemnation of the system. All that is noble in man is opposed to it; all that is base, oppressive, and cruel, pleads for it.

"The spirit of the New Testament is against slavery, and the principles of the New Testament, if fairly applied, would abolish it. In the New Testament no man is commanded to purchase and own a slave; no man is commended as adding anything to the evidences of his Christian character, or as performing the appropriate duty of a Christian, for owning one. No where in the New Testament is the institution referred to as a good one, or as a desirable one. It is commonly — indeed, it is almost universally — conceded that the proper application of the principles of the New Testament would abolish slavery everywhere, or that, the state of things which will exist when the Gospel shall be fairly applied to all the relations of life, slavery will not be found among those relations.

"Let slavery be removed from the church, and let the voice of the church, with one accord, be lifted up in favor of freedom; let the church be wholly detached from the institution, and let there be adopted by all its ministers and members an interpretation of the Bible—as I believe there may be and ought to be—that shall be in accordance with the deep-seated principles of our nature in favor of freedom, and with our own aspirations for liberty, and with the sentiments of the world in its onward progress in regard to human rights, and not only would a very material objection against the Bible be taken away—and one which would be fatal if it were well founded—but the establishment of a very strong argument *in favor* of the Bible, as a revelation from God, would be the direct result of such a position."

Thomas Scott, the celebrated English Presbyterian Commentator, says:

"To number the persons of men with beasts, sheep, and horses, as the stock of a farm, or with bales of goods, as the cargo of a ship, is, no doubt, a most detestable and anti-Christian practice."

From a resolution denunciatory of slavery, unanimously adopted by the General Assembly of the Presbyterian Church, in 1818, we make the following extract:

"We consider the voluntary enslaving of one part of the human race by another as a gross violation of the most precious and sacred rights of human nature, as utterly inconsistent with the law of God, which requires us to love our neighbor as ourselves, and as totally irreconcilable with the spirit and principles of the Gospel of Christ, which enjoins that 'all things whatsoever ye would that men should do to you, do ye even so to them.' . . . We rejoice that the church to which we belong commenced, as early as any other in this country, the good work of endeavoring to put an end to slavery, and that in the same work many of its members have ever since been, and now are, among the most active, vigorous, and efficient laborers. . . . We earnestly exhort them to continue, and, if possible, to increase, their exertions to effect a total abolition of slavery."

A Committee of the Synod of Kentucky, in an address to the Presbyterians of that State, says:

"That our negroes will be worse off, if emancipated, is, we feel, but a specious pretext for lulling our own pangs of conscience, and answering the argument of the philanthropist. None of us believe that God has so created a whole race that it is better for them to remain in perpetual bondage."

EPISCOPAL TESTIMONY

Bishop Horsley says:

"Slavery is injustice, which no consideration of policy can extenuate."

Bishop Butler says:

"Despicable as the negroes may appear in our eyes, they are the creatures of God, and of the race of mankind, for whom Christ died, and it is inexcusable to keep them in ignorance of the end for which they were made, and of the means whereby they may become partakers of the general redemption."

Bishop Porteus says:

"The Bible classes men-stealers or slave-traders among the murderers of fathers and mothers, and the most profane criminals on earth."

John Jay, Esq., of the City of New York — a most exemplary Episcopalian—in a pamphlet entitled, "Thoughts on the Duty of the Episcopal Church, in Relation to Slavery," says:

"Alas! for the expectation that she would conform to the spirit of her ancient mother! She has not merely remained a mute and careless spectator of this great conflict of truth and justice with hypocrisy and cruelty, but her very priests and deacons may be seen ministering at the altar of slavery, offering their talents and influence at its unholy shrine, and openly repeating the awful blasphemy, that the precepts of our Saviour sanction the system of American slavery. Her Northern clergy, with rare exceptions, whatever they may feel on the subject, rebuke it neither in public nor in private, and her periodicals, far from advancing the progress of abolition, at times oppose our societies, impliedly defending slavery, as not incompatible with Christianity, and occasionally withholding information useful to the cause of freedom."

A writer in a late number of "The Anti-Slavery Church man," published in Geneva, Wisconsin, speaking of a certain portion of the New Testament, says:

"This passage of Paul places necessary work in the hands of Gospel ministers. If they preach the whole Gospel, they must preach what this passage enjoins — and if they do this, they must preach against American slavery. Its being connected with politics does not shield them. Political connections cannot place sin under protection. They cannot throw around it guards that the public teachers of morals may not pass. Sin is a violation of God's law — and God's law must be proclaimed and enforced at all hazards. This is the business of the messenger of God, and if anything stands in its way, it is his right, rather it is his solemn commission, to go forward — straightway to overpass the lines that would shut him out, and utter his warnings. Many sins there are, that, in like manner, might be shielded. Fashion, and rank, and business, are doing their part to keep much sin in respectability, and excuse it from the attacks of God's ministers. But what are these, that they should seal a minister's lips — what more are the wishes of politicians?"

For further testimony from this branch of the Christian system, if desired, we refer the reader to the Rev. Dudley A. Tyng, the Rev. Evan M. Johnson, and the Rev. J. McNamara, — all Broad Church Episcopalians, whose magic eloquence and irresistible arguments bid fair, at an early day, to win over to the paths of progressive freedom, truth, justice and humanity, the greater number of their High and Low Church brethren.

BAPTIST TESTIMONY

Concerning a certain text, the Rev. Mr. Brisbane, once a slaveholding Baptist in South Carolina, says:

"Paul was speaking of the law as having been made for menstealers. Where is the record of that law? It is in Exodus xxi. 16, and in these words: 'He that stealeth a man, and selleth him, or if he be found in his possession, he shall surely be put to death.' Here it will be perceived that it was a crime to sell the man, for which the seller must suffer death. But it was no less a crime to hold him as a slave, for this also was punishable with death. A man may be kidnapped out of slavery into freedom. There was no law against that. And why? Because kidnapping a slave and placing him in a condition of freedom, was only to restore him to his lost rights. But if the man who takes him becomes a slaveholder, or a slave seller, then he is a criminal, liable to the penalty of death, because he robs the man of liberty. Perhaps some will say this law was only applicable to the first holder of the slave, that is, the original kidnapper, but not to his successors who might have purchased or inherited him. But what is kidnapping? Suppose I propose to a neighbor to give him a certain sum of money if he will steal a white child in Carolina and deliver him to me. He steals him; I pay him the money upon his delivering the child to me. Is it not my act as fully as his? Am I not also the thief? But does it alter the case whether I agree before hand or not, to pay him for the child? He steals him, and then sells him to me. He is found by his parents in my hands. Will it avail me to say I purchased him and paid my money for him? Will it not be asked, Do you not know that a white person is not merchantable? And shall I not have to pay the damage for detaining that child in my service as a slave? Assuredly, not only in the eyes of the law, but in the judgment of the whole community, I would be regarded a criminal.

"So when one man steals another and offers him for sale, no one, in view of the Divine law, can buy him, for the reason that the Divine law forbids that man shall in the first place be made a merchantable article. The inquiry must be, if I buy, I buy in violation of the Divine law, and it will not do for me to plead that I bought him. I have him in possession, and that is enough, God condemns me for it as a man-stealer. My having him in possession is evidence against me, and the Mosaic law says, if he be found in my hands, I must die. Now, when Paul said the law was made for men-stealers, was it not also saying the law was made for slaveholders? I am not intending to apply this term in harsh spirit. But I am bound, as I fear God to speak what I am satisfied is the true meaning of the apostle."

In his "Elements of Moral Science," the Rev. Francis Wayland, D.D., one of the most erudite and distinguished Baptists now living, says:

"Domestic slavery proceeds upon the principle that the master has a right to control the actions, physical and intellectual, of the slave, for his own, that is, the master's individual benefit; and, of course, that the happiness of the master, when it comes in competition with the happiness of the slave, extinguishes in the latter the right to pursue it. It supposes, at best, that the relation between master and slave, is not that which exists between man and man, but is a modification, at least, of that which exists between man and the brutes.

"Now, this manifestly supposes that the two classes of beings are created with dissimilar rights: that the master possesses rights which have never been conceded by the slave; and that the slave has no rights at all over the means of happiness which God has given him, whenever these means of happiness can be rendered available to the service of his master. It supposes that the Creator intended one human being to govern the physical, intellectual and moral actions of as many other human beings as by purchase he can bring within his physical power; and that one human being may thus acquire a right to sacrifice the happiness of any number of other human beings, for the purpose of promoting his own. Slavery thus violates the personal liberty of man as a physical, intellectual, and moral being.

"It purports to give to the master a right to control the physical labor of the slave, not for the sake of the happiness of the slave, but for the sake of the happiness of the master. It subjects the amount of labor, and the kind of labor, and the remuneration for labor, entirely to the will of the one party, to the entire exclusion of the will of the other party.

"But if this right in the master over the slave be conceded, there are of course conceded all other rights necessary to insure its possession. Hence, inasmuch as the slave can be held in this condition only while he remains in the lowest state of mental imbecility, it supposes the master to have the right to control his intellectual development, just as far as may be necessary to secure entire subjection. Thus, it supposes the slave to have no right to use his intellect for the production of his own happiness; but, only to use it in such manner as may conduce to his master's profit."

And, moreover, inasmuch as the acquisition of the knowledge of his duty to God could not be freely made without the acquisition of other knowledge, which might, if universally diffused, endanger the control of the master, slavery supposes the master to have the right to determine how much knowledge of his duty a slave shall obtain, the manner in which he shall obtain it, and the manner in which he shall discharge that duty after he shall have obtained a knowledge of it. It thus subjects the duty of man to God entirely to the will of man; and this for the sake of pecuniary profit. It renders the eternal happiness of the one party subservient to the temporal happiness of the other. And this principle is commonly carried into effect in slaveholding countries.

If argument were necessary to show that such a system as this must be at variance with the ordinance of God, it might be easily drawn from the effects which it produces both upon *morals* and *national wealth*.

Its effects must be disastrous upon the *morals* of both parties. By presenting objects on whom passion may be satiated without resistance and without redress, it cultivates in the master, pride, anger, cruelty, selfishness and licentiousness. By accustoming the slave to subject his moral principles to the will of another, it tends to abolish in him all moral distinction; and thus fosters in him lying, deceit, hypocrisy, dishonesty, and a willingness to yield himself up to minister to the appetites of his master.

The effects of slavery on *national wealth*, may be easily seen from the following considerations:

Instead of imposing upon all the necessity of labor, it restricts the number of laborers, that is of producers, within the smallest possible limit, by rendering labor disgraceful. It takes from the laborers the natural stimulus to labor, namely, the desire in the individual of improving his condition; and substitutes, in the place of it, that motive which is the least operative and the least constant, namely, the fear of punishment without the consciousness of moral delinquency. It removes, as far as possible, from both parties, the disposition and the motives to frugality. Neither the master learns frugality from the necessity of labor, nor the slave from the benefits which it confers. And here, while the one party wastes from ignorance of the laws of acquisition, and the other because he can have no motive to economy, capital must accumulate but slowly, if indeed it accumulate at all.

No country, not of great fertility, can long sustain a large slave population. Soils of more than ordinary fertility can not sustain it long, after the richness of the soil has been exhausted. Hence, slavery in this country is acknowledged to have impoverished many of our most valuable districts; and, hence, it is continually migrating from the older settlements, to those new and untilled regions, where the accumulated manure of centuries of vegetation has formed a soil, whose productiveness may, for a while, sustain a system at variance with the laws of nature. Many of our free and of our slaveholding States were peopled at about the same time. The slaveholding States had every advantage, both in soil and climate, over their neighbors. And yet the accumulation of capital has been greatly in favor of the latter. If anyone doubts whether this difference be owing to the use of slave labor, let him ask himself what would have been the condition of the slaveholding States, at this moment, if they had been inhabited, from the beginning, by an industrious yeomanry; each one holding his own land, and each one tilling it with the labor of his own hands.

The moral precepts of the Bible are diametrically opposed to slavery. They are, Thou shalt love thy *neighbor* as *thyself,* and *all things whatsoever* ye would that men should do unto you, do ye even so unto them.

The application of these precepts is universal. Our neighbor is *every one whom we may benefit.* The obligation respects *all things whatsoever.* The precept, then, manifestly, extends to *men, as men,* or *men in every condition;* and if to all things whatsoever, certainly to a thing so important as the right to personal liberty.

Again. By this precept, it is made our duty to cherish as tender and delicate a respect for the right which the meanest individual possesses over the means of happiness bestowed upon him by God, as we cherish for our own right over our own means of happiness, or as we desire any other individual to cherish for it. Now, were this precept obeyed, it is manifest that slavery could not in fact exist for a single instant. The principle of the precept is absolutely subversive of the principle of slavery. That of the one is the entire equality of right; that of the other, the entire absorption of the rights of one in the rights of the other.

If anyone doubts respecting the bearing of the Scripture precept upon this case, a few plain questions may throw additional light upon the subject. For instance, —

"Do the precepts and the spirit of the Gospel allow me to derive my support from a system which extorts labor from my fellow-men, without allowing them any voice in the equivalent which they shall receive; and which can only be sustained by keeping them in a state of mental degradation, and by shutting them out, in a great degree, from the means of salvation?

"Would the master be willing that another person should subject him to slavery, for the same reasons, and on the same grounds, that he holds his slave in bondage?

"Would the Gospel allow us, if it were in our power, to reduce our fellow-citizens of our own color to slavery? If the gospel be diametrically opposed to the *principle* of slavery, it must be opposed to the *practice* of slavery; and therefore, were the principles of the gospel fully adopted, slavery could not exist.

"The very course which the gospel takes on this subject, seems to have been the only one that could have been taken, in order to effect the universal abolition of slavery. The gospel was designed, not for one race, or for one time, but for all races, and for all times. It looked not at the abolition of this form of evil for that age alone, but for its universal abolition. Hence, the important object of its Author was, to gain it a lodgment in every part of the known world; so that, by its universal diffusion among all classes of society, it might quietly and peacefully modify and subdue the evil passions of men; and thus, without violence, work a revolution in the whole mass of mankind.

"If the system be wrong, as we have endeavored to show, if it be at variance with our duty both to God and to man, it must be abandoned. If it be asked when, I ask again, when shall a man begin to cease doing wrong? Is not the answer, *immediately*? If a man is injuring *us*, do we ever doubt as to the time when *he* ought to cease? There is then no doubt in respect to the time when we ought to cease inflicting injury upon others."

Abraham Booth, an eminent theological writer of the Baptist persuasion, says:

"I have not a stronger conviction of scarcely anything, than that slaveholding (except when the slave has forfeited his liberty by crimes against society) is wicked and inconsistent with Christian character. To me it is evident, that whoever would purchase an innocent black man to make him a slave, would with equal readiness purchase a white one for the same purpose, could he do it with equal impunity, and no more disgrace."

At a meeting of the General Committee of the Baptists of Virginia, in 1789, the following resolution was offered by Eld. John Leland, and adopted:

"*Resolved,* That slavery is a violent deprivation of the rights of nature, and inconsistent with republican government, and therefore we recommend it to our brethren to make use of every measure to extirpate this horrid evil from the land; and pray Almighty God that our honorable legislature may have it in their power to proclaim the great jubilee, consistent with the principles of good policy."

METHODIST TESTIMONY

John Wesley, the celebrated founder of Methodism, says:

"Men buyers are exactly on a level with men stealers."

Again, he says:

"American Slavery is the vilest that ever saw the sun; it constitutes the sum of all villanies."

The learned Dr. Adam Clarke, author of a voluminous commentary on the Scriptures, says:

"Slave-dealers, whether those who carry on the traffic in human flesh and blood; or those who steal a person in order to sell him into bondage; or those who buy such stolen men or women, no matter of what color, or what country; or the nations who legalize or connive at such traffic; all these are men-stealers, and God classes them with the most flagitious of mortals."

One of the rules laid down in the Methodist Discipline, as amended in 1784, was as follows:

"Every member of our Society who has slaves in his possession, shall, within twelve months after notice given to him by the assistant, legally execute and record an instrument, whereby he emancipates and sets free every slave in his possession."

Another rule was in these words:

"No person holding slaves shall in future be admitted into Society, or to the Lord's Supper, till he previously complies with these rules concerning slavery."

The answer to the question—"What shall be done with those who buy or sell slaves, or give them away"—is couched in the following language:

"They are immediately to be expelled, unless they buy them on purpose to free them."

In 1785, the voice of this church was heard as follows:

"We do hold in the deepest abhorrence the practice of slavery, and shall not cease to seek its destruction, by all wise and prudent means."

In 1797, the Discipline contained the following wholesome paragraph:

"The preachers and other members of our Society are requested to consider the subject of negro slavery, with deep attention, and that they impart to the General Conference, through the medium of the Yearly Conferences, or otherwise, any important thoughts on the subject, that the Conference may have full light, in order to take further steps towards eradicating this enormous evil from that part of the Church of God with which they are connected. The Annual Conferences are directed to draw up addresses for the gradual emancipation of the slaves, to the legislatures of those States in which no general laws have been passed for that purpose. These addresses shall urge, in the most respectful but pointed manner, the necessity of a law for the gradual emancipation of slaves. Proper committees shall be appointed by the Annual Conferences, out of the most respectable of our friends, for conducting the business; and presiding elders, elders, deacons, and traveling preachers, shall procure as many proper signatures as possible to the addresses, and give all the assistance in their power, in every respect, to aid the committees, and to forward the blessed undertaking. Let this be continued from year to year, till the desired end be accomplished."

CATHOLIC TESTIMONY

It has been only about twenty years since Pope Gregory XVI. immortalized himself by issuing the famous Bull against slavery, from which the following is an extract:

"Placed as we are on the Supreme seat of the apostles, and acting, though by no merits of our own, as the vicegerent of Jesus Christ, the Son of God, who, through his great mercy, condescended to make himself man, and to die for the redemption of the world, we regard as a duty devolving on our pastoral functions, that we endeavor to turn aside our faithful flocks entirely from the inhuman traffic in negroes, or any other human beings whatever. . . . In progress of time, as the clouds of heathen superstition became gradually dispersed, circumstances reached that point, that during several centuries there were no slaves allowed amongst the great majority of the Christian nations; but with grief we are compelled to add, that there afterwards arose, even among the faithful, a race of men, who, basely blinded by the appetite and desire of sordid lucre, did not hesitate to reduce, in remote regions of the earth, Indians, negroes, and other wretched beings, to the misery of slavery; or, finding the trade established and augmented, to assist the shameful crime of others. Nor did many of the most glorious of the Roman Pontiffs omit severely to reprove their conduct, as injurious to their souls' health, and disgraceful to the Christian name. Among these may be especially quoted the bull of Paul III., which bears the date of the 29th of May, 1537, addressed to the Cardinal Archbishop of Toledo, and another still more comprehensive, by Urban VIII., dated the 22d of April, 1636, to the collector Jurius of the Apostolic chamber in Portugal, most severely castigating by name those who presumed to subject either East or West Indians to slavery, to sell, buy, exchange, or give them away, to separate them from their wives and children, despoil them of their goods and property, to bring or transmit them to other places, or by any means to deprive them of liberty, or retain them in slavery; also most severely castigating those who should presume or dare to afford council, aid, favor or assistance, under any pretext, or borrowed color, to those doing the aforesaid; or should preach or teach that it is lawful, or should otherwise presume or dare to cooperate, by any possible means, with the aforesaid. . . . Wherefore, we, desiring to divert this disgrace from the whole confines of Christianity, having summoned several of our venerable brothers, their Eminences the Cardinals, of the H. R. Church, to our council, and, having maturely deliberated on the whole matter, pursuing the footsteps of our predecessors, admonished by our apostolical authority, and urgently invoke in the Lord, all Christians, of whatever condition, that none henceforth dare to subject to slavery, unjustly persecute, or despoil of their goods, Indians, negroes, or other classes of men, or be accessories to others, or furnish them aid or assistance in so doing; and on no account henceforth to exercise that inhuman traffic by which negroes are reduced to slavery, as if they were not men, but automata or chattels, and are sold in defiance of all the laws of justice and humanity, and devoted to severe and intolerable labors. We further reprobate, by our apostolical authority, all the above-described offences as utterly unworthy of the Christian name; and by the same authority we rigidly prohibit and interdict all and every individual, whether ecclesiastical or laical, from presuming to defend that commerce in negro slaves under pretence or borrowed color, or to teach or publish in any manner, publicly or privately, things contrary to the admonitions which we have given in these letters.

"And, finally, that our letters, may be rendered more apparent to all, and that no person may allege any ignorance thereof, we decree that it shall be published according to custom, and copies be properly affixed to the gates of St. Peter and of the Apostolic Chancel, every and in like manner to the General Court of Mount Citatorio, and in the field of the Campus Florae and also through the city, by one of our heralds, according to aforesaid custom.

"Given at Rome, at the Palace of Santa Maria Major, under the seal of the fisherman, on the 3d day of December, 1837, and in the ninth year of our pontificate.

"Countersigned by Cardinal A. Lambruschini."

We have already quoted the language of Pope Leo X., who says:

"Not only does the Christian religion, but nature herself cry out against the State of slavery."

The Abbe Raynal says:

"He who supports slavery is the enemy of the human race. He divides it into two societies of legal assassins, the oppressors and the oppressed. I shall not be afraid to cite to the tribunal of reason and justice those governments which tolerate this cruelty, or which even are not ashamed to make it the basis of their power."

From the proceedings of a Massachusetts Anti-slavery Convention in 1855, we make the following extract:

"Henry Kemp, a Roman Catholic, came forward to defend the Roman Church in reply to Mr. Foster. He claimed that the Catholic Church is thoroughly anti-slavery—as thoroughly as even his friend Foster."

Thus manfully do men of pure hearts and noble minds, whether in Church or State, and without regard to sect or party, lift up their voices against the wicked and pernicious institution of human slavery. Thus they speak, and thus they are obliged to speak, if they speak at all; it is only the voice of Nature, Justice, Truth, and Love, that issues from them. The divine principle in man prompts him to speak and strike for Freedom; the diabolical principle within him prompts him to speak and strike for slavery.

From those churches which are now—as all churches ought to be, and will be, before the world becomes Christianized — thoroughly imbued with the principles of freedom, we do not, as already intimated, deem it particularly necessary to bring forward new arguments in opposition to slavery. If, however, the reader would be pleased to hear from the churches to which we chiefly allude— and, by the bye, he might hear from them with much profit to himself—we respectfully refer him to Henry Ward Beecher, George B. Cheever, Joseph P. Thompson, Theodore Parker, E. H. Chapin, and H. W. Bellows, of the North, and to M. D. Conway, John G. Fee, James S. Davis, Daniel Wilson, and W. E. Lincoln, of the South. All these reverend gentlemen, ministers of different denominations, feel it their duty to preach against slavery, and, to their honor be it said, they do preach against it with unabated zeal and success. Our earnest prayer is, that Heaven may enable them, their contemporaries and successors, to preach against it with such energy and effect, as will cause it to disappear forever from the soil of our Republic.

Chapter 7

Free Figures and Slaves

UNDER THIS HEADING WE PROPOSE to introduce the remainder of the more important statistics of the Free and of the Slave States; — especially those that relate to Commerce, Manufactures, Internal Improvements, Education and Religion. Originally it was our intention to devote a separate chapter to each of the industrial and moral interests above-named: but other considerations have so greatly encroached on our space, that we are compelled to modify our design. To the thoughtful and discriminating reader, however, the chief statistics which follow will be none the less interesting for not being the subjects of annotations.

At present, all we ask of pro-slavery men, no matter in what part of the world they may reside, is to look these figures fairly in the face. We wish them to do it, in the first instance, not on the platforms of public debate, where the exercise of eloquence is too often characterized by violent passion and subterfuge, but in their own private apartments, where no eye save that of the All-seeing One will rest upon them, and where, in considering the relations which they sustain to the past, the present, and the future, an opportunity will be afforded them of securing that most valuable of all possessions attainable on earth, a conscience void of offence toward God and man.

Each separate table or particular compilation of statistics will afford food for at least an hour's profitable reflection; indeed, the more these figures are studied, and the better they are understood, the sooner will the author's object be accomplished, — the sooner will the genius of Universal Liberty dispel the dark clouds of slavery.

Table No. XXVI.

Tonnage, Exports and Imports of the Free States — 1855

	Tonnage	Exports	Imports
California	92,623	$8,224,066	$5,951,379
Connecticut	137,170	878,874	636,826
Illinois	53,797	547,053	54,509
Indiana	3,698		
Iowa			
Maine	806,587	4,851,207	2,927,443
Massachusetts	970,727	28,190,925	45,113,774
Michigan	69,490	568,091	281,379
New Hampshire	30,330	1,523	17,786
New Jersey	121,020	687	1,473
New York	1,404,221	113,731,238	164,776,511
Ohio	91,607	847,143	600,656
Pennsylvania	397,768	6,274,338	15,300,935
Rhode Island	51,038	336,023	536,387
Vermont	6,915	2,895,468	591,593
Wisconsin	15,624	174,057	48,159
TOTAL	4,252,615	$167,520,693	$236,838,810
Corrected			*$236,847,810*

Table No. XXVII.

Tonnage, Exports and Imports of the Slave States — 1855

	Tonnage	Exports	Imports
Alabama	36,274	$14,270,585	$619,964
Arkansas			
Delaware	19,186	68,087	5,821
Florida	14,835	1,403,594	45,998
Georgia	29,505	7,543,519	273,716
Kentucky	22,680		
Louisiana	204,149	55,367,962	12,900,821
Maryland	234,805	10,395,984	7,788,949
Mississippi	2,475		1,661
Missouri	60,592		
North Carolina	60,077	433,818	243,083
South Carolina	60,935	12,700,250	1,588,542
Tennessee	8,404		
Texas	8,812	916,961	262,568
Virginia	92,788	4,379,928	855,405
TOTAL	855,517	$107,480,688	$24,586,528

Table No. XXVIII.

Product of Manufactures in the Free States — 1850

	Val. of Annual products	Capital invested	Hands employed
California	$12,862,522	$1,006,197	3,964
Connecticut	45,110,102	23,890,348	47,770
Illinois	17,236,073	6,385,387	12,065
Indiana	18,922,651	7,941,602	14,342
Iowa	3,551,783	1,292,875	1,707
Maine	24,664,135	14,700,452	28,078
Massachusetts	151,137,145	83,357,642	165,938
Michigan	10,976,894	6,534,250	9,290
New Hampshire	23,164,503	18,242,114	27,092
New Jersey	39,713,586	22,184,730	37,311
New York	237,597,249	99,904,405	199,349
Ohio	62,647,259	29,019,538	51,489
Pennsylvania	155,044,910	94,473,810	146,766
Rhode Island	22,093,258	12,923,176	20,881
Vermont	8,570,920	5,001,377	8,445
Wisconsin	9,293,068	3,382,148	6,089
TOTAL	$842,586,058	$430,240,051	780,576

Table No. XXIX.

Product of Manufactures in the Slave States — 1850

	Val. of Annual products	Capital invested	Hands employed
Alabama	$4,538,878	$3,450,606	4,936
Arkansas	607,436	324,065	903
Delaware	4,649,296	2,978,945	3,888
Florida	668,338	547,060	991
Georgia	7,086,525	5,460,483	8,378
Kentucky	24,588,483	12,350,734	24,385
Louisiana	7,320,948	5,318,074	6,437
Maryland	32,477,702	14,753,143	30,124
Mississippi	2,972,038	1,833,420	3,173
Missouri	23,749,265	9,079,695	16,850
North Carolina	9,111,245	7,252,225	12,444
South Carolina	7,063,513	6,056,865	7,009
Tennessee	9,728,438	6,975,279	12,032
Texas	1,165,538	539,290	1,066
Virginia	29,705,387	18,109,993	29,109
TOTAL	$165,433,030	$95,029,877	161,725
Corrected	*$165,413,027*	*$95,029,879*	*161,733*

Table No. XXX.

Miles of Canals and Railroads in the Free States — 1854-1857

	Canals, miles, 1854	Railroads, miles, 1857	Cost of Railroads, 1855
California		22	
Connecticut	61	600	$25,224,191
Illinois	100	2,524	55,663,656
Indiana	367	1,806	29,585,923
Iowa		253	2,300,000
Maine	50	442	13,749,021
Massachusetts	100	1,285	59,167,781
Michigan		600	22,370,397
New Hampshire	11	645	15,860,949
New Jersey	147	472	13,840,030
New York	989	2,700	111,882,503
Ohio	921	2,869	67,798,202
Pennsylvania	936	2,407	94,657,675
Rhode Island		85	2,614,484
Vermont		515	17,998,835
Wisconsin		629	5,600,000
TOTAL	3,682	17,855	$538,313,647

Table No. XXXI.

Miles of Canals and Railroads in the Slave States — 1854-1857

	Canals, miles, 1854	Railroads, miles, 1857	Cost of Railroads, 1855
Alabama	51	484	$3,986,208
Arkansas			
Delaware	14	120	600,000
Florida		86	250,000
Georgia	28	1,062	17,034,802
Kentucky	486	306	6,179,072
Louisiana	101	263	1,731,000
Maryland	184	597	12,654,333
Mississippi		410	4,520,000
Missouri		189	1,000,000
North Carolina	13	612	6,847,213
South Carolina	50	706	13,547,093
Tennessee		508	10,436,610
Texas		57	16,466,250
Virginia	181	1,479	
TOTAL	1,116	6,859	$95,252,581
Corrected	*1,108*	*6,879*	

Table No. XXXII.

Bank Capital in the Free and in the Slave States — 1855

Free States		Slave States	
California		Alabama	$2,296,400
Connecticut	$15,597,891	Arkansas	
Illinois	2,513,790	Delaware	1,393,175
Indiana	7,281,934	Florida	
Iowa		Georgia	13,413,100
Maine	7,301,252	Kentucky	10,369,717
Massachusetts	54,492,660	Louisiana	20,179,107
Michigan	980,416	Maryland	10,411,874
New Hampshire	3,626,000	Mississippi	240,165
New Jersey	5,314,885	Missouri	1,215,398
New York	83,773,288	North Carolina	5,205,073
Ohio	7,166,581	South Carolina	16,603,253
Pennsylvania	19,864,825	Tennessee	6,717,848
Rhode Island	17,511,162	Texas	
Vermont	3,275,656	Virginia	14,033,838
Wisconsin	1,400,000		
TOTAL	230,100,340	TOTAL	102,078,948

Table No. XXXIII.

Militia Force of the Free and the Slave States — 1852

Free States		Slave States	
California		Alabama	76,662
Connecticut	51,649	Arkansas	17,137
Illinois	170,359	Delaware	9,229
Indiana	53,918	Florida	12,122
Iowa		Georgia	57,312
Maine	62,588	Kentucky	81,840
Massachusetts	119,690	Louisiana	43,823
Michigan	63,938	Maryland	46,864
New Hampshire	32,151	Mississippi	36,084
New Jersey	39,171	Missouri	61,000
New York	265,293	North Carolina	79,448
Ohio	176,455	South Carolina	55,209
Pennsylvania	276,070	Tennessee	71,252
Rhode Island	14,443	Texas	19,766
Vermont	23,915	Virginia	125,128
Wisconsin	32,203		
TOTAL	1,381,843	TOTAL	792,876

Table No. XXXIV.

Post Office Operations in the Free States — 1855

	Stamps sold	Total Postage collected	Cost of Trans. the mails
California	$81,437	$234,591	$135,386
Connecticut	79,284	179,230	81,462
Illinois	105,252	279,887	280,038
Indiana	60,578	180,405	190,480
Iowa	28,198	82,420	84,428
Maine	60,165	151,358	82,218
Massachusetts	259,062	532,184	153,091
Michigan	49,763	142,188	148,204
New Hampshire	38,387	95,609	46,631
New Jersey	31,495	109,697	80,084
New York	542,498	1,383,157	481,410
Ohio	167,958	452,643	421,870
Pennsylvania	217,293	583,013	251,833
Rhode Island	30,291	58,624	13,891
Vermont	36,314	92,816	64,437
Wisconsin	33,538	112,903	92,842
TOTAL	$1,719,513	$4,670,725	$2,608,295
Corrected	*$1,821,513*	*$4,670,725*	*$2,608,305*

Table No. XXXV.
Post Office Operations in the Slave States — 1855

	Stamps sold	Total Postage collected	Cost of Trans. the mails
Alabama	$44,514	$104,514	226,816
Arkansas	8,941	30,664	117,659
Delaware	7,298	19,644	9,243
Florida	8,764	19,275	77,553
Georgia	73,880	149,063	216,003
Kentucky	55,694	130,067	144,161
Louisiana	50,778	133,753	133,810
Maryland	77,743	191,485	192,743
Mississippi	31,182	78,739	170,785
Missouri	53,742	139,652	185,096
North Carolina	34,235	72,759	148,249
South Carolina	47,368	91,600	192,216
Tennessee	48,377	103,686	116,091
Texas	24,530	70,436	209,936
Virginia	96,799	217,861	245,592
TOTAL	$666,845	$1,553,198	$2,385,953
Corrected	*$663,845*	*$1,553,198*	*$2,385,953*

Table No. XXXVI.
Public Schools of the Free States—1850

	Number	Teachers	Pupils
California	2	2	49
Connecticut	1,656	1,787	71,269
Illinois	4,052	4,248	125,725
Indiana	4,822	4,860	161,500
Iowa	740	828	29,556
Maine	4,042	5,540	192,815
Massachusetts	3,679	4,443	176,475
Michigan	2,714	3,231	110,455
New Hampshire	2,381	3,013	75,643
New Jersey	1,473	1,574	77,930
New York	11,580	13,965	675,221
Ohio	11,661	12,886	484,153
Pennsylvania	9,061	10,024	413,706
Rhode Island	416	518	23,130
Vermont	2,731	4,173	93,457
Wisconsin	1,423	1,529	58,817
TOTAL	62,433	72,621	2,769,901

Table No. XXXVII.
Public Schools in the Slave States — 1850

	Number	Teachers	Pupils
Alabama	1,152	1,195	28,380
Arkansas	353	355	8,493
Delaware	194	214	8,970
Florida	69	73	1,878
Georgia	1,251	1,265	32,705
Kentucky	2,234	2,306	71,429
Louisiana	664	822	25,046
Maryland	898	986	33,111
Mississippi	782	826	18,746
Missouri	1,570	1,620	51,754
North Carolina	2,657	2,730	104,095
South Carolina	724	739	17,838
Tennessee	2,680	2,819	104,117
Texas	349	360	7,946
Virginia	2,930	2,997	67,353
TOTAL	18,507	19,307	581,861

Table No. XXXVIII.

Libraries Other than Private in the Free States — 1850

	Number	Volumes
California		
Connecticut	164	165,318
Illinois	152	62,486
Indiana	151	68,403
Iowa	32	5,790
Maine	236	121,969
Massachusetts	1,462	684,015
Michigan	417	107,943
New Hampshire	129	85,759
New Jersey	128	80,885
New York	11,013	1,760,820
Ohio	352	186,826
Pennsylvania	393	363,400
Rhode Island	96	104,342
Vermont	96	64,641
Wisconsin	72	21,020
TOTAL	14,911	3,888,234
Corrected	*14,893*	*3,883,617*

Table No. XXXIX.
Libraries Other than Private in the Slave States — 1850

	Number	Volumes
Alabama	56	20,623
Arkansas	3	420
Delaware	17	17,950
Florida	7	2,660
Georgia	38	31,788
Kentucky	80	79,466
Louisiana	10	26,800
Maryland	124	125,042
Mississippi	117	21,737
Missouri	97	75,056
North Carolina	38	29,592
South Carolina	26	107,472
Tennessee	34	22,896
Texas	12	4,230
Virginia	54	88,462
TOTAL	695	649,577
Corrected	*713*	*654,194*

Table No. XL.
Newspapers and Periodicals Published
in the Free States — 1850

	Number	Copies printed annually
California	7	761,200
Connecticut	46	4,267,932
Illinois	107	5,102,276
Indiana	107	4,316,828
Iowa	29	1,512,800
Maine	49	4,203,064
Massachusetts	202	64,820,564
Michigan	58	3,247,736
New Hampshire	38	3,067,552
New Jersey	51	4,098,678
New York	428	115,385,473
Ohio	261	30,473,407
Pennsylvania	309	84,898,672
Rhode Island	19	2,756,950
Vermont	35	2,567,662
Wisconsin	46	2,665,487
TOTAL	1,790	334,146,281

Table No. XLI.
Newspapers and Periodicals Published
in the Slave States — 1850

	Number	Copies printed annually
Alabama	60	2,662,741
Arkansas	9	377,000
Delaware	10	421,200
Florida	10	319,800
Georgia	51	4,070,868
Kentucky	62	6,582,838
Louisiana	55	12,416,224
Maryland	68	19,612,724
Mississippi	50	1,752,504
Missouri	61	6,195,560
North Carolina	51	2,020,564
South Carolina	46	7,145,930
Tennessee	50	6,940,750
Texas	34	1,296,924
Virginia	87	9,223,068
TOTAL	704	81,038,693

Table No. XLII.

Illiterate White Adults in the Free States—1850

	Native	Foreign	Total
California	2,201	2,917	5,118
Connecticut	826	4,013	4,739
Illinois	34,107	5,947	40,054
Indiana	67,275	8,265	70,540
Iowa	7,043	1,077	8,120
Maine	1,999	4,148	6,147
Massachusetts	1,055	26,484	27,539
Michigan	4,903	3,009	7,912
New Hampshire	893	2,064	2,957
New Jersey	8,370	5,878	14,248
New York	23,241	68,052	91,293
Ohio	51,968	9,062	61,030
Pennsylvania	41,944	24,989	66,928
Rhode Island	981	2,359	3,340
Vermont	565	5,624	6,189
Wisconsin	1,459	4,902	6,361
TOTAL	248,725	173,790	422,515
Corrected	*248,830*	*178,790*	

Table No. XLIII.
Illiterate White Adults in the Slave States—1850

	Native	Foreign	Total
Alabama	33,618	139	33,757
Arkansas	16,792	27	16,819
Delaware	4,132	404	4,536
Florida	3,564	295	3,859
Georgia	40,794	406	41,200
Kentucky	64,340	2,347	66,687
Louisiana	14,950	6,271	21,221
Maryland	17,364	3,451	20,815
Mississippi	13,324	81	13,405
Missouri	34,420	1,861	36,281
North Carolina	73,226	340	73,566
South Carolina	15,580	104	15,684
Tennessee	77,017	505	77,522
Texas	8,037	2,488	10,525
Virginia	75,868	1,137	77,005
TOTAL	493,026	19,856	512,882

Table No. XLIV.

National Political Power of the Free States—1857

	Senators	Rep. in lower House Cong.	Electoral votes
California	2	2	4
Connecticut	2	4	6
Illinois	2	9	11
Indiana	2	11	13
Iowa	2	2	4
Maine	2	6	8
Massachusetts	2	11	13
Michigan	2	4	6
New Hampshire	2	3	5
New Jersey	2	5	7
New York	2	33	35
Ohio	2	21	23
Pennsylvania	2	25	27
Rhode Island	2	2	4
Vermont	2	3	5
Wisconsin	2	3	5
TOTAL	32	144	176

Table No. XLV.
National Political Power of the Slave States — 1857

	Senators	Rep. in lower House Cong.	Electoral votes
Alabama	2	7	9
Arkansas	2	2	4
Delaware	2	1	3
Florida	2	1	3
Georgia	2	8	10
Kentucky	2	10	12
Louisiana	2	4	6
Maryland	2	6	8
Mississippi	2	5	7
Missouri	2	7	9
North Carolina	2	8	10
South Carolina	2	6	8
Tennessee	2	10	12
Texas	2	2	4
Virginia	2	13	15
TOTAL	30	90	120

Table No. XLVI.

Popular Vote for President by the Free States — 1856

	Republican Fremont	American Fillmore	Democratic Buchanan	Total
California	20,339	35,113	51,925	107,377
Connecticut	42,715	2,615	34,995	80,325
Illinois	96,189	37,444	105,348	238,981
Indiana	94,375	22,386	118,670	235,431
Iowa	43,954	9,180	36,170	89,304
Maine	67,379	3,325	39,080	109,784
Massachusetts	108,190	19,626	39,240	167,056
Michigan	71,762	1,660	52,136	125,558
New Hampshire	38,345	422	32,789	71,556
New Jersey	28,338	24,115	46,943	99,396
New York	276,907	124,604	195,878	597,389
Ohio	187,497	28,126	170,874	386,497
Pennsylvania	147,510	82,175	230,710	460,395
Rhode Island	11,467	1,675	6,580	19,722
Vermont	39,561	545	10,569	50,675
Wisconsin	66,090	579	52,843	119,512
TOTAL	1,340,618	393,590	1,224,750	2,958,958

Table No. XLVII.
Popular Vote for President by the Slave States — 1856

	Republican Fremont	American Fillmore	Democratic. Buchanan	Total
Alabama		28,552	46,739	75,291
Arkansas		10,787	21,910	32,697
Delaware	308	6,175	8,004	14,487
Florida		4,833	6,358	11,191
Georgia		42,228	56,578	98,806
Kentucky	314	67,416	74,642	142,372
Louisiana		20,709	22,164	42,873
Maryland	281	47,460	39,115	86,856
Mississippi		24,195	35,446	59,641
Missouri		48,524	58,164	106,688
North Carolina		36,886	48,246	85,132
South Carolina*				
Tennessee		66,178	73,638	139,816
Texas		15,244	28,757	44,001
Virginia	291	60,278	89,826	150,395
TOTAL	1,194	479,465	609,587	1,090,246

* No popular vote.

Table No. XLVIII.
Value of Churches in the Free and
in the Slave States — 1850

Free States		Slave States	
California	$288,400	Alabama	
Connecticut	3,599,330	Arkansas	$1,244,741
Illinois	1,532,305	Delaware	149,686
Indiana	1,568,906	Florida	340,345
Iowa	235,412	Georgia	192,600
Maine	1,794,209	Kentucky	1,327,112
Massachusetts	10,504,888	Louisiana	2,295,353
Michigan	793,180	Maryland	1,940,495
New Hampshire	1,433,266	Mississippi	3,974,116
New Jersey	3,712,863	Missouri	832,622
New York	21,539,561	North Carolina	1,730,135
Ohio	5,860,059	South Carolina	907,785
Pennsylvania	11,853,291	Tennessee	2,181,476
Rhode Island	1,293,600	Texas	1,246,951
Vermont	1,251,655	Virginia	408,944
Wisconsin	512,552		2,902,220
TOTAL	$67,773,477	TOTAL	$21,674,581

Table No. XLIX.
Patents Issued on New Inventions in the
Free and in the Slave States — 1856

Free States		Slave States	
California	13	Alabama	11
Connecticut	142	Arkansas	
Illinois	93	Delaware	8
Indiana	67	Florida	3
Iowa	14	Georgia	13
Maine	42	Kentucky	26
Massachusetts	331	Louisiana	30
Michigan	22	Maryland	49
New Hampshire	43	Mississippi	8
New Jersey	78	Missouri	32
New York	592	North Carolina	9
Ohio	139	South Carolina	10
Pennsylvania	267	Tennessee	23
Rhode Island	18	Texas	4
Vermont	35	Virginia	42
Wisconsin	33		
TOTAL	1,929	TOTAL	268

Table No. L.

Bible Cause and Tract Cause in the Free States — 1855

	Contributions for the Bible Cause	Contributions for the Tract Cause
California	$1,900	$ 5
Connecticut	24,528	15,872
Illinois	28,403	3,786
Indiana	6,755	1,491
Iowa	4,216	2,005
Maine	5,449	2,981
Massachusetts	43,444	11,492
Michigan	5,554	1,114
New Hampshire	6,271	1,288
New Jersey	15,475	3,546
New York	123,386	61,233
Ohio	25,758	9,576
Pennsylvania	25,360	12,121
Rhode Island	2,669	2,121
Vermont	5,709	2,867
Wisconsin	4,790	474
TOTAL	$319,667	$131,972

Table No. LI.

Bible Cause and Tract Cause in the Slave States—1855

	Contributions for the Bible Cause	Contributions for the Tract Cause
Alabama	$3,351	477
Arkansas	2,950	110
Delaware	1,037	163
Florida	1,957	5
Georgia	4,532	1,468
Kentucky	5,956	1,366
Louisiana	1,810	1,099
Maryland	8,909	5,365
Mississippi	1,067	267
Missouri	4,711	936
North Carolina	6,197	1,419
South Carolina	3,984	3,222
Tennessee	8,383	1,807
Texas	3,985	127
Virginia	9,296	6,894
TOTAL	$68,125	$24,725

Table No. LII.
Missionary Cause and Colonization* Cause
in the Free States — 1855-1856

	Contributions for Miss'y purposes, 1855	Contributions for Coloniza. pur., 1856
California	$ 192	$ 1
Connecticut	48,044	9,233
Illinois	10,040	543
Indiana	4,705	34
Iowa	1,750	3
Maine	13,929	1,719
Massachusetts	128,505	1,422
Michigan	4,935	4
New Hampshire	11,963	1,130
New Jersey	19,946	3,261
New York	172,115	24,371
Ohio	19,890	2,687
Pennsylvania	43,412	4,287
Rhode Island	9,440	2,125
Vermont	11,094	304
Wisconsin	2,216	806
TOTAL	$502,174	$51,930
Corrected	$504,031	$53,786

* For colonizing free blacks in Liberia.

Table No. LIII.

Missionary Cause and Colonization* Cause
in the Slave States — 1855-1856

	Contributions for Miss'y purposes, 1855	Contributions for Coloniza. pur., 1856
Alabama	$5,963	$1,113
Arkansas	455	1
Delaware	1,003	250
Florida	340	13
Georgia	9,846	5,323
Kentucky	6,953	4,436
Louisiana	334	871
Maryland	20,677	406
Mississippi	4,957	2,177
Missouri	2,712	313
North Carolina	6,010	969
South Carolina	15,248	129
Tennessee	4,971	1,611
Texas	349	6
Virginia	22,106	10,000
TOTAL	$101,934	$27,618
Corrected	*$103,779*	*$29,474*

* For colonizing free blacks in Liberia.

Table No. LIV.

Deaths in the Free States — 1850

	Number of deaths	Ratio to the Number living
California		
Connecticut	5,781	64
Illinois	11,619	73
Indiana	12,728	78
Iowa	2,044	94
Maine	7,545	77
Massachusetts	19,414	51
Michigan	4,520	88
New Hampshire	4,268	74
New Jersey	6,467	76
New York	44,339	70
Ohio	28,949	68
Pennsylvania	28,318	82
Rhode Island	2,241	66
Vermont	3,132	100
Wisconsin	2,884	106
TOTAL	184,249	73

Table No. LV.
Deaths in the Slave States — 1850

	Number of deaths	Ratio to the Number living
Alabama	9,084	85
Arkansas	2,987	70
Delaware	1,209	76
Florida	933	94
Georgia	9,920	92
Kentucky	15,206	65
Louisiana	11,948	43
Maryland	9,594	61
Mississippi	8,711	70
Missouri	12,211	56
North Carolina	10,207	85
South Carolina	7,997	84
Tennessee	11,759	85
Texas	3,046	70
Virginia	19,053	75
TOTAL	133,865	72

Table No. LVI.

Free White Male Persons over Fifteen Years of Age Engaged in
Agricultural and Other Outdoor Labor in the Slave-states — 1850

	No. engaged in Agriculture	No. engaged in other outdoor labor	Total
Alabama	67,742	7,229	74,971
Arkansas	28,436	5,596	34,032
Delaware	6,225	4,184	10,409
Florida	5,472	2,598	8,070
Georgia	82,107	11,054	93,161
Kentucky	110,119	26,308	136,427
Louisiana	11,524	13,827	25,351
Maryland	24,672	17,146	41,818
Mississippi	50,028	5,823	55,851
Missouri	64,292	19,900	84,192
North Carolina	76,338	21,876	98,214
South Carolina	37,612	6,991	44,603
Tennessee	115,844	16,795	132,639
Texas	24,987	22,713	47,700
Virginia	97,654	33,928	131,582
TOTAL	803,052	215,968	1,019,020

Too hot in the South, and too unhealthy there—white men "can't stand it"—negroes only can endure the heat of Southern climes! How often are our ears insulted with such wickedly false assertions as these! In what degree of latitude—please tell us—in what degree of latitude do the rays of the sun become too calorific for white men? Certainly in no part of the United States, for in the extreme South we find a very large number of non-slaveholding whites over the age of fifteen, who derive their entire support from manual labor in the open fields. The sun, that bugbear of slaveholding demagogues, shone on more than one million of free white laborers —mostly agriculturists—in the slave States in 1850, exclusive of those engaged in commerce, trade, manufactures, the mechanic arts, and mining. Yet, notwithstanding all these instances of exposure to his wrath, we have had no intelligence whatever of a single case of *coup de soleil*. Alabama is not too hot; sixty-seven thousand white sons of toil till her soil. Mississippi is not too hot; fifty-five thousand free white laborers are hopeful devotees of her outdoor pursuits. Texas is not too hot; forty-seven thousand free white persons, males, over the age of fifteen, daily perform their rural vocations amidst her unsheltered air.

It is stated on good authority that, in January, 1856, native ice, three inches thick, was found in Galveston Bay; we have seen it ten inches thick in North Carolina, with the mercury in the thermometer at two degrees below zero. In January, 1857, while the snow was from three to five feet deep in many parts of North Carolina, the thermometer indicated a degree of coldness seldom exceeded in any State in the Union — thirteen degrees below zero. The truth is, instead of its being too hot in the South for white men, it is too cold for negroes; and we long to see the day arrive when the latter shall have entirely receded from their uncongenial homes in America, and given full and undivided place to the former.

Too hot in the South for white men! It is not too hot for white women. In different counties in North Carolina, have we seen the poor white wife of the poor white husband, following him in the harvest-field from morning till night, binding up the grain as it fell from his cradle. In the immediate neighborhood from which we hail, there are not less than thirty young women, non-slaveholding whites, between the ages of fifteen and twenty-five—some of whom are so well known to us that we could call them by name — who labor in the fields every summer; two of them in particular, near neighbors to our mother, are in the habit of hiring themselves out during harvest-time, the very hottest season of the year, to bind wheat and oats—each of them keeping up with the reaper; and this for the paltry consideration of twenty-five cents per day.

That any respectable man—any man with a heart or a soul in his composition—can look upon these poor toiling white women without feeling indignant at that accursed system of slavery which has entailed on them the miseries of poverty, ignorance, and degradation, we shall not do ourself the violence to believe. If they and their husbands, and their sons and daughters, and brothers and sisters, are not righted in some of the more important particulars in which they have been wronged, the fault shall lie at other doors than our own. In their behalf, chiefly, have we written and compiled this work; and until our object shall have been accomplished, or until life shall have been extinguished, there shall be no abatement in our efforts to aid them in regaining the natural and inalienable prerogatives out of which they have been so infamously swindled. We want to see no more plowing, or hoeing, or raking, or grain-binding, by white women in the Southern States; employment in cotton-mills and other factories would be far more profitable and congenial to them, and this they shall have within a short period after slavery shall have been abolished.

Too hot in the South for white men! What is the testimony of reliable Southerners themselves? Says Cassius M. Clay, of Kentucky:

"In the extreme South, at New Orleans, the laboring men—the stevedores and hackmen on the levee, where the heat is intensified by the proximity of the red brick buildings— are all white men, and they are in the full enjoyment of health. But how about Cotton? I am informed by a friend of mine—himself a slaveholder, and therefore good authority—that in Northwestern Texas, among the German settlements, who true to their national instincts, will not employ the labor of a slave: they produce more cotton to the acre, and of a better quality, and selling at prices from a cent to a cent and a half a pound higher than that produced by slave labor."

Says Gov. Hammond, of South Carolina:

"The steady heat of our summers is not so prostrating as the short, but frequent and sudden, bursts of Northern summers."

In an extract which may be found in our second chapter, and to which we respectfully refer the reader, it will be seen that this same South Carolinian, speaking of "not less than fifty thousand" non-slaveholding whites, says—"most of these now follow agricultural pursuits."

Says Dr. Cartwright of New Orleans:

"Here in New Orleans, the larger part of the drudgery-work requiring exposure to the sun, as railroad-making, street-paving, dray-driving, ditching and building, is performed by white people."

To the statistical tables which show the number of deaths in the free and in the slave States in 1850, we would direct special attention. Those persons, particularly the propogandists of negro slavery, who, heretofore, have been so dreadfully exercised on account of what they have been pleased to term "the insalubrity of Southern climes," will there find something to allay their fearful apprehensions. A critical examination of said tables will disclose the fact that, in proportion to population, deaths occur more frequently in Massachusetts than in any Southern State except Louisiana; more frequently in New York than in any of the Southern States, except Maryland, Missouri, Kentucky, Louisiana, and Texas; more frequently in New Jersey, in Pennsylvania, and in Ohio, than in either Georgia, Florida, or Alabama. Leaving Wisconsin and Louisiana out of the account, and then comparing the bills of mortality in the remaining Northern States, with those in the remaining Southern

States, we find the difference decidedly in favor of the latter; for, according to this calculation, while the ratio of deaths is as only one to 74.60 of the living population in the Southern States, it is as one to 72.39 in the Northern.

Says Dr. J. C. Nott, of Mobile:

"Heat, moisture, animal and vegetable matter are said to be the elements which produce the diseases of the South, and yet the testimony in proof of the health of the banks of the lower portion of the Mississippi River, is too strong to be doubted,—not only the river itself but also the numerous bayous which meander through Louisiana. Here is a perfectly flat alluvial country, covering several hundred miles, interspersed with interminable lakes, lagoons and jungles, and still we are informed by Dr. Cartwright, one of the most acute observers of the day, that this country is exempt from miasmatic disorders, and is extremely healthy. His assertion has been confirmed to me by hundreds of witnesses, and we know from our own observation, that the population present a robust and healthy appearance."

But the best part is yet to come. In spite of all the blatant assertions of the oligarchy, that the climate of the South was arranged expressly for the negroes, and that the negroes were created expressly to inhabit it as the healthful servitors of other men, a carefully kept register of all the deaths that occurred in Charleston, South Carolina, for the space of six years, shows that, even in that locality which is generally regarded as so unhealthy, the annual mortality was much greater among the blacks, in proportion to population, than among the whites. Dr. Nott himself shall state the facts. He says:

"The average mortality for the last six years in Charleston for all ages is 1 in 51, including all classes. Blacks alone 1 in 44; whites alone, 1 in 58—a very remarkable result, certainly. This mortality is perhaps not an unfair test, as the population during the last six years has been undisturbed by emigration and acclimated in a greater proportion than at any former period."

Numerous other authorities might be cited in proof of the general healthiness of the climate south of Mason and Dixon's line. Of 127 remarkable cases of American longevity, published in a recent edition of Blake's Biographical Dictionary, 68 deceased centenarians are credited to the Southern States, and 59 to the Northern — the list being headed with Betsey Trantham, of Tennessee — a white woman, who died in 1834, at the extraordinarily advanced age of 154 years.

Table No. LVII.

Natives of the Slave States in the Free States, and Natives of the Free States in the Slave States. — 1850

	Natives of the Slave States		Natives of the Free States
California	24,055	Alabama	4,947
Connecticut	1,390	Arkansas	7,965
Illinois	144,809	Delaware	6,996
Indiana	176,581	Florida	1,718
Iowa	31,392	Georgia	4,249
Maine	458	Kentucky	31,340
Massachusetts	2,980	Louisiana	14,567
Michigan	3,634	Maryland	23,815
New Hampshire	215	Mississippi	4,517
New Jersey	4,110	Missouri	55,664
New York	12,625	North Carolina	2,167
Ohio	152,319	South Carolina	2,427
Pennsylvania	47,180	Tennessee	6,571
Rhode Island	982	Texas	9,982
Vermont	140	Virginia	28,999
Wisconsin	6,353		
TOTAL	609,223	TOTAL	205,924

This last table, compiled from the 116th page of the Compendium of the Seventh Census, shows, in a most lucid and startling manner, how negroes, slavery and slaveholders are driving the native non-slaveholding whites away from their homes, and keeping at a distance other decent people. From the South the tide of emigration still flows in a westerly and north-westerly direction, and it will continue to do so until slavery is abolished. The following remarks, which we extract from an editorial article that appeared in the Memphis (Tenn.) *Bulletin* near the close of the year 1856, are worth considering in this connection:

"We have never before observed so large a number of immigrants going westward as are crossing the river at this point daily, the two ferry boats — sometimes three — going crowded from early morn until the boats cease making their trips at night. It is no uncommon sight to see from twenty to forty wagons encamped on the bluff for the night, notwithstanding there has been a steady stream going across the river all day, and yet the cry is, still they come."

About the same time the Cassville (Geo.) *Standard* spoke with surprise of the multitude of emigrants crowding the streets of that town bound for the far West.

Prof. B. S. Hedrick, of Chapel Hill, North Carolina, says:

"Of my neighbors, friends and family, nearly one-half have left the State since I was old enough to remember. Many is the time I have stood by the loaded emigrant wagon, and given the parting hand to those whose faces I was never to look upon again. They were going to seek homes in the free West, knowing, as they did, that free and slave labor could not both exist and prosper in the same community.

"If anyone thinks that I speak without knowledge, let him refer to the last census. He will there find that in 1850 there were fifty-eight thousand native North Carolinians living in the free States of the West — thirty-three-thousand in Indiana alone. There were, at the same time, one hundred and eighty thousand Virginians living in the free States. Now, if these people were so much in love with the 'institution,' why did they not remain where they could enjoy its blessings?

"From my knowledge of the people of North Carolina, I believe that the majority of them who will go to Kansas during the next five years, would prefer that it should be a free State. I am sure that if I were to go there I should vote to exclude slavery."

For daring to have political opinions of his own, and because he did not deem it his duty to conceal the fact that he loved liberty better than slavery, the gallant author of the extract above quoted was peremptorily dismissed from his post of analytical and agricultural chemist in the University of North Carolina, ignominiously subjected to the indignities of a mob, and then savagely driven beyond the borders of his native State. His villainous persecutors, if not called to settle their accounts in another world within the next ten years, will probably survive to repent of the enormity of their pro-slavery folly.

Table No. LVIII.

Value of the Slaves at $400 per Head. — 1850*

	Value of the Slaves at $400 per head	Val. of Real and Per. Estate, less the val. of slaves at $400 p. head
Alabama	$137,137,600	$81,066,732
Arkansas	18,840,000	21,001,025
Delaware	916,000	17,939,863
Florida	15,724,000	7,474,734
Georgia	152,672,800	182,752,914
Kentucky	84,392,400	217,236,056
Louisiana	97,923,600	136,075,164
Maryland	36,147,200	183,070,164
Mississippi	123,951,200	105,000,000
Missouri	34,968,800	102,278,907
North Carolina	115,419,200	111,381,272
South Carolina	153,993,600	134,264,094
Tennessee	95,783,600	111,671,104
Texas	23,264,400	32,097,940
Virginia	189,011,200	202,634,638
TOTAL	$1,280,145,600	$1,655,945,137
Corrected	*$1,280,146,000*	*$1,645,945,007*

* It is intended that this Table shall be considered in connection with Tables XX and XXI

TABLES 34 and 35 show that, on account of the pitiable poverty and ignorance of slavery, the mails were transported throughout the Southern States, during the year 1855, at an extra cost to the General Government of more than six hundred thousand dollars! In the free States, postages were received to the amount of more than two millions of dollars over and above the cost of transportation.

To Dr. G. Bailey, editor of the *National Era*, Washington city, D. C., we are indebted for the following useful and interesting statistics, to which some of our readers will doubtless have frequent occasion to refer:

PRESIDENTS OF THE UNITED STATES

March 4, 1789-March 3, 1797 George Washington, *Virginia*
March 4, 1797-March 3, 1801 John Adams, *Massachusetts*
March 4, 1801-March 3, 1809 Thomas Jefferson, *Virginia*
March 4, 1809-March 3, 1817 James Madison, *Virginia*
March 4, 1817-March 3, 1825 James Monroe, *Virginia*
March 4, 1825-March 3, 1829 John Q. Adams, *Massachusetts*
March 4, 1829-March 3, 1837 Andrew Jackson, *Tennessee*
March 4, 1837-March 3, 1841 Martin Van Buren, *New York*
March 4, 1841-March 3, 1845 William H. Harrison, *Ohio*
March 4, 1845-March 3, 1849 James K. Polk, *Tennessee*
March 4, 1849-March 3, 1853 Zachary Taylor, *Louisiana*
March 4, 1853-March 3, 1857 Franklin Pierce, *New Hampshire*
March 4, 1857-March 3, 1861 James Buchanan, *Pennsylvania*

At the close of the term for which Mr. Buchanan is elected, it will have been seventy-two years since the organization of the present Government. In that period, there have been eighteen elections for President, the candidates chosen in twelve of them being Southern men and slaveholders, in six of them Northern men and non-slaveholders.

No Northern man has ever been re-elected, but five Southern men have been thus honored.

Gen. Harrison, of Ohio, died one month after his inauguration, Gen. Taylor, of Louisiana, about four months after his inauguration. In the former case, John Tyler, of Virginia, became acting President, in the latter, Millard Fillmore, of New York.

Of the seventy-two years, closing with Mr. Buchanan's term, should he live it out, Southern men and slaveholders have occupied the Presidential chair forty-eight years and three months, or a little more than two-thirds of the time.

THE SUPREME COURT

The judicial districts are organized so as to give five judges to the slave States, and four to the free, although the population, wealth, and business of the latter are far in advance of those of the former. The arrangement affords, however, an excuse for constituting the Supreme Court, with a majority of judges from the slaveholding States.

Chief Justice—R. B. Taney, *Maryland*

Associate Justice—J. M. Wayne, *Georgia*

Associate Justice—John Catron, *Tennessee*

Associate Justice—P. V. Daniel, *Virginia*

Associate Justice—John A. Campbell, *Alabama*

Associate Justice—John McLean, *Ohio*

Associate Justice—S. Nelson, *New York*

Associate Justice—R. C. Grier, *Pennsylvania*

Associate Justice—B. R. Curtis, *Massachusetts*

Reporter—B. C. Howard, *Maryland*

Clerk—W. T. Carroll, *D. C.*

SECRETARIES OF STATE

The highest office in the Cabinet is that of Secretary of State, who has under his charge the foreign relations of the country. Since the

year 1789, there have been twenty-two appointments to the office
—fourteen from slave States, eight from free. Or, counting by years,
the post has been filled by Southern men and slaveholders very
nearly forty years out of sixty-seven, as follows:

Appointed.
Sept. 26, 1789, Thomas Jefferson, *Virginia*
Jan. 2, 1794, E. Randolph, *Virginia*
Dec. 10, 1795, T. Pickering, *Massachusetts*
May 13, 1800, J. Marshall, *Virginia*
March 5, 1801, James Madison, *Virginia*
March 6, 1809, R. Smith, *Maryland*
April 2, 1811, James Monroe, *Virginia*
Feb. 28, 1815, James Monroe, *Virginia*
March 5, 1815, J. Q. Adams, *Massachusetts*
March 7, 1825, Henry Clay, *Kentucky*
March 6, 1829, Martin Van Buren, *New York*
May 24, 1831, E. Livingston, *Louisiana*
May 29, 1833, Louis McLane, *Delaware*
June 27, 1834, J. Forsyth, *Georgia*
March 5, 1841, Daniel Webster, *Massachusetts*
July 24, 1843, A. P. Upshur, *Virginia*
March 6, 1844, J. C. Calhoun, *South Carolina*
March 5, 1845, James Buchanan, *Pennsylvania*
March 7, 1849, J. M. Clayton, *Delaware*
July 20, 1850, Daniel Webster, *Massachusetts*
Dec. 9, 1851, E. Everett, *Massachusetts*
March 5, 1853, W. L. Marcy, *New York*

PRESIDENTS PRO TEM. OF THE SENATE

Since the year 1809, every President *pro tem.* of the Senate of the
United States has been a Southern man and slaveholder, with the
exception of Samuel L. Southard, of New Jersey, who held the
office for a very short time, and Mr. Bright, of Indiana, who has held

it for one or two sessions, we believe, having been elected, however, as a known adherent of the slave interest, believed to be interested in slave "property."

SPEAKERS OF THE HOUSE OF REPRESENTATIVES

April, 1789-March 3, 1791 F. A. Muhlenberg, *Penn.*
Oct. 24, 1791-March 2, 1793 J. Trumbull, *Connecticut*
Dec. 2, 1793-March 3, 1795 F. A. Muhlenberg, *Penn.*
Dec. 7, 1795-March 3, 1797 Jonathan Dayton, *New Jersey*
May 15, 1797-March 3, 1799 Jonathan Dayton, *New Jersey*
Dec. 2, 1799-March 3, 1801 Theodore Sedgwick, *Mass.*
Dec. 7, 1801-March 3, 1807 Nathaniel Macon, *N. Car.*
Oct. 26, 1807-March 3, 1811 J. B. Varnum, *Massachusetts*
March 4, 1811-Jan. 19, 1814 Henry Clay, *Kentucky*
Jan. 19, 1814-March 2, 1815 Langdon Cheves, *S. Car.*
Dec. 4, 1815-Nov. 13, 1820 Henry Clay, *Kentucky*
Nov. 15, 1820-March 3, 1821 J. W. Taylor, *New York*
Dec. 3, 1821-March 3, 1823 P. B. Barbour, *Virginia*
Dec. 1, 1823-March 3, 1825 Henry Clay, *Kentucky*
Dec. 5, 1825-March 3, 1827 J. W. Taylor, *New York*
Dec. 3, 1827-June 2, 1834 A. Stevenson, *Virginia*
June 2, 1834-March 3, 1835 John Bell, *Tennessee*
Dec. 7, 1835-March 3, 1839 James K. Polk, *Tennessee*
Dec. 16, 1839-March 3, 1841 R. M. T. Hunter, *Virginia*
May 31, 1841-March 3, 1843 John White, *Tennessee*
Dec. 4, 1843-March 3, 1845 J. W. Jones, *Virginia*
Dec. 1, 1845-March 3, 1847 J. W. Davis, *Indiana*
Dec. 6, 1847-March 3, 1849 R. C. Winthrop, *Mass.*
Dec. 22, 1849-March 3, 1851 Howell Cobb, *Georgia*
Dec. 1, 1851-March 3, 1853 Linn Boyd, *Kentucky*
Dec. 1, 1853-March 3, 1855 Linn Boyd, *Kentucky*
Feb. 28, 1856-March 3, 1857 Nathaniel P. Banks, *Mass.*

POSTMASTERS-GENERAL

Appointed—

Sept. 26, 1789, S. Osgood, *Massachusetts*

Aug. 12, 1791, T. Pickering, *Massachusetts*

Feb. 25, 1795, J. Habersham, *Georgia*

Nov. 28, 1801, G. Granger, *Connecticut*

March 17, 1814, R. J. Meigs, *Ohio*

June 25, 1823, John McLean, *Ohio*

March 9, 1829, W. T. Barry, *Kentucky*

May 1, 1835, A. Kendall, *Kentucky*

May 18, 1840, J. M. Niles, *Connecticut*

March 6, 1841, F. Granger, *New York*

Sept. 13, 1841, C. A. Wickliffe, *Kentucky*

March 5, 1845, C. Johnson, *Tennessee*

March 7, 1849, J. Collamer, *Vermont*

July 20, 1850, N. K. Hall, *New York*

Aug. 31, 1852, S. D. Hubbard, *Connecticut*

March 5, 1853, J. Campbell, *Pennsylvania*

Sectionalism does not seem to have had much to do with this Department or with that of the Interior, created in 1848-49.

SECRETARIES OF THE INTERIOR

Appointed—

March 7, 1849, T. Ewing, *Ohio*

July 20, 1850, J. A. Pearce, *Maryland*

Aug. 15, 1850, T. M. T. McKennon, *Pennsylvania*

Sept. 12, 1850, A. H. H. Stuart, *Virginia*

March 5, 1853, R. McClelland, *Michigan*

ATTORNEYS-GENERAL

Appointed—

Sept. 26, 1789, E. Randolph, *Virginia*

June 27, 1794, W. Bradford, *Pennsylvania*

Dec. 10, 1795, C. Lee, *Virginia*

Feb. 20, 1801, T. Parsons, *Massachusetts*

March 5, 1800, L. Lincoln, *Massachusetts*

March 2, 1805, R. Smith, *Maryland*

Dec. 23, 1805, J. Breckinridge, *Kentucky*

Jan. 20, 1807, C. A. Rodney, *Pennsylvania*

Dec. 11, 1811, W. Pinkney, *Maryland*

Feb. 10, 1814, W. Rush, *Pennsylvania*

Nov. 13, 1817, W. Wirt, *Virginia*

March 9, 1829, J. McPherson Berrien, *Georgia*

July 20, 1831, Roger B. Taney, *Maryland*

Nov. 15, 1833, B. F. Butler, *New York*

July 7, 1838, F. Grundy, *Tennessee*

Jan. 10, 1840, H. D. Gilpin, *Pennsylvania*

March 5, 1841, J. J. Crittenden, *Kentucky*

Sept. 13, 1841, H. S. Legare, *South Carolina*

July 1, 1843, John Nelson, *Maryland*

March 5, 1845, J. Y. Mason, *Virginia*

Oct. 17, 1846, N. Clifford, *Maine*

June 21, 1848, Isaac Toucey, *Connecticut*

March 7, 1849, R. Johnson, *Maryland*

July 20, 1850, J. J. Crittenden, *Kentucky*

March 5, 1853, C. Cushing, *Massachusetts*

SECRETARIES OF THE TREASURY

The post of Secretary of the Treasury, although one of great importance, requires financial abilities of a high order, which are more frequently found in the North than in the South, and affords little opportunity for influencing general politics, or the questions springing out of Slavery. We need not therefore be surprised to learn that Northern men have been allowed to discharge its duties some forty-eight years out of sixty-seven, as follows:

Appointed—
Sept. 11, 1789, A. Hamilton, *New York*
Feb. 3, 1795, O. Wolcott, *Connecticut*
Dec. 31, 1800, S. Dexter, *Massachusetts*
May 14, 1801, A. Gallatin, *Pennsylvania*
Feb. 9, 1814, G. W. Campbell, *Tennessee*
Oct. 6, 1814, A. J. Dallas, *Pennsylvania*
Oct. 22, 1816, W. H. Crawford, *Georgia*
March 7, 1825, R. Rush, *Pennsylvania*
March 6, 1829, S. D. Ingham, *Pennsylvania*
Aug. 8, 1831, L. McLane, *Delaware*
May 29, 1833, W. J. Duane, *Pennsylvania*
Sept. 23, 1833, Roger B. Taney, *Maryland*
June 27, 1834, L. Woodbury, *New Hampshire*
March 5, 1841, Thomas Ewing, *Ohio*
Sept. 13, 1841, W. Forward, *Pennsylvania*
March 3, 1843, J. C. Spencer, *New York*
June 15, 1844, G. M. Bibb, *Kentucky*
March 5, 1845, R. J. Walker, *Mississippi*
March 7, 1849, W. M. Meredith, *Pennsylvania*
June 20, 1850, Thomas Corwin, *Ohio*
March 5, 1843, James Guthrie, *Kentucky*

SECRETARIES OF WAR AND THE NAVY

The Slaveholders, since March 8th, 1841, a period of nearly sixteen years, have taken almost exclusive supervision of the Navy, Northern men having occupied the Secretaryship only two years. Nor has any Northern man been Secretary of War since 1849. Considering that nearly all the shipping belongs to the free States, which also supply the seamen, it does seem remarkable that Slaveholders should have monopolized for the last sixteen years the control of the Navy.

SECRETARIES OF WAR

Appointed—

Sept. 12, 1789, Henry Knox, *Massachusetts*

Jan. 2, 1795, T. Pickering, *Massachusetts*

Jan. 27, 1796, J. McHenry, *Maryland*

May 7, 1800, J. Marshall, *Virginia*

May 13, 1800, S. Dexter, *Massachusetts*

Feb. 3, 1801, R. Griswold, *Connecticut*

March 5, 1801, H. Dearborn, *Massachusetts*

March 7, 1802, W. Eustis, *Massachusetts*

Jan. 13, 1813, J. Armstrong, *New York*

Sept. 27, 1814, James Monroe, *Virginia*

March 3, 1815, W. H. Crawford, *Georgia*

April 7, 1817, G. Graham, *Virginia*

March 5, 1817, J. Shelby, *Kentucky*

Oct. 8, 1817, J. C. Calhoun, *South Carolina*

March 7, 1825, J. Barbour, *Virginia*

May 26, 1828, P. B. Porter, *Pennsylvania*

March 9, 1829, J. H. Eaton, *Tennessee*

Aug. 1, 1831, Lewis Cass, *Ohio*

March 3, 1837, B. F. Butler, *New York*

March 7, 1837, J. R. Poinsett, *South Carolina*

March 5, 1841, James Bell, *Tennessee*

Sept. 13, 1841, John McLean, *Ohio*

Oct. 12, 1841, J. C. Spencer, *New York*

March 8, 1843, J. W. Porter, *Pennsylvania*

Feb. 15, 1844, W. Wilkins, *Pennsylvania*

March 5, 1845, William L. Marcy, *New York*

March 7, 1849, G. W. Crawford, *Georgia*

July 20, 1850, E. Bates, *Missouri*

Aug. 15, 1850, C. M. Conrad, *Louisiana*

March 5, 1853, Jefferson Davis *Mississippi*

SECRETARIES OF THE NAVY

Appointed —

May 3, 1798, G. Cabot, *Massachusetts*
May 21, 1798, B. Stoddart, *Massachusetts*
July 15, 1801, R. Smith, *Maryland*
May 3, 1805, J. Crowninshield, *Massachusetts*
March 7, 1809, P. Hamilton, *South Carolina*
Jan. 12, 1813, W. Jones, *Pennsylvania*
Dec. 17, 1814, B. W. Crowninshield, *Massachusetts*
Nov. 9, 1818, Smith Thompson, *New York*
Sept. 1, 1823, John Rogers, *Massachusetts*
Sept. 16, 1823, S. L. Southard, *New Jersey*
March 9, 1819, John Branch, *North Carolina*
May 23, 1831, L. Woodbury, *New Hampshire*
June 30, 1834, M. Dickerson, *New Jersey*
June 20, 1838, J. K. Paulding, *New York*
March 5, 1841, G. F. Badger, *North Carolina*
Sept. 13, 1841, A. P. Upshur, *Virginia*
July 24, 1843, D. Henshaw, *Massachusetts*
Feb. 12, 1844, T. W. Gilmer, *Virginia*
March 14, 1844, James Y. Mason, *Virginia*
March 10, 1845, G. Bancroft, *Massachusetts*
Sept. 9, 1846, James Y. Mason, *Virginia*
March 7, 1849, W. B. Preston, *Virginia*
July 20, 1850, W. A. Graham, *N. Carolina*
July 22, 1852, J. P. Kennedy, *Maryland*
March 3, 1853, J. C. Dobbin, *N. Carolina*

RECAPITULATION

Presidency. — Southern men and Slaveholders, 48 years 3 months; Northern men, 23 years 9 months.

Pro. Tem. Presidency of the Senate. — Since 1809, held by Southern men and Slaveholders, except for three or four sessions by Northern men.

Speakership of the House. — Filled by Southern men and Slave-holders forty-three years, Northern men, twenty-five.

Supreme Court. — A majority of the Judges, including Chief Justice, Southern men and Slaveholders.

Secretaryship of State. — Filled by Southern men and Slaveholders forty years, Northern, twenty-seven.

Attorney Generalship. — Filled by Southern men and Slaveholders forty-two years, Northern men, twenty-five.

War and Navy. — Secretaryship of the Navy, Southern men and Slaveholders, the last sixteen years, with an interval of two years.

William Henry Hurlbut, of South Carolina, a gentleman of enviable literary attainments, and one from whom we may expect a continuation of good service in the eminently holy crusade now going on against slavery and the devil, furnished not long since, to the *Edinburgh Review,* in the course of a long and highly interesting article, the following summary of oligarchal usurpations — showing that *slaveholders have occupied the principal posts of the Government nearly two-thirds of the time*:

Presidents	11 out of 16
Judges of the Supreme Court	17 out of 28
Attorneys-General	14 out of 19
Presidents of the Senate	61 out of 77
Speakers of the House	21 out of 33
Foreign Ministers	80 out of 134

As a matter of general interest, and as showing that, while there have been but 11 non-slaveholders directly before the people as candidates for the Presidency, there have been *at least* 16 slaveholders who were willing to serve their country in the capacity of chief magistrate, the following table may be here introduced:

Result of the Presidential Elections in the United States from 1796 to 1856

	Name of Candidate	Elect'l Vote
1796	John Adams	71
1796	Thomas Jefferson	68
1800	Thomas Jefferson	73
1800	John Adams	64
1804	Thomas Jefferson	162
1804	Charles C. Pinckney	14
1808	James Madison	128
1808	Charles C. Pinckney	45
1812	James Madison	122
1812	De Witt Clinton	89
1816	James Monroe	183
1816	Rufus King	34
1820	James Monroe	218
1820	No opposition but one vote	
1824	Andrew Jackson*	99
1824	John Q. Adams	84
1824	W. H. Crawford	41
1824	Henry Clay	37
1828	Andrew Jackson	178
1828	John Q. Adams	83
1832	Andrew Jackson	219
1832	Henry Clay	49
1832	John Floyd	11
1832	William Wirt	7
1836	Martin Van Buren	170
1836	William H. Harrison	73
1836	Hugh L. White	26
1836	Willie P. Mangum	11

1836	Daniel Webster	14
1840	William H. Harrison	234
1840	Martin Van Buren	60
1844	James K. Polk	170
1844	Henry Clay	105
1848	Zachary Taylor	163
1848	Lewis Cass	127
1852	Franklin Pierce	254
1852	General Winfield Scott	42
1856	James Buchanan	174
1856	John C. Fremont	114
1856	Millard Fillmore	8

* No choice by the people; John Q. Adams elected by the House of Representatives.

AID FOR KANSAS

As a sort of accompaniment to tables, 50, 51, 52 and 53, we will here introduce a few items which will more fully illustrate the liberality of Freedom and the niggardliness of Slavery.

From an editorial article that appeared in the Richmond (Va.,) *Dispatch*, in July, 1856, bewailing the close-fistedness of slavery, we make the following extract:

"Gerrit Smith, the Abolitionist, has just pledged himself to give $1,500 a month for the next twelve months to aid in establishing Freedom in Kansas. He gave, but a short time since, at the Kansas relief meeting in Albany, $3,000. Prior to that, he had sent about $1,000 to the Boston Emigrant Committee. Out of his own funds, he subsequently equipped a Madison county company, of one hundred picked men, and paid their expenses to Kansas. At Syracuse he subscribed $10,000 for Abolition purposes, so that his entire contributions amount to at least $40,000."

An Eastern paper says:

"The sum of $500 was contributed at a meeting at New Bedford on Monday evening, to make Kansas free. The following sums have been contributed for the same purpose: $2,000 in Taunton: $600 in Raynham: $800 in Clinton: $300 in Danbury, Ct. In Wisconsin, $2,500 at Janesville: $500 at Dalton: $500 at the Women's Aid Meeting in Chicago: $2,000 in Rockford, Ill."

A telegraphic dispatch, dated Boston, January 2, 1857, informs us that "The Secretary of the Kansas Aid Committee acknowledges the receipt of $42,678."

Exclusive of the amounts above, the readers of the New York *Tribune* have contributed about $30,000 for the purpose of securing Kansas to Freedom; and, with the same object in view, other individuals and societies have, from time to time, made large contributions, of which we have failed to keep a memorandum. The legislature of Vermont has appropriated $20,000; and other free State legislatures are prepared to appropriate millions, if necessary. Free men have determined that Kansas shall be free, and free it soon shall be, and ever so remain. Harmoniously the work proceeds.

Now let us see how slavery has rewarded the poor, ignorant, deluded, and degraded mortals — swaggering lick-spittles — who have labored so hard to gain for it "a local habitation and a name" in the disputed territory. One D. B. Atchison, Chairman of the Executive Committee of Border Ruffians, shall tell us all about it. Over date of October 13th, 1856, he says:

"Up to this moment, from all the States except Missouri, we have only received the following sums, and through the following persons:

A. W. Jones, Houston, Miss.	$152
H. D. Clayton, Eufala, Ala.	500
Capt. Deedrick, South Carolina	500
	$1,152."

On this subject, further comment is unnecessary.

Numerous other contrasts, equally disproportionate, might be drawn between the vigor and munificence of freedom and the impotence and stinginess of slavery. We will, however, in addition to the above, advert to only a single instance. During the latter part of the summer of 1855, the citizens of the black towns of Norfolk and Portsmouth, in Virginia, were sorely plagued with yellow fever. Many of them fell victims to the disease, and most of those who survived, and who were not too unwell to travel, left their homes, horror-stricken and dejected. To the horror of mankind in general, and to the glory of freemen in particular, contributions in money, provisions, clothing, and other valuable supplies, poured in from all parts of the country, for the relief of the sufferers. Portsmouth alone, according to the report of her relief association, received $42,547 in cash from the free States, and only $12,182 in cash from all the slave States, exclusive of Virginia, within whose borders the malady prevailed. Including Virginia, the sum total of all the slave State contributions amounted to only $33,398. Well did the Richmond *Examiner* remark at the time — "we fear that generosity of Virginians is but a figure of speech." Slavery! thy name is shame!

IN CONNECTION with tables 44 and 45, it will be well to examine the following statistics of Congressional representation, which we transcribe from Reynold's Political Map of the United States:

UNITED STATES SENATE

16 free States, with a white population of 13,238,670, have 32 Senators.

15 slave States, with a white population of 6,186,477, have 30 Senators.

As a ratio of population per senator, 413,708 free men of the North enjoy but the same political privileges in the U. S. Senate as is given to 206,215 people in the South.

HOUSE OF REPRESENTATIVES

The free States have a total of 144 members.

The slave States have a total of 90 members.

One free State Representative represents 91,935 white men and women.

One slave State Representative represents 68,725 white men and women.

Slave Representation gives to slavery an advantage over freedom of 30 votes in the House of Representatives.

Custom-house Receipts. — 1854.

Free States	$60,010,489
Slave States	5,136,969
Balance in favor of the Free States	$54,873,520

A contrast quite distinguishable!

That the apologists of slavery cannot excuse the shame and the shabbiness of themselves and their country, as we have frequently heard them attempt to do, by falsely asserting that the North has enjoyed over the South the advantages of priority of settlement, will fully appear from the following table:

FREE STATES

1614. New York first settled by the Dutch.

1620. Massachusetts settled by the Puritans.

1623. New Hampshire settled by the Puritans.

1624. New Jersey settled by the Dutch.

1635. Connecticut settled by the Puritans.

1636. Rhode Island settled by Roger Williams.

1682. Pennsylvania settled by William Penn.

1791. Vermont admitted into the Union.

1802. Ohio admitted into the Union.

1816. Indiana admitted into the Union.

1818. Illinois admitted into the Union.

1820. Maine admitted into the Union.

1836. Michigan admitted into the Union.

1846. Iowa admitted into the Union.

1848. Wisconsin admitted into the Union.

1850. California admitted into the Union.

SLAVE STATES

1607. Virginia first settled by the English.

1627. Delaware settled by the Swedes and Fins.

1635. Maryland settled by Irish Catholics.

1650. North Carolina settled by the English.

1670. South Carolina settled by the Huguenots.

1733. Georgia settled by Gen. Oglethorpe.

1782. Kentucky admitted into the Union.

1796. Tennessee admitted into the Union.

1811. Louisiana admitted into the Union.

1817. Mississippi admitted into the Union.

1819. Alabama admitted into the Union.

1821. Missouri admitted into the Union.

1836. Arkansas admitted into the Union.

1845. Florida admitted into the Union.

1846. Texas admitted into the Union.

In the course of an exceedingly interesting article on the early settlements in America, R. K. Browne, formerly editor and proprietor of the San Francisco *Evening Journal,* says:

"Many people seem to think that the Pilgrim Fathers were the first who settled upon our shores, and therefore that they ought to be entitled, in a particular manner, to our remembrance and esteem.

"This is *not the case,* and we herewith present to our readers a list of settlements made in the present United States, prior to that of Plymouth.

1564. A Colony of French Protestants under Ribault settled in Florida.

1565. St. Augustine founded by Pedro Melendez. (St. Augustine is the oldest town in the United States).

1584. Sir Walter Raleigh obtains a patent and sends two vessels to the American coast, which receives the name of Virginia.

1607. The first effectual settlement made at Jamestown, Va., by the London Company.

1614. A fort erected by the Dutch upon the site of New York.

1615. Fort Orange built near the site of Albany, N. Y.

1619. The first General Assembly called in Virginia.

1620. The Pilgrims land on Plymouth Rock."

The reports of the Comptrollers of the States of New York and North Carolina, for the year 1856, are now before us. From each report we have gleaned a single item, which, when compared, the one with the other, speaks volumes in favor of freedom and against slavery. We refer to the average value per acre of lands in the two States; let slavocrats read, reflect, and repent.

In 1856, there were assessed for taxation in the State of

NEW YORK

Acres of land	30080000
Valued at	$1,112,133,136
Average value per acre	$36.97

In 1856, there were assessed for taxation in the State of

NORTH CAROLINA

Acres of land	32450560
Valued at	$98,800,636
Average value per acre	$3.06

It is difficult for us to make any remarks on the official facts above. Our indignation is struck almost dumb at this astounding and revolting display of the awful wreck that slavery is leaving behind it in the South. We will, however, go into a calculation for the purpose of ascertaining as nearly as possible, in this one particular, how much North Carolina has lost by the retention of slavery. As we have already seen, the average value per acre of land in the State of New York is $36.97; in North Carolina it is only $3.06; why is it so much less, or even any less, in the latter than in the former? The answer is, *slavery*. In soil, in climate, in minerals, in water-power for manufactural purposes, and in area of territory, North Carolina has the advantage of New York, and, with the exception of slavery, no plausible reason can possibly be assigned why land should not be *at least* as valuable in the valley of the Yadkin as it is along the banks of the Genesee.

The difference between $36.97 and $3.06 is $33.91, which, multiplied by the whole number of acres of land in North Carolina, will show, in this one particular, the enormous loss that Freedom has sustained on account of Slavery in the Old North State. Thus:

32,450,560 acres at $33.91. . . . $1,100,398,489.

Let it be indelibly impressed on the mind, however, that this amount, large as it is, is only a moity of the sum that it has cost to maintain slavery in North Carolina. From time to time, hundreds upon hundreds of millions of dollars have left the State, either in search of profitable, permanent investment abroad, or in the shape of profits to Northern merchants and manufactures, who have become the moneyed aristocracy of the country by supplying to the South such articles of necessity, utility, and adornment, as would have been produced at home but for the pernicious presence of the peculiar institution.

A reward of Eleven Hundred Millions of Dollars is offered for the conversion of the lands of North Carolina into free soil. The lands themselves, desolate and impoverished under the fatal foot of slavery, offer the reward. How, then, can it be made to appear that the abolition of slavery in North Carolina, and, indeed, throughout all the Southern States — for slavery is exceedingly inimical to them all — is not demanded by every consideration of justice, prudence, and good sense? In 1850, the total value of all the slaves of the State, at the rate of four hundred dollars per head, amounted to less than one hundred and sixteen millions of dollars. Is the sum of one hundred and sixteen millions of dollars more desirable than the sum of eleven hundred millions of dollars? When a man has land for sale, does he reject thirty-six dollars per acre and take three? Non-slaveholding whites! look well to your interests! Many of you have lands; comparatively speaking, you have nothing else. Abolish slavery, and you will enhance the value of every league, your own and your neighbors', from three to thirty-six dollars per acre. Your little tract containing two hundred acres, now valued at the pitiful sum of only six hundred dollars, will then be worth seven thousand. Your children, now deprived of even the meagre advantages of common schools, will then reap the benefits of a collegiate education. Your rivers and smaller streams, now wasting their waters in idleness, will then turn the wheels of multitudinous mills. Your bays and harbors, now unknown to commerce, will then swarm with ships from every enlightened quarter of the globe. Non-slaveholding whites! look well to your interests!

Would the slaveholders of North Carolina lose anything by the abolition of slavery? Let us see. According to their own estimate, their slaves are worth, in round numbers, say, one hundred and twenty millions of dollars. There are in the State twenty-eight thousand slaveholders, owning, it may be safely assumed, an average of at least five hundred acres of land each — fourteen millions of acres in all. This number of acres, multiplied by thirty-three dollars and ninety-one cents, the difference in value between free soil and slave soil, makes the enormous sum of four hundred and seventy-four millions of dollars — showing that, by the abolition of slavery, the slaveholders themselves would realize a net profit of not less than three hundred and fifty-four millions of dollars!

Compensation to slaveholders for the negroes now in their possession! The idea is preposterous. The suggestion is criminal. The demand is unjust, wicked, monstrous, damnable. Shall we pat the bloodhounds of slavery for the sake of doing them a favor? Shall we fee the curs of slavery in order to make them rich at our expense? Shall we pay the whelps of slavery for the privilege of converting them into decent, honest, upright men?

No, never! The non-slaveholders expect to gain, and will gain, something by the abolition of slavery; but slaveholders themselves will, by far, be the greater gainers; for, in proportion to population, they own much larger and more fertile tracts of land, and will, as a matter of course, receive the lion's share of the increase in the value of not only real estate, but also of other genuine property, of which they are likewise the principal owners. How ridiculously absurd, therefore, is the objection, that, if we liberate the slaves, we ruin the masters! Not long since, a gentleman in Baltimore, a native of Maryland, remarked in our presence that he was an abolitionist because he felt that it was right and proper to be one; "but," inquired he, "are there not, in some of the States, many widows and orphans who would be left in destitute circumstances, if their negroes were taken from them?" In answer to the question, we replied that slavery had already reduced thousands and tens of thousands of non-slaveholding widows and orphans to the lowest depths of poverty and ignorance, and that we did not believe one slaveholding widow and three orphans were of more, or even of as much consequence as five non-slaveholding widows and fifteen orphans. "You are right," exclaimed the gentleman, "I had not viewed the subject in that light before; I perceive you go in for the greatest good to the greatest number." Emancipate the negroes, and the ex-slaveholding widow would still retain her lands and tenements, which, in consequence of being surroundend by the magic influences of liberty, would soon render her far more wealthy and infinitely more respectable, than she could possibly ever become while trafficking in human flesh.

The fact is, every slave in the South costs the State in which he resides at least three times as much as he, in the whole course of his life, is worth to his master. Slavery benefits no one but its immediate, individual owners, and them only in a pecuniary point of view, and at the sacrifice of the dearest rights and interests of the whole mass of non-slaveholders, white and black. Even the masters themselves, as we have already shown, would be far better off without it than with it. To all classes of society the institution is a curse; an especial curse is it to those who own it not. Non-slaveholding whites! look well to your interests!

Chapter 8

Southern Literature

IT IS WITH SOME DEGREE OF HESITATION that we add a chapter on
Southern Literature — not that the theme is inappropriate to this
work; still less, that it is an unfruitful one; but our hesitation results
from our conscious inability, in the limited time and space at our
command, to do the subject justice. Few, except those whose experience has taught them, have any adequate idea of the amount of
preparatory labor requisite to the production of a work into which
the statistical element largely enters; especially is this so, when the
statistics desired are not readily accessible through public and
official documents. The author who honestly aims at entire accuracy
in his statements, may find himself baffled for weeks in his pursuit
of a single item of information, not of much importance in itself
perhaps, when separately considered, but necessary in its connection with others, to the completion of a harmonious whole. Not
unfrequently, during the preparation of the preceding pages, have
we been subjected to this delay and annoyance.

The following brief references to the protracted preparatory
labors and inevitable delays to which authors are subjected, may
interest our readers, and induce them to regard with charity any
deficiencies, either in detail or in general arrangement, which,
owing to the necessary haste of preparation, these concluding pages
of our work may exhibit:

Goldsmith was engaged nine years in the preparation of "*The
Traveller*," and five years in gathering and arranging the incidents
of his "*Deserted Village*," and two years in their versification.

Bancroft, the American Historian, has been more than thirty
years engaged upon his History of the United States, from his

projection of the work to the present date; and that History is not yet completed.

Hidreth, a no less eminent historian, from the time he began to collect materials for his History of the United States to the date of its completion, devoted no less than twenty-five years to the work.

Webster, our great lexicographer, gave thirty-five years of his life in bringing his Unabridged Dictionary of the English Language to the degree of accuracy and completeness in which we now find it.

Dr. John W. Mason, after ten years' labor in the accumulation of materials for a Life of Alexander Hamilton, was compelled to relinquish the work on account of impaired health.

Mr. James Banks, of Fayetteville, North Carolina, who recently delivered a lecture upon the Life and Character of Flora McDonald, was eighteen years in the collection of his materials.

Oulibicheff, a distinguished Russian author, spent twenty-five years in writing the Life of Mozart.

Examples of this kind might be multiplied to an almost indefinite extent. Indeed, almost all the poets, prose-writers, painters, sculptors, composers, and other devotees of Art, who have won undying fame for themselves, have done so through long years of earnest and almost unremitted toil.

We are quite conscious that the fullness and accuracy of statement which are desirable in this chapter cannot be attained in the brief time allowed us for its completion; but, though much will necessarily be omitted that ought to be said, we shall endeavor to make no statement of facts which are not well authenticated, and no inferences from the same which are not logically true. We can only promise to do the best in our power, with the materials at our command, to exhibit the inevitable influence of slavery upon Southern Literature, and to demonstrate that the accursed institution so cherished by the oligarchy, is no less prejudicial to our advancement in letters, than it is destructive of our material prosperity.

What is the actual condition of Literature at the South? Our question includes more than simple authorship in the various departments of letters, from the compilation of a primary reader to the production of a Scientific or Theological Treatise. We comprehend in it all the activities engaged in the creation, publication, and sale of books and periodicals, from the penny primer to the heavy folio, and from the dingy, coarse-typed weekly paper, to the large, well-filled daily.

It were unjust to deny a degree of intellectual activity to the South. It has produced a few good authors—a few competent editors, and a moderately large number of clever magazinists, paragraphists, essayists and critics. Absolutely, then, it must be conceded that the South has something that may be called a literature; it is only when we speak of her in comparison with the North, that we say, with a pardonably strong expression, "The South has no literature." This was virtually admitted by more than one speaker at the late "Southern Convention" at Savannah. Said a South Carolina orator on that occasion: "It is important that the South *should have* a literature of her own, to defend her principles and her rights;" a sufficiently plain concession that she has not, now, such a literature. But *facts* speak more significantly than the rounded periods of Convention orators. Let us look at facts, then.

First, turning our attention to the periodical literature of the South, we obtain these results: By the census of 1850, we ascertain that the entire number of periodicals, daily, semi-weekly, weekly, semi-monthly, monthly and quarterly, published in the slave States, including the District of Columbia, were seven hundred and twenty-two. These had an aggregate *yearly* circulation of ninety-two million one hundred and sixty-seven thousand one hundred and twenty-nine. (92,167,129). The number of periodicals, of every class, published in the non-slaveholding States (exclusive of California) was one thousand eight hundred and ninety-three, with an aggregate yearly circulation of three hundred and thirty-three million three hundred and eighty-six thousand and eighty-one. (333,386,081).

We are aware that there may be inaccuracies in the foregoing estimates; but the compilers of the census, not we, are responsible for them. Besides, the figures are unquestionably as fair for the South as for the North; we accept them, therefore, as a just basis of our comparisons. Nearly seven years have elapsed since these statistics were taken, and these seven years have wrought an immense change in the journalism of the North, without any corresponding change in that of the South. It is noteworthy that, as a general thing, the principal journals of the free States are more comprehensive in their scope, more complete in every department, and enlist, if not a higher order of talent, at least *more* talent, than they did seven years ago. This improvement extends not only to the metropolitan, but to the country papers also. In fact, the very highest literary ability, in finance, in political economy, in science, in statism, in law, in theology, in medicine, in the belles-lettres, is laid under contribution by the journals of the non-slaveholding States. This is true only to a very limited degree of Southern journals. Their position, with but few exceptions, is substantially the same that it was ten years ago. They are neither worse nor better—the imbecility and inertia which attaches to everything which slavery touches, clings to them now as tenaciously as it did when Henry A. Wise thanked God for the paucity of newspapers in the Old Dominion, and the platitudes of "Father" Ritchie were recognized as the political gospel of the South. They have not, so far as we can learn, increased materially in number, nor in the aggregate of their yearly circulation. In the free States, no week passes that does not add to the number of their journals, and extend the circle of their readers and their influence. Since the census tables to which we have referred were prepared, two of the many excellent weekly journals of which the city of New York can boast, have sprung into being, and attained an aggregate circulation more than twice as large as that of the entire newspaper press of Virginia in 1850—and exceeding, by some thousands, the aggregate circulation of the two hundred and fifty journals of which Alabama, Arkansas, Kentucky, Georgia, North Carolina and Florida, could boast at the time abovementioned.

In this connection, we beg leave to introduce the following letter, kindly furnished us by the proprietors of the N. Y. Tribune, in answer to enquiries which we addressed to them:

TRIBUNE OFFICE, NEW YORK, 30th May, 1857
MR. H. R. HELPER,
Sir:
In answer to your inquiry we inform you that we employ in our building one hundred and seventy-six persons regularly: this does not include our carriers and cartmen, nor does it include the men employed in the Job Office in our building. During the past year we have used in printing *The Tribune*, Forty-four thousand nine hundred and seventy nine (44,979) reams of paper, weighing two million three hundred and ten thousand one hundred and thirty (2,310,130) pounds. We publish one hundred and seventy-six thousand copies of our weekly edition, which goes to press, the second form, at 7 1-2 o'clock, A. M. and is finished at 2 A. M. the next morning. Our mailers require eighteen to nineteen hours to mail our Weekly, which makes from thirty to thirty-two cart loads.
Very respectfully,
GREELEY & MCELRATH.

Throughout the non-slaveholding States, the newspaper or magazine that has *not* improved during the last decade of years, is an exception to the general rule. Throughout the entire slaveholding States, the newspaper or magazine that *has* improved during that time, is no less an exception to the general rule that there obtains. Outside of the larger cities of the South, there are not, probably, half a dozen newspapers in the whole slaveholding region that can safely challenge a comparison with the country-press of the North. What that country-press was twenty years ago, the country-press of the South is now.

We do not deny that the South has produced able journalists; and that some of the newspapers of her principal cities exhibit a degree of enterprise and talent that cannot fail to command for them the respect of all intelligent men. But these journals, we regret to say, are marked exceptions to the general condition of the Southern press; and even the best of these fall far below the standard of excellence attained by the leading journals of the North. In fact, whether our comparison embraces quantity only, or extends to both quantity and quality, it is found to be immeasurably in favor of the non-slaveholding States, which in journalism, as in all other industrial pursuits, leave their slavery-cursed competitors at an infinite distance behind them, and thus vindicate the superiority of free institutions, which, recognizing labor as honorable, secure its rewards for all.

The literary vassalage of the South to the North constitutes in itself a most significant commentary upon the diatribes of the former concerning "a purely Southern literature." To begin at the beginning — the Alphabetical Blocks and Educational tables from which our Southern abecedarian takes his initial lesson, were projected and manufactured in the North. Going forward a step, we find the youngling intent in spelling short sentences, or gratifying his juvenile fondness for the fine arts by copying the wood-cuts from his Northern primer. Yet another step, and we discover him with his Sanders' Reader, his Mitchell's Geography, his Emerson's Arithmetic, all produced by Northern mind and Northern enterprise. There is nothing *wrong* in this; it is only a little ridiculous in view of the fulminations of the Southern proslavery press against the North. Occasionally however we are amused by the efforts of the oligarchs to make their own school-books, or to root out of all educational text-books every reference to the pestilential heresy of freedom. A "gentleman" in Charleston, S. C. is devoting his energies to the preparation of a series of pro-slavery elementary works, consisting of primers, readers, &c. — and lo! they are all printed, stitched and bound north of Mason and Dixon's line! A single *fact* like this is sufficient to overturn whole folios of *theory* concerning the divinity of slavery. The truth is, that, not school-books alone, but works of almost every class produced by the South, depend upon Northern enterprise and skill for their introduction to the public. Mr. DeBow, the eminent Statistician, publishes a Southern Review, purporting to be issued from New Orleans. It is printed and bound in the city of New York. We clip the following paragraph from a recent number of the Vicksburgh (Miss.) *Whig*:

"SOUTHERN ENTERPRISE.—Even the Mississippi Legislature, at its late session allowed its laws to go to Boston to be printed, and made an appropriation of $3,000 to pay one of its members to go there and read the proof sheets instead of having it done in the State, and thereby assisting in building up a Southern publishing house. What a commentary on the Yankee-haters!"

The Greensboro (N. C.) *Patriot* thus records a similar contribution, on the part of that State, to "the creation of a purely Southern Literature:

"We have heard it said, that those who had the control of the printing of the revised Statutes of North Carolina, in order to save a few dimes, had the work executed in Boston, in preference to giving the job to a citizen of this State. We impugn not the motives of the agents in this matter; but it is a little humiliating that no work except the commonest labor, can be done in North Carolina; that everything which requires a little skill, capital, or ingenuity, must be sent North. In the case under consideration, we have heard it remarked, that when the whole bill of expenses connected with the printing of the Revised Statutes in Boston was footed up, it only amounted to a few thousand dollars more than the job would have cost in this State. But then we have the consolation of knowing that the book *came from the North*, and that it was printed among the *abolitionists* of Boston; the *peculiar friends* of North Carolina and the South generally.—Of course we ought to be willing to pay a few extra thousands in consideration of these important facts!"

Southern divines give us elaborate "Bible Arguments;" Southern statists heap treatise upon treatise through which the Federal Constitution is tortured into all monstrous shapes; Southern novelists bore us *ad infinitum* with pictures of the beatitudes of plantation life and the negro-quarters; Southern verse-wrights drone out their drowsy dactyls or grow ventricous with their turgid heroics all in defence of slavery,—priest, politician, novelist, bardling, severally ringing the changes upon "the Biblical institution," "the conservative institution," "the humanizing institution," "the patriarchal institution"—and then—have their books printed on Northern paper, with Northern types, by Northern artisans, stitched, bound and made ready for the market by Northern industry; and yet fail to see in all this, as a true philosophical mind *must* see, an overwhelming refutation of their miserable sophisms in behalf of a system against which humanity in all its impulses and aspirations, and civilization in all its activities and triumphs, utter their perpetual protest.

From a curious article in the "American Publishers' Circular" on "Book Making in America," we give the following extracts:

"It is somewhat alarming to know that the number of houses now actually engaged in the publishing of books, not including periodicals, amounts to more than three hundred. About three-fourths of these are engaged in Boston, New York, Philadelphia, and Baltimore —the balance being divided between Cincinnati, Buffalo, Auburn, Albany, Louisville, Chicago, St. Louis, and a few other places. There are more than three thousand book-sellers who dispense the publications of these three hundred, besides six or seven thousand apothecaries, grocers, and hardware dealers, who connect literature with drugs, molasses, and nails.

"The best printing in America is probably now done in Cambridge; the best cloth binding in Boston, and the best calf and morocco in New York and Philadelphia. In these two latter styles we are, as yet, a long distance from Heyday, the pride of London. His finish is supreme. There is nothing between it and perfection.

"Books have multiplied to such an extent in our country, that it now takes 750 paper mills, with 2,000 engines in constant operation, to supply the printers, who work day and night, endeavoring to keep their engagements with publishers. These tireless mills produced 270,000,000 pounds of paper the past year, which immense supply has sold for about $27,000,000. A pound and a quarter of rags were required for a pound of paper, and 400,000,000 pounds were therefore consumed in this way last year. The cost of manufacturing a twelve months' supply of paper for the United States, aside from labor and rags, is computed at $4,000,000. . . .

"The Harper establishment, the largest of our publishing houses, covers half an acre of ground. If old Mr. Caxton, who printed those stories of the Trojan war so long ago, could follow the Ex-Mayor of New York in one of his morning rounds in Franklin Square, he would be, to say the least, a little surprised. He would see in one room the floor loaded with the weight of 150 tons of presses. The electrotyping process would puzzle him somewhat; the drying and pressing process would startle him; the bustle would make his head ache; and the stock-room would quite finish him. An edition of Harpers' Monthly Magazine alone consists of 175,000. Few persons have any idea how large a number this is as applied to the edition of a book. It is computed that if these magazines were to rain down, and one man should attempt to pick them up like chips, it would take him a fortnight to pick up the copies of one single number, supposing him to pick up one every second, and to work ten hours a day."

"The rapidity with which books are now manufactured is almost incredible. A complete copy of one of Bulwer's novels, published across the water in three volumes, and reproduced here in one, was swept through the press in New York in fifty hours, and offered for sale smoking hot in the streets. The fabulous edifice proposed by a Yankee from Vermont, no longer seems an impossibility. 'Build the establishment according to my plan,' said he; 'drive a sheep in at one end, and he shall immediately come out at the other, four quarters of lamb, a felt hat, a leather apron, and a quarto Bible.'"

The business of the Messrs. Harper, whose establishment is referred to in the foregoing extract, is probably more generally diffused over every section of this country than that of any other publishing house. From enquiries recently made of them we learn that they issue, on an average, 3,000 bound volumes per day, throughout the year, and that each volume will average 500 pages—making a total of about one million of volumes, and not less than five hundred millions of pages per annum. This does not include the Magazine and books in pamphlet form, each of which contains as much matter as a bound volume. — Their bills for paper exceed $300,000 annually, and as the average cost is fifteen cents per pound, they consume more than two millions of pounds—say one thousand tons of white paper.

There are regularly employed in their own premises about 550 persons, including printers, binders, engravers, and clerks. These are all paid in full once a fortnight in bankable money. Besides these, there are numerous authors and artists in every section of the country, who furnish manuscripts and illustrations, on terms generally satisfactory to all the parties interested.

The Magazine has a monthly circulation of between 175,000 and 200,000, or about two millions of copies annually. Each number of the Magazine is closed up about the fifth of the month previous to its date. Three or four days thereafter the mailing begins, commencing with more distant subscribers, all of whom are supplied before any copies are sold for delivery in New York. The intention of the publishers is, that it shall be delivered as nearly as possible on the same day in St. Louis, New Orleans, Cincinnati, Philadelphia, Boston, and New York. It takes from ten to twelve days to dispatch the whole edition, (which weighs between four and five tons,) by mail and express.

Their new periodical, "Harpers' Weekly," has, in a little more than four months, reached a sale of nearly 70,000 copies. The mailing of this commences on Tuesday night, and occupies about three days.

Ex-Mayor Harper, whom we have found to be one of the most affable and estimable gentlemen in the city of New York, informed us, sometime ago, that, though he had no means of knowing positively, he was of the opinion that about eighty per cent of all their publications find final purchasers in the free States—the remainder, about twenty per cent, in the slave States. Yet it is probable that, with one or two exceptions, no other publishing house in the country has so large a percentage of Southern trade.

Of the "more than three hundred houses engaged in the publication of books," to which the writer in the "American Publishers' Circular" refers, upwards of nine-tenths of the number are in the non-slaveholding States, and these represent not less than ninety-nine hundredths of the whole capital invested in the business. Baltimore has twice as many publishers as any other Southern city; and nearly as many as the whole South beside. The census returns of 1850 give but twenty-four publishers for the entire South, and ten of these were in Maryland. The relative disproportion which then existed in this branch of enterprise, between the North and the South, still exists; or, if it has been changed at all, that change is in favor of the North. So of all the capital, enterprise and industry involved in the manufacture of the *material* that enters into the composition of books. All the paper manufactories of the South do not produce enough to supply a single publishing house in the city of New York.—Perhaps "a Southern Literature" does not necessarily involve the enterprises requisite to the *manufacture* of books; but experience has shown that there is a somewhat intimate relation between the author, printer, paper-maker and publisher; in other words, that the intellectual activity which expresses itself in books, is measurable by the mechanical activities engaged in their manufacture.—Thus a State that is fruitful in authors will almost necessarily be fruitful in publishers; and the number of both classes will be proportioned to the *reading* population. The poverty of Southern literature is legitimately shown, therefore, in the paucity of Southern publishers. We do not deny a high degree of cultivated talent to the South; we are familiar with the names of her sons whose genius has made them eminent; all that we insist upon is, that the same accursed influence which has smitten her industrial enterprises with paralysis, and retarded indefinitely her material advancement, has exerted a corresponding influence upon her literature. How it has done this we shall more fully indicate before we close the chapter.

At the "Southern Convention" held some months since at Savannah, a good deal was said about "Southern literature," and many suggestions made in reference to the best means for its promotion. One speaker thought that "they could get text-books at home without going to either Old England or New England for them." Well— they can try. The effort will not harm them; nor the North either. The orator was confident "that the South had talent enough to do anything that needs to be done, and independence enough to do it." The *talent* we shall not deny; the *independence* we are ready to believe in when we see it. When she throws off the incubus of slavery under which she goes staggering like the Sailor of Bagdad under the weight of the Old Man of the Sea, she will prove her independence, and demonstrate her ability "to do anything that needs to be done." Till then she is but a fettered giant, whose vitals are torn by the dogs which her own folly has engendered.

Another speaker, on the occasion referred to, half-unconsciously it would seem, threw a gleam of light upon the subject under discussion, which, had not himself and his hearers been bat-blind, would have revealed the clue that conducts from the darkness in which they burrow to the day of redemption for the South. Said he:

"Northern publishers employ the talent of the South and of the whole country to write for them, and pour out thousands annually for it; but Southern men expect to get talent without paying for it. The *Southern Quarterly Review* and the *Literary Messenger* are literally struggling for existence, for want of material aid. . . . It is not the South that builds up Northern literature—*they do it themselves.* There is talent and mind and poetic genius enough in the South to build up a literature of a high order; but Southern publishers cannot get money enough to assist them in their enterprises, and, therefore, the South has no literature."

Here are truths. "Southern men expect to get talent without

paying for it." A very natural expectation, considering that they have been accustomed to have all their material wants supplied by the uncompensated toil of their slaves. In this instance it may seem an absurd one, but it results legitimately from the system of slavery. That system, in fact, operates in a two-fold way against the Southern publisher: first, by its practical repudiation of the scriptural axiom that the laborer is worthy of his hire; and secondly, by restricting the circle of readers through the ignorance which it inevitably engenders. How is it that the people of the North build up their literature?—Two words reveal the secret: *intelligence*—*compensation*. They are *a reading people*—the poorest artsisan or day-laborer has his shelf of books, or his daily or weekly paper, whose contents he seldom fails to master before retiring at night; and *they are accustomed to pay for all the books and papers which they peruse.* Readers and payers—these are the men who insure the prosperity of publishers. Where a system of enforced servitude prevails, it is very apt to beget loose notions about the obligation of paying for anything; and many minds fail to see the distinction, morally, between compelling Sambo to pick cotton without paying him wages, or compelling Lippincott & Co. to manufacture books for the planter's pleasure or edification upon the same liberal terms. But more than this—where a system of enforced servitude prevails, a fearful degree of ignorance prevails also, as its necessary accompaniment. The enslaved masses are, of course, thrust back from the fountains of knowledge by the strong arm of law, while the poor non-slaveholding classes are almost as effectually excluded from the institutions of learning by their poverty—the sparse population of slaveholding districts being unfavorable to the maintenance of free schools, and the exigencies of their condition forbidding them to avail themselves of any more costly educational privileges.

Northern publishers can "employ the talent of the South and of the whole country to write for them, and pour out thousands annually for it," simply because a *reading* population, accustomed to *pay* for the service which it receives, enables them to do so. A similar population at the South would enable Southern publishers to do the same. Substitute free labor for slave labor, the institutions of freedom for those of slavery, and it would not long remain true that "Southern publishers cannot get money enough to assist them in their enterprises, and therefore the South has no literature." This is the discovery which the South Carolina orator from whom we quote, but narrowly escaped making, when he stood upon its very edge, and rounded his periods with the truths in whose unapprehended meanings was hidden this germ of redemption for a nation.

The self-stultification of folly, however, was never more evident than it is in the current gabble of the oligarchs about a "Southern literature." They do not mean by it a healthy, manly, normal utterance of unfettered minds, without which there can be no proper literature; but an emasculated substitute therefor, from which the element of freedom is eliminated; husks, from which the kernel has escaped—a body, from which the vitalizing spirit has fled—a literature which ignores manhood by confounding it with brutehood; or, at best, deals with all similes of freedom as treason against the "peculiar institution." There is not a single great name in the literary annals of the old or new world that could drawf itself to the stature requisite to gain admission into the Pantheon erected by these devotees of the Inane for their Lilliputian deities. Thank God, a "Southern literature," in the sense intended by the champions of slavery, is a simple impossibility, rendered such by that absence of mind which they demand in its producers as a prerequisite to admission into the guild of Southern authorship. The tenuous thoughts of such authorlings could not survive a single breath of manly criticism. The history of the rise, progress, and decline of their literature could be easily written on a child's smooth palm, and leave space enough for its funeral oration and epitaph. The latter might appropriately be that which, in one of our rural districts, marks the grave of a still-born infant:

"If so early I am done for, I wonder what I was begun for!"

We desire to see the South bear its just proportion in the literary activities and achievements of our common country. It has never yet done so, and it never will until its own manhood is vindicated in the abolition of slavery. The impulse which such a measure would give to all industrial pursuits that deal with the elements of material prosperity, would be imparted also to the no less valuable but more intangible creations of the mind. Take from the intellect of the South the incubus which now oppresses it, and its rebound would be glorious; the era of its diviner inspirations would begin; and its triumphs would be a perpetual vindication of the superiority of free institutions over those of slavery.

To Duyckinck's Cyclopedia of American Literature — a sort of *Omnium-gatherum* that reminds one of Jeremiah's figs — we are indebted for the following facts: The whole number of "American authors" whose place of nativity is given, is five hundred and sixty-nine. Of these seventy-nine were foreign born, eighty-seven were natives of the South, and four hundred and three—a vast majority of the whole, first breathed the vital air in the free North. Many of those who were born in the South, received their education in the North, quite a number of whom became permanent residents thereof. Still, for the purposes of this computation, we count them on the side of the South. Yet how significant the comparison which this computation furnishes! Throwing the foreign born (adopted citizens, mostly residents of the North) out of the reckoning, and the record stands, — Northern authors *four hundred and three;* Southern, *eighty-seven*—a difference of three hundred and sixteen in favor of the North! And this, probably, indicates very fairly the relative intellectual activity of the two sections.

We accept the facts gleaned from Duyckinck's work as a basis, simply, of our estimate: not as being absolutely accurate in themselves, though they are doubtless reliable in the main, and certainly as fair for the South as they are for the North. We might dissent from the judgment of the compiler in reference to the propriety of applying the term "literature" to much that his compilation contains; but as tastes have differed from the days of the venerable dame who kissed her cow—not to extend our researches into the condition of things anterior to that interesting event—we will not insist upon *our* view of the matter, but take it for granted that he has disentombed from forgotten reviews, newspapers, pamphlets, and posters, a fair relative proportion of "authors" for both North and South, for which "American Literature" is unquestionably under infinite obligations to him!

Griswold's "Poets and Poetry of America" and Thomas Buchanan Read's "Female Poets of America" furnish evidence, equally conclusive, of the benumbing influence of slavery upon the intellect of a country. Of course, these compilers say nothing about Slavery, and probably never thought of it in connection with their respective works, but none the less significant on that account is the testimony of the *facts* which they give. From the last edition of Griswold's compilation, (which contains the names of none of our female writers, he having included them in a separate volume) we find the names of one hundred and forty-one writers of verse: of these *one* was foreign-born, *seventeen* natives of the slaveholding, and *one hundred and twenty-three* of the non-slaveholding States. Of our female poets, whose nativity is given by Mr. Read, *eleven* are natives of the South; and *seventy-three* of the North! These simple arithmetical figures are God's eternal Scripture against the folly and madness of Slavery, and need no aid of rhetoric to give emphasis to the startling eloquence of their revelations.

But, after all, literature is not to be estimated by cubic feet or pounds averdupois, nor measured by the bushel or the yardstick. Quality, rather than quantity, is the true standard of estimation. The fact, however, matters little for our present purpose; for the South, we are sorry to say, is as much behind the North in the former as in the latter. We do not forget the names of Gayarre, Benton, Simms, and other eminent citizens of the Slave States, who have by their contributions to American letters conferred honor upon themselves and upon our common country, when we affirm, that those among our authors who enjoy a cosmopolitan reputation, are, with a few honorable exceptions, natives of the Free North; and that the names which most brilliantly illustrate our literature, in its every department, are those which have grown into greatness under the nurturing influence of free institutions. "Comparisons are odious," it is said; and we will not, unnecessarily, render them more so, in the present instance, by contrasting, name by name, the literary men of the South with the literary men of the North. We do not depreciate the former, nor overestimate the latter. But let us ask, whence come our geographers, our astronomers, our chemists, our meteorologists, our ethnologists, and others, who have made their names illustrious in the domain of the Natural Sciences? Not from the Slave States, certainly. In the Literature of Law, the South can furnish no name that can claim peership with those of Story and of Kent; in History, none that tower up to the altitude of Bancroft, Prescott, Hildreth, Motley and Washington Irving; in Theology, none that can challenge favorable comparison with those of Edwards, Dwight, Channing, Taylor, Bushnell, Tyler and Wayland: in Fiction, none that take rank with Cooper, and Mrs. Stowe; and but few that may do so with even the second class novelists of the North;* in Poetry, none that can command position with Bryant, Halleck, and Percival, with Whittier, Longfellow, and Lowell, with Willis, Stoddard and Taylor, with Holmes, Saxe, and Burleigh; and — we might add twenty other Northern names before we found their Southern peer, with the exception of poor Poe, who, within a narrow range of subjects, showed himself a poet of consummate art, and occupies a sort of debatable ground between our first and second-class writers.

We might extend this comparison to our writers in every department of letters, from the compiler of school-books to the author of the most profound ethical treatise, and with precisely the same

---

* We Southerners all glory in the literary reputation of Mr. Simms; yet we must confess his inferiority to Cooper, and prejudice alone will refuse to admit, that, while in the *art* of the novelist he is the superior of Mrs. Stowe in genius he must take position below her.

result. But we forbear. The task is distasteful to our State pride, and would have been entirely avoided had not a higher principle urged us to its performance. It remains for us now to enquire,

What has produced this literary pauperism of the south? One single word, most pregnant in its terrible meanings, answers the question. That word is — SLAVERY! But we have been so long accustomed to the ugly thing itself, and have become so familiar with its no less ugly fruits, that the common mind fails to apprehend the connection between the one, as cause, and the other as effect; and it therefore becomes necessary to give a more detailed answer to our interrogatory.

Obviously, then, the conditions requisite to a flourishing literature are wanting at the South. These are —

I. Readers. The people of the South are not a reading people. Many of the adult population never learned to read; still more, do not care to read. We have been impressed, during a temporary sojourn in the North, with the difference between the middle and laboring classes in the Free States, and the same classes in the Slave States, in this respect. Passing along the great routes of travel in the former, or taking our seat in the comfortable cars that pass up and down the avenues of our great commercial metropolis, we have not failed to contrast the employment of our fellow-passengers with that which occupies the attention of the corresponding classes on our various Southern routes of travel. In the one case, a large proportion of the passengers seem intent upon mastering the contents of the newspaper, or some recently published book. The merchant, the mechanic, the artisan, the professional man, and even the common laborer, going to or returning from their daily avocations, are busy with their morning or evening paper, or engaged in an intelligent discussion of some topic of public interest. This is their leisure hour, and it is given to the acquisition of such information as may be of immediate or ultimate use, or to the cultivation of a taste for elegant literature. In the other case, newspapers and books seem generally ignored, and noisy discussions of village and

State politics, the tobacco and cotton-crops, filibusterism in Cuba, Nicaragua, or Sonora, the price of negroes generally, and especially of "fine-looking wenches," the beauties of lynch-law, the delights of horse-racing, the excitement of street fights with bowie-knives and revolvers, the "manifest destiny" theory that justifies the stealing of all territory contiguous to our own, and kindred topics, constitute the warp and woof of conversation. All this is on a level with the general intelligence of the Slave States. It is true, these States have their educated men,—the majority of whom owe their literary culture to the colleges of the North. Not that there are no Southern colleges—for there are institutions, so called, in a majority of the Slave States.—Some of them, too, are not deficient in the appointments requisite to our higher educational institutions; but as a general thing, Southern colleges are colleges only in *name*, and will scarcely take rank with a third-rate Northern academy, while our academies, with a few exceptions, are immeasurably inferior to the public schools of New York, Philadelphia, and Boston. The truth is, there is a vast inert mass of stupidity and ignorance, too dense for individual effort to enlighten or remove, in all communities cursed with the institution of slavery. Disguise the unwelcome truth as we may, slavery is the parent of ignorance, and ignorance begets a whole brood of follies and of vices, and every one of these is inevitably hostile to literary culture. The masses, if they think of literature at all, think of it only as a costly luxury, to be monopolized by the few.

The proportion of white adults over twenty years of age, in each State, who cannot read and write, to the *whole* white population, is as follows:

Connecticut	1 to every 568	Louisiana	1 to every 38½
Vermont	1 to every 473	Maryland	1 to every 27
N. Hampshire	1 to every 310	Mississippi	1 to every 20
Massachusetts	1 to every 166	Delaware	1 to every 18
Maine	1 to every 108	South Carolina	1 to every 17
Michigan	1 to every 97	Missouri	1 to every 16
Rhode Island	1 to every 67	Alabama	1 to every 15
New Jersey	1 to every 58	Kentucky	1 to every 13½
New York	1 to every 56	Georgia	1 to every 13
Pennsylvania	1 to every 50	Virginia	1 to every 12½
Ohio	1 to every 43	Arkansas	1 to every 11½
Indiana	1 to every 18	Tennessee	1 to every 11
Illinois	1 to every 17	North Carolina	1 to every 7

In this table, Illinois and Indiana are the only Free States which, in point of education, are surpassed by any of the Slave States; and this disgraceful fact is owing, principally, to the influx of foreigners, and to immigrants from the Slave States. New York, Rhode Island, and Pennsylvania have also a large foreign element in their population, that swells very considerably this percentage of ignorance. For instance, New York shows, by the last census, a population of 98,722 who cannot read and write, and of this number 68,052 are foreigners; Rhode Island, 3,607, of whom 2,359 are foreigners; Pennsylvania, 76,272, of whom 24,989 are foreigners. On the other hand, the ignorance of the Slave States is principally *native* ignorance, but comparatively few emigrants from Europe seeking a home upon a soil cursed with "the peculiar institution." North Carolina has a foreign population of only 340, South Carolina only

104, Arkansas only 27, Tennessee only 505, and Virginia only 1,137, who cannot read and write; while the aggregate of *native* ignorance in these five States (exclusive of the *slaves,* who are debarred all education by *law*) is 278,948! No longer ago than 1837, Governor Clarke, of Kentucky, in his message to the Legislature of that State, declared that "by the computation of those most familiar with the subject, *one-third of the adult population of the State are unable to write their names;*" and Governor Campbell, of Virginia, reported to the Legislature, that "from the returns of ninety-eight clerks, it appeared that of 4,614 applications for marriage licenses in 1837, no less than 1,047 were made by men unable to write."

In the Slave States the proportion of free white children between the ages of five and twenty, who are found at any school or college, is not quite *one-fifth* of the whole; in the Free States, the proportion is more than *three-fifths.*

We could fill our pages with facts like these to an almost indefinite extent, but it cannot be necessary. No truth is more demonstrable, no truth has been more abundantly demonstrated, than this: that Slavery is hostile to general education; its strength, its very life, is in the ignorance and stolidity of the masses; it naturally and necessarily represses general literary culture. To talk, therefore, of the "creation of a purely Southern Literature," without *readers* to demand, or *writers* to produce it, is the mere babble of idiocy.

II. Another thing essential to the creation of a literature is MENTAL FREEDOM. How much of *that* is to be found in the region of Slavery? We will not say that there is *none;* but if it exists, it exists as the outlawed antagonist of human chattelhood. He who believes that the despotism of the accursed institution expends its malignant forces upon the *slave,* leaving intact the white and (so called) free population, is the victim of a most monstrous delusion. One end of the yoke that bows the African to the dust, presses heavily upon the neck of his Anglo-Saxon master. The entire mind of the South either stultifies itself into acquiescence with Slavery, succumbs to its authority, or chafes in indignant protest against its monstrous pretensions and outrageous usurpations. A free press is an institution almost unknown at the South. Free speech is considered as treason against slavery: and when people dare neither speak nor print their thoughts, free thought itself is well nigh extinguished. All that can be said in *defence* of human bondage, may be spoken freely; but question either its morality or its policy, and the terrors of lynch law are at once invoked to put down the pestilent heresy. The legislation of the Slave States for the suppression of the freedom of speech and the press, is disgraceful and cowardly to the last degree, and can find its parallel only in the meanest and bloodiest despotisms of the Old World. No institution that could bear the light would thus sneakingly seek to burrow itself in utter darkness. Look, too, at the mobbings, lynchings, robberies, social and political proscriptions, and all manner of nameless outrages, to which men in the South have been subjected, simply upon the suspicion that they were the enemies of Slavery. We could fill page after page of this volume with the record of such atrocities. But a simple reference to them is enough. Our countrymen have not yet forgotten why John C. Underwood was, but a few months since, banished from his home in Virginia, and the accomplished Hedreck driven from his College professorship in North Carolina. They believed Slavery inimical to the best interest of the South, and for daring to give expression to this belief in moderate yet manly language, they were ostracised by the despotic Slave Power, and compelled to seek a refuge from its vengeance in States where the principles of freedom are better understood. Pending the last Presidential election, there were thousands, no, tens of thousands of voters in the Slave States, who desired to give their suffrages for the Republican nominee, John C. Fremont, himself a Southerner, but a non-slaveholder. The Constitution of the United States guaranteed to these men an expression of their preference at the ballot-box. But were they permitted such an expression? Not at all. They were denounced, threatened, overawed, by the Slave Power—and it is not too much to say that there was really no *Constitutional election*, —that is, no such free expression of political preferences as the Constitution aims to secure—in a majority of the Slave States.

From a multiplicity of facts like these, the inference is unavoidable, that Slavery tolerates no freedom of the press—no freedom of speech—no freedom of opinion. To expect that a whole-souled, manly literature can flourish under such conditions is as absurd as it would be to look for health amid the pestilential vapors of a dungeon, or for the continuance of animal life without the aid of oxygen.

III. Mental activity — force — enterprise — are requisite to the creation of literature. Slavery tends to sluggishness—imbecility—inertia. Where free thought is treason, the masses will not long take the trouble of thinking at all. Desuetude begets Incompetence—the *dare-not* soon becomes the *cannot.* The mind thus enslaved, necessarily loses its interest in the processes of other minds; and its tendency is to sink down into absolute stolidity or sottishness. Our remarks find melancholy confirmation in the abject servilism in which multitudes of the non-slave-holding whites of the South are involved. In them, ambition, pride, self-respect, hope, seem alike extinct. Their slaveholding fellows are, in some respects, in a still more unhappy condition—helpless, nerveless, ignorant, selfish; yet vain-glorious, self-sufficient and brutal. Are these the chosen architects who are expected to build up "a purely Southern literature?"

The truth is, slavery destroys, or vitiates, or pollutes, whatever it touches. No interest of society escapes the influence of its clinging curse. It makes Southern religion a stench in the nostrils of Christendom—it makes Southern politics a libel upon all the principles of Republicanism — it makes Southern literature a travesty upon the honorable profession of letters. Than the better class of Southern authors themselves, none will feel more keenly the truth of our remarks. They write books, but can find for them neither publishers nor remunerative sales at the South The executors of Calhoun seek, for his works, a Northern publisher. Benton writes history and prepares voluminous compilations, which are given to the world through a Northern publisher. Simms writes novels and poems, and they are scattered abroad from the presses of a Northern publisher. Eighty per cent of all the copies sold are probably bought by Northern readers.

When will Southern authors understand their own interests? When will the South, as a whole, abandoning its present suicidal policy, enter upon that career of prosperity, greatness, and true renown, to which God by his word and his providences, is calling it? "If thou take away from the midst of thee the yoke, the putting forth of the finger and speaking vanity; and if thou draw out thy soul to the hungry and satisfy the afflicted soul; then shall thy light rise in obscurity and thy darkness be as the noonday: And the Lord shall guide thee continually and satisfy thy soul in drought, and make fat thy bones; and thou shalt be like a watered garden, and like a spring of water, whose waters fail not. And they that shall be of thee shall build the old waste places; thou shalt raise up the foundations of many generations; and thou shalt be called, The repairer of the breach, The restorer of paths to dwell in."

Our limits, not our materials, are exhausted. We would gladly say more, but can only, in conclusion, add as the result of our investigations in this department of our subject, that *Literature and Liberty are inseparable; the one can never have a vigorous existence without being wedded to the other.*

Our work is done. It is the voice of the non-slaveholding whites of the South, through one identified with them by interest, by feeling, by position. That voice, by whomsoever spoken, must yet be heard and heeded. The time hastens—the doom of slavery is written—the redemption of the South draws nigh.

In taking leave of our readers, we know not how we can give more forcible expression to our thoughts and intentions than by saying that, in concert with the intelligent free voters of the North, we, the non-slaveholding whites of the South, expect to elevate John C. Fremont, Cassius M. Clay, James G. Birney, or some other South-

ern non-slaveholder, to the Presidency in 1860; and that the patriot
thus elevated to that dignified station will, through our cordial
cooperation, be succeeded by William H. Seward, Charles Sumner,
John Mclean, or some other non-slaveholder of the North; — and
furthermore, that if, in these or in any other similar cases, the
oligarchs do not quietly submit to the will of a constitutional majority of the people, as expressed at the ballot-box, the first battle
between freedom and slavery will be fought at home — and may
God defend the right!

Index

quantity, 32, 34, 44, 53, 64, 128, 312

race, 2, 73, 87, 96, 98, 113, 148, 155, 164, 175, 178, 181, 193, 200, 201, 204, 221, 222, 229, 232, 233
railroads, 9, 76, 206, 240, 241
Randolph, Edmund, 170, 172
Randolph, John, 169
Randolph, Peyton, 172
Randolph, Thomas M., 170
Raynal, Abbe, 233
Raynor, Kenneth, 142
Read, Mr., 312
reading, 110, 161, 307, 309, 314
real estate, 102, 107, 109–111, 295
reasons, 11, 12, 14, 92, 102, 140, 157, 208, 217, 228
Reid, Hon. Mr., 196
religion: apostles, 231; bible, 168, 220–222, 227, 260, 261, 303, 305; bishops, 222; churches, 39, 76, 219–223, 230–232, 234, 258; clergy, 222; doctrines, 197; general, 97, 98, 104, 132, 168, 169, 203, 204, 213, 216, 219, 233, 235, 319; Jesus Christ, 204, 221, 222, 231; priests, 222, 304; Roman Catholic, 145, 219, 231, 234
representatives, 93, 114, 134–136, 146, 159, 183, 196, 199, 204, 279, 287, 290
Republic, 80, 97, 135, 136, 141, 150, 158, 159, 161, 191, 198, 212, 234
Republican, 80, 143, 167, 168, 174,

198, 199, 215, 217, 229, 256, 257, 318
resolution, 146, 172, 221, 229
resources, 10, 15, 65, 85, 94, 195
Revolutionary Fathers, 97
Revolutionary War, 96
Rhode Island, 19, 21, 23, 25, 45, 47, 49, 55, 57, 59, 68, 117, 119, 130, 236, 238, 240, 242–244, 246, 248, 250, 252, 254, 256, 258–260, 262, 264, 272, 290, 316
Richmond, 63, 77, 87–91, 287, 289
Richmond Enquirer, 77, 88, 90
Richmond Examiner, 289
Rio Grande, 17, 132
Ritchie, Mr., 79, 88
Rives, Mr., 86, 88
Rockford, Ill., 288
Rocky Mountains, 207
Roman Pontiffs, 232
Ruffin, Hon. Judge, 189
ruin, 13, 85, 86, 141, 148, 193, 295
rules, 1, 30, 35, 37, 65, 70, 87, 115, 187, 215, 230, 301

sacred, 13, 30, 80, 81, 98, 104, 107, 109, 141, 159, 165, 166, 187, 200, 205, 212, 221
sale, 9, 33, 34, 40, 78, 110, 215, 224, 294, 299, 305, 306
San Francisco Evening Journal, 291
Savannah, 36, 299, 308
science, 14, 15, 74, 97, 127, 180, 186, 194, 195, 225, 300

www.ingramcontent.com/pod-product-compliance
Lightning Source LLC
Chambersburg PA
CBHW030939150426
42812CB00064B/3057/J